Bertrand Russell

Twayne's English Authors Series

Kinley E. Roby, Editor

Northeastern University

TEAS 421

BERTRAND RUSSELL
(1872–1970)
Photograph courtesy of
The Bertrand Russell Archives,
McMaster University, Ontario

Bertrand Russell

By Paul Grimley Kuntz

Emory University

Twayne Publishers • Boston

Bertrand Russell

Paul Grimley Kuntz

Copyright © 1986 by G. K. Hall & Co.
All Rights Reserved
Published by Twayne Publishers
A Division of G. K. Hall & Co.
70 Lincoln Street
Boston, Massachusetts 02111

Copyediting supervised by Lewis DeSimone
Book production by Elizabeth Todesco
Book design by Barbara Anderson

Typeset in 11 pt. Garamond
by Modern Graphics, Inc., Weymouth, Massachusetts

Printed on permanent/durable acid-free paper
and bound in the United States of America.

Library of Congress Cataloging in Publication Data

Kuntz, Paul Grimley, 1915–
  Bertrand Russell.

  (Twayne's English authors series; TEAS 421)
  Bibliography: p. 171
  Includes index.
  1. Russell, Bertrand, 1872–1970. I. Title.
II. Series.
B1649.R94K86   1986   192   85–24699
ISBN 0–8057–6916–1

For Marion and all our children and children's children: Iran, Matthew, Kristin, Jonathan, George, Ann, and those yet to be named.

Contents

About the Author
Preface
Chronology
Abbreviations

Chapter One
Bertrand Russell: Hero of Free Thought   1

Chapter Two
The Quest for Certainty
in Belief, Knowledge, Truth   11

Chapter Three
The New Logic of Relations: The Order of
Thought and the Order of Things   30

Chapter Four
Words and the World: Shall Philosophy Be
No More Than Analysis of the Order of Language?   54

Chapter Five
Metaphysics: Knowledge of the Real Order?   75

Chapter Six
Manifest Evils: Imperatives of the Moral Order   94

Chapter Seven
Rational Man and Irrational Society:
Can Mankind Resolve the Disorders of Our Age?   117

Chapter Eight
Russell's Religion: Could His God
Be the Ground of Order?   134

Notes and References   155
Selected Bibliography   171
Index   179

About the Author

Paul Grimley Kuntz was born in Philadelphia in 1915 and became interested in Bertrand Russell while in high school. The first book that fascinated him was *The Problems of Philosophy*. Kuntz's father had purchased the volume from Home University Library in 1912, the date of the first issue. The problem of certainty had raised doubts in the boy's mind and this was the only book that showed him that there was a subject in which claims are met with counterclaims. "Is there any knowledge in the world so certain that no reasonable man could doubt it?" The initial question remains provocative.

He was educated at Haverford College, where, appropriate to a Quaker education, he read Russell's *Why Men Fight*. After graduating with a B.A. in 1937 Kuntz took three degrees from Harvard University (S.T.B. in 1940, S.T.M. in 1941—the *S* stands for "science" and not "sacred" and meant in relation to theology a philological method—and Ph.D. in 1946). His dissertation was on Russell's friend George Santayana. After early teaching at Smith College he spent eighteen years at Grinnell College. Since 1966 he has been professor of philosophy at Emory University.

Kuntz is coauthor of *Philosophy and the Study of Alternative Beliefs, Lotze's System of Philosophy,* and *The Concept of Order.* Most recently he published *Alfred North Whitehead* (Twayne, 1984), to which *Bertrand Russell* is a companion volume. Kuntz has written about a hundred articles on order/disorder.

With his wife, Dr. Marion Leathers Kuntz, he has organized conferences in the history of ideas at the Medieval Institute of Western Michigan University. Among the great ideas are "hierarchy," "harmony," "balance," "opposition," "analogy," and "truth." Several of the Kuntzes' studies of these modes of order have been published, and half a dozen more are nearing publication.

The major point of Kuntz's philosophy is that the study of order has been central to philosophies of East and West; and although now neglected, when explored, this is the key to understanding our knowledge and the value of the cosmos.

Preface

The Logical, Metaphysical, and Moral Unity of Bertrand Russell's Philosophy

Bertrand Russell as an international figure, a writer meriting the Nobel Prize, and the most prominent representative of Anglo-American realistic philosophy continues to fascinate a wide audience. His career is the longest (1872–1970) and is also the most diverse in the history of philosophy. Therefore, it has been very easy to pick one side, at one level, during one period, and represent this as the whole Russell. Examples are common: Russell the practical atheist, Russell the pacifist, Russell the positivist and linguistic analyst, Russell the prophet of the sexual revolution, Russell the sinner, and Russell the saint. Because the interpreters take only the most obvious statements (and Russell did often achieve clarity of expression by oversimplification), there is little effort to read deeply enough to find the common threads throughout his long career and tie together his diverse activities. I should not argue that Russell arrived at and sustained a *system* of philosophy, but he is not as Ali Baba's brother, Cassim, utterly chopped in pieces by the forty thieves. Russell himself, in a diary of 1894, shared the concern of metaphysics "to undo the work of [divisive] thought and to restore the original concrete unity."[1] There are many opposites in Russell, and the pattern is often one of swinging back and forth, statable as Russell in dialogue with himself.

My thesis about the whole Russell is that it is a major error to fail to recognize the structure relating the parts. My work is to correct such an authoritative handling as that in *The Encyclopedia of Philosophy*[2] in which there are no connections among the three parts done by three authors. The epistemology is cut up into periods, the moral concern remains a complete dualism, and the metaphysics is reduced to isolated puzzles. Unfortunately, this treatment perpetuates the incoherence of the twentieth-century mind and fails to do justice to Russell's consistent concern with objective truth and with the explicit virtues of the liberal humanitarian, as well as his concern that life and thought be grounded in respect for the world order that he called "cosmic piety."

My thesis of how Russell intended to unify thought through the new logic of relations is fully supported by the essay "On the Notion of Order."[3] Russell's Platonistic period allegedly collapses into a nominalistic opposite, logical atomism. But in *Philosophy of Logical Atomism*, we find an ontology not so simple: "There are particulars and qualities and relations of various orders, a whole hierarchy."[4] The secondary literature, such as Quine's interpretation, has been largely atomistic and ignores the correspondence of structures. Among the interpreters who have stressed structure there are a few who have not extended their articles to cover more than part of Russell's account of scientific knowledge. Russell, faced with an interpreter who ascribed to him a complete dualism of the physical and the psychic, rebuked this criticism: "Rightly or wrongly [I argued in *Analysis of Matter*] that there can be *similarity as to structure,* and that our knowledge of the physical world is only that of structure."[5]

Bertrand Russell is one of the great writers of philosophy in an age that has included William James, F. H. Bradley, Henri Bergson, George Santayana, José Ortega y Gasset, and Martin Heidegger. It is more likely that the common reader of English will have a book of Russell than of any other philosopher except Plato or Aristotle in translation. Russell's books have come steadily since the last years of the nineteenth century; about forty are available in paperback, and about twenty are available in boards. Perhaps another twenty are at present out of print, but they can be found in college and public libraries.

The reader must not expect here a complete book on the works of Russell in so short a text, for Russell is not merely a logician to be numbered with Aristotle, Leibniz, and Peirce but a great innovator in the philosophic analysis of language and knowledge. He wrote on many phases of public life—on the reform of society, on problems of peace and war, on marriage, education, and religion. I shall try to interpret his thought sympathetically in following one theme that is common to all these disciplines of philosophy both theoretical and practical.

This theme is *order,* which is given a precise definition in mathematical logic and which is central to Russell's theory of knowledge and truth, mind and matter, the individual and the authority of state and church.

The most unforgettable lectures I ever heard were those in the William James series of 1940, given at Harvard after Russell had been denied a position at City College of New York. These were published as *Inquiry into Meaning and Truth*. The main point that motivates this book is that philosophy is not about words but about the world. On this point the analysts and positivists have misled us; and the metaphysicians, from Plato on down through history, have been right.

The reader may well pass from chapter 1 directly to the exposition of Russell's practical philosophy in chapters 6, 7, and 8. Then the theoretical matters of chapters 2, 3, 4, and 5 may take on a more human significance. But from the perspective of theory (of knowledge, logic, linguistic analysis, and being), it is the abstract that is far more simple and therefore the more intelligible aspect of the cosmos. The great beauty of reading Russell is that he is equally excellent in both the mathematical language of symbolic logic and in simple common English. If readers allow Russell to teach them, they can learn from him to move either from the abstract to the concrete or from the concrete to the abstract. This is necessary to become, like Russell, a person who bridges the gap between the two cultures of the sciences and the humanistic arts.

My thanks are to Lord Russell, to the editors of this series, to my students and colleagues, to many librarians, and to members of my family who, to my delight, question what I write and help me write better. Special thanks for editorial assistance are due to Steven Keith, Patricia Redford, William Brooks, Vicki Shadix, Mary Ann Kontaratos, Anne Owens, and Ivia Cofresí.

My professional indebtedness is especially to Prof. Robert Arrington, Prof. William Alston, Prof. Nicholas Capaldi, and Dr. Kenneth Blackwell of the Bertrand Russell Center, McMaster University.

At crucial junctures in the project I was aided and supported by Prof. Donald Philip Verene, chairman of the Department of Philosophy, and by the department itself. The project has been supported by Prof. Claudia Adkinson and the Emory Research Committee. To all of them, but especially to my wife, Dr. Marion Leathers Kuntz, I owe deepest thanks.

Since Russell is, of all major philosophers, the most forward looking and future oriented, this study is dedicated to our grandchildren, actual and potential.

Paul Grimley Kuntz

Emory University

Chronology

1872   18 May, Bertrand Arthur William Russell born near Trelleck, Monmouthshire, son of John, Viscount Amberley, and Katherine (daughter of Baron Stanley of Alderley).

1874–1876   Death of Lady Amberley and of Bertrand's sister, followed by the death of Viscount Amberley. Bertrand and his elder brother are provided with "a Christian education" at Pembroke Lodge, Richmond Park, the home of their grandparents, Lord John, first Earl Russell, and Countess Russell ("Lady John").

1890   Scholar of Trinity College, Cambridge.

1893–1894   First class honors in mathematics and first class honors in moral sciences.

1894   Attaché at the British embassy in Paris. Marries Alys Whitall Pearsall Smith of Philadelphia (marriage dissolved 1921; she dies in 1951).[1]

1895   Elected fellow of Trinity College, Cambridge (fellowship dissertation, *An Essay on the Foundations of Geometry*, 1897). The Russells in Berlin, gathering materials for a book published in the subsequent year, *German Social Democracy*.

1896   First of many visits to the United States. Lectures at Johns Hopkins and at Bryn Mawr.

1899   Substitutes at Cambridge for J. M. E. McTaggart, lecturing on Leibniz (results published at Cambridge, *A Critical Exposition of the Philosophy of Leibniz*, 1900). Influenced by G. E. Moore, he reverses his admiration for Kant and Hegel.

1900   The "most important year" in Russell's intellectual life; with the Whiteheads the Russells attend the First International Congress of Philosophy at Paris, where they meet Giuseppe Peano and other Continental mathematical logicians.

1902 Joins the Co-efficients at invitation of Beatrice (Mrs. Sidney) Webb to discuss political policy with Sir Edward Grey, Haldane, the Webbs, and a dozen others. "Russell flung out of the club" because, according to H. G. Wells, only he sympathizes with Russell's antiimperialist sentiments.[2]

1903–1913 After Russell's *The Principles of Mathematics* and Whitehead's *Treatise on Universal Algebra* five years earlier, the two authors abandon plans for separate second volumes and collaborate on producing *Principia Mathematica;* volume 1 published in 1910, volume 2 in 1912, volume 3 in 1913 (volume 4 on geometry, Whitehead's prime responsibility, abandoned because of the war).

1905 "On Denoting" published in *Mind:* Russell's "Theory of Descriptions" his "greatest philosophical discovery, more important than anything he said later" (G. E. Moore).

1907 Stands unsuccessfully for Parliament.

1908 Fellow of the Royal Society, London (F.R.S.).

1910 Lecturer in mathematical logic, Trinity College. Fails of nomination for Parliament; Liberal party rejects him because of his agnostic views.

1911 President of the Aristotelian Society. Separation from Alys Russell.

1913 Address to the Heretics, Trinity College, "The Philosophy of Bergson."[3]

1914 Visiting professor at Harvard University, and delivers Lowell Lectures in Boston published as *Our Knowledge of the External World As a Field for Scientific Method in Philosophy* (1914). Herbert Spencer Lecture at Oxford on "Scientific Method in Philosophy."

1915 Devotes himself to the pacifist efforts of the No Conscription Fellowship. Argues his conviction—"I could not feel that the victory of either side would solve any problem"—in four books and many pamphlets, thus first making him known beyond academic circles.

1916   June, fined one hundred pounds (and ten pounds costs) for a pamphlet that allegedly interfered with military conscription; refuses to pay and his belongings at Trinity distrained on; a friend buys his library for him. Because convicted he is deprived of lectureship at Trinity College; when offered a post at Harvard, he is refused a passport.[4]

1918   February, prosecuted a second time, for a *Tribunal* article allegedly casting aspersions on the American army; sentenced to four or six months in prison, which he spends writing *Introduction to Mathematical Philosophy* (1919). "The Philosophy of Logical Atomism," eight lectures given in London and published with questions and answers in the *Monist*. Acknowledges that for the past four years he has been under the influence of his student, Ludwig Wittgenstein, and takes a position similar in many points to *Tractatus Logico-Philosophicus* (which Russell publishes, with an introduction, in 1922).

1920   Trip of five weeks to Russia; talks with Lenin, Trotsky, and Gorky (publishes *Bolshevism: Practice and Theory*, 1920).

1920–1921   Professor of philosophy, National University of Peking (publishes *The Problem of China*, 1922). Visits Japan also.

1921   Marries a second time, to Dora Winifred Black, Fellow of Girton College (children: John Conrad, Katharine Jane; marriage dissolved, 1935). Living at Chelsea and Land's End, devoting himself to journalism.

1922   Labour candidate for Parliament. Moncure D. Conway Memorial Lecture, "Free Thought and Official Propaganda."

1923   Labour candidate for Parliament.

1924   Lecture tour in the United States (also in 1927, 1929, 1931). Discussion "Bolshevism and the West" and "How to Be Free and Happy" in New York.

1926   Tarner Lectures at Trinity (published as *The Analysis of Matter,* 1927).

1927   The Russells open an experimental school for young children at Beacon Hill, near Petersfield (educational theories in *On Education,* 1926, and *Education and the Social Order,* 1932). Lecture to National Secular Society, "Why I Am Not a Christian."

1931   On death of elder brother, becomes third Earl Russell of Kingston Russell.

1936   Marries a third time, to Patricia Helen Spence (one son: Conrad Sebastian Robert; marriage dissolved, 1951).

1938–1939   Lecturer, University of Chicago; professor of philosophy, University of California at Los Angeles.

1939–1940   Appointed professor of philosophy at the City College of the City of New York: denounced by clergy and religious organizations; City Council condemns him as "an enemy of religion and morality." "A taxpayer's suit brought by a Brooklyn housewife resulted in a judicial order to rescind the appointment on March 30; appeal was denied, and the appointment remained invalidated."[5]

1940   William James Lecturer at Harvard. Publishes *An Inquiry into Meaning and Truth.* Signs a five-year contract to lecture at Barnes Foundation, Merion, Pennsylvania.

1942   Dismissed by Barnes Foundation; sues for breach of contract and is awarded twenty thousand dollars damages in 1943. The lectures designed for delivery and partly given, published as *A History of Western Philosophy* (1945).

1944   Returns to England after six years in the United States. Fellow of Trinity College, Cambridge; topic of course: Non-Demonstrative Inference.

1948   In airplane crash on trip to Norway; saves himself by swimming until rescued. Publishes *Human Knowledge: Its Scope and Limits,* his "philosophic testament," "the nearest thing to a systematic philosophy" he has yet written.[6]

1948–1949 First Reith Lecturer, BBC (basis for *Authority and the Individual,* 1949). Addresses Westminster School: "Atomic Energy and the Problems of Europe."

1949 Receives Order of Merit.

1950 Receives Nobel Prize in literature "in recognition of his many-sided and significant authorship in which he has constantly figured as a defender of humanity and freedom of thought."

1951 Lectures at Columbia University, "The Impact of Science on Society." Marries a fourth time, to Edith Finch.

1954 Sounds warning to world of race suicide because of hydrogen bomb. Works to neutralize Britain in struggle between United States and Soviet Union, to reduce armaments of world powers, and so on.[7]

1957 In "Open Letter to Eisenhower and Krushchev," draws lessons from history that all who set out to conquer the world bring their own nations to ruin and that no ideology has ever succeeded in conquering the allegiance of the race; therefore those who hold the faith of either Jefferson or Marx cannot hope to be unequivocally triumphant.[8]

1959 Writes introduction to Ernest Gellner's *Words and Things,* denouncing linguistic philosophy of Oxford and deploring the influence of the later Wittgenstein. "The later Wittgenstein . . . seems to have grown tired of serious thinking and to have invented a doctrine which would make such an activity unnecessary. I do not for one moment believe that the doctrine which has these lazy consequences is true. . . . The desire to understand the world is, they think, an outdated folly."[9]

1961 Summoned with others of the Committee of 100 for inciting the public to commit a breach of peace (a forthcoming sit-down demonstration); sentence of two months' imprisonment is reduced to seven days and served in Brixton Prison, where he was incarcerated forty-three years earlier.[10]

1967   Publication begun of *Autobiography*.

1970   2 February, dies at Plas Penrhyn, Monmouthshire, at age ninety-seven.

Abbreviations

It is common in books about Russell to abbreviate the titles, and I have continued the practice in this text. Care needs to be paid to the editions cited, for there are nearly always English editions, and sometimes both American and English paperbacks, usually with different paginations. I list the works alphabetically by abbreviation, citing the paperback edition of *The ABC of Relativity* because there is no other now available.

Ai   *The Autobiography of Bertrand Russell.* Vol. 1, *1872–1914.* Boston: Little, Brown, 1967.

Aii   *The Autobiography of Bertrand Russell.* Vol. 2, *1914–1944.* Boston: Little, Brown, 1968.

Aiii   *The Autobiography of Bertrand Russell.* Vol. 3, *1944–1969.* Boston: Little, Brown, 1969.

ABCA   *The ABC of Atoms.* New York: E. P. Dutton, 1923.

ABCR   *The ABC of Relativity.* Edited by Felix Pirani. New York: New American Library, 1959.

AI   *Authority and the Individual* Boston: Beacon Press, 1949.

AMat   *The Analysis of Matter.* New York: Dover, 1954.

AMd   *The Analysis of Mind.* London: G. Allen & Unwin, 1921.

AP   *The Amberley Papers.* With Patricia Russell. 2 vols. London: Hogarth Press, 1937.

APh   *The Art of Philosophizing.* New York: Philosophical Library, 1968.

BRA   *Bertrand Russell's America.* Edited by Barry Feinberg and Ronald Kasrils. New York: Viking Press, 1973.

BRSM   *Bertrand Russell Speaks His Mind.* London: Arthur Barker, 1960).

BW   *Basic Writings.* London: G. Allen & Unwin, 1961.

CH   *The Conquest of Happiness.* New York: New American Library, 1951.

CS   *Common Sense and Nuclear Warfare.* London: G. Allen & Unwin, 1959.

CSBR   *The Collected Stories of Bertrand Russell.* Edited by Barry Feinberg. London: G. Allen & Unwin, 1972.

DBR   *Dear Bertrand Russell: A Selection of His Correspondence with the General Public, 1950–1968.* Edited by Barry Feinberg and Ronald Kasrils. Boston: Houghton Mifflin, 1969.

DRDJ   *Dear Russell—Dear Jourdain: A Commentary on Russell's Logic Based on His Correspondence with Philip Jourdain.* New York: Columbia University Press, 1977.

EA   *Essays in Analysis.* Edited by Douglas Lackey. New York: George Braziller, 1973.

EFG   *An Essay on the Foundations of Geometry.* 1897. Reprint, with introduction by Morris Kline. New York: Dover, 1956.

EGL   *Education and the Good Life.* New York: Boni & Liveright, 1926. As *On Education Especially in Early Childhood.* London: G. Allen & Unwin, 1926.

ESO   *Education and the Social Order.* London: G. Allen & Unwin, 1932.

FF   *Fact and Fiction.* London: G. Allen & Unwin, 1961.

FMW   *The Free Man's Worship.* In *BW,* pp. 66–72.

FO   *Freedom and Organization.* London: G. Allen & Unwin, 1934.

GSD   *German Social Democracy.* London: G. Allen & Unwin, 1965.

HK   *Human Knowledge: Its Scope and Limits.* New York: Simon & Schuster, 1948.

HMF   *Has Man a Future?* Baltimore: Penguin, 1961.

HS   *Human Society in Ethics and Politics.* London: G. Allen & Unwin, 1954.

HWP   *History of Western Philosophy.* New York: Simon & Schuster, 1945.

IFS   *Icarus or the Future of Science.* New York: Dutton, 1924.

IMP   *Introduction to Mathematical Philosophy.* 2d ed. London: G. Allen & Unwin, 1920.

IMT   *Inquiry into Meaning and Truth.* London: G. Allen & Unwin, 1940.

IPI   *In Praise of Idleness and Other Essays.* London: G. Allen & Unwin, 1935.

ISS   *Impact of Science on Society.* London: G. Allen & Unwin, 1952.

ITL-P   Introduction to *Tractatus Logico-Philosophicus,* by Ludwig Wittgenstein. London: Routledge & Kegan Paul, 1922.

JWT   *Justice in Wartime.* London: G. Allen & Unwin, 1916.

LA   *Logical Atomism.* In *LK,* pp. 321–43.

LK   *Logic and Knowledge.* London: G. Allen & Unwin, 1956.

ML   *Mysticism and Logic and Other Essays.* 2d ed. London: G. Allen & Unwin, 1917.

MM   *Marriage and Morals.* London: G. Allen & Unwin, 1929.

MPD   *My Philosophical Development.* London: G. Allen & Unwin, 1959.

NEP   *Nightmares of Eminent Persons.* London: Bodley Head, 1954.

NHCW   *New Hopes for a Changing World.* London: G. Allen & Unwin, 1951.

OKEW   *Our Knowledge of the External World.* London: G. Allen & Unwin, 1926.

P   *Power: A New Social Analysis.* London: G. Allen & Unwin, 1938.

PC   *The Problem of China.* London: G. Allen & Unwin, 1922.

PE   *Philosophical Essays.* Rev. ed. London: G. Allen & Unwin, 1966.

Ph   *Philosophy.* New York: W. W. Norton, 1927. Published in Great Britain as *An Outline of Philosophy.*

PI   *Political Ideals.* London: G. Allen & Unwin, 1963.

PIC   *The Prospects of Industrial Civilization.* London: G. Allen & Unwin, 1923.

PL   *Critical Exposition of the Philosophy of Leibniz.* 2d ed. London: G. Allen & Unwin, 1937.

PLA   *Philosophy of Logical Atomism.* In *LK,* pp. 175–281.

PM   *Principia Mathematica.* With Alfred North Whitehead. 2d ed. 3 vols. Cambridge: At the University Press, 1925–27.

PMath   *Principles of Mathematics.* 2d ed. London: G. Allen & Unwin, 1937.

PMem   *Portraits from Memory and Other Essays.* 2d ed. London: G. Allen & Unwin, 1956.

PP   *The Problems of Philosophy.* New York: Oxford University Press, 1959.

PSR   *Principles of Social Reconstruction.* London: G. Allen & Unwin, 1916.

PTB   *The Practice and Theory of Bolshevism.* 2d ed. London: G. Allen & Unwin, 1949. Also abbreviated BPT.

RF   *Roads to Freedom: Socialism, Anarchism and Syndicalism.* London: G. Allen & Unwin, 1918.

RS   *Religion and Science.* London: Oxford University Press, 1935.

SE   *Sceptical Essays.* London: G. Allen & Unwin, 1928.

SO   *Scientific Outlook.* New York: W. W. Norton, 1962.

SP   *Selected Papers.* With special introduction. New York: Modern Library, 1927.

SS   *Satan in the Suburbs and Other Stories.* New York: Simon & Schuster, 1953.

UE   *Unpopular Essays.* New York: Simon & Schuster, 1950.

UH   *Understanding History and Other Essays.* New York: Philosophical Library, 1957.

UV   *Unarmed Victory.* Baltimore: Penguin, 1963.

VLR   *The Vital Letters of Russell, Krushchev, Dulles.* London: Macgibbon & Kee, 1958.

WCV   *War Crimes in Vietnam.* With C. Farley, Ralph Schoenman, and R. Stetler, Jr. London: G. Allen & Unwin, 1967.

WNC   *Why I Am Not a Christian and Other Essays on Religion and Related Subjects.* Edited by Paul Edwards. New York: Simon & Schuster, 1957.

WW   *Wisdom of the West.* Edited by Paul Foukes. New York: Crescent, 1959.

WWP   *Which Way to Peace?* London: Michael Joseph, 1936.

Chapter One

Bertrand Russell: Hero of Free Thought

Noble Heritage

Some accounts of Bertrand Russell's family begin with his ancestors' coming to England with William of Normandy in 1066.[1] But since there is little of the medieval Catholic in him and much of the modern Protestant, it seems best to begin with John Russell (ca. 1485–1555). This son of a country squire was one of the new men who served Henry VIII and was rewarded by being created Lord Russell of Chenies and Knight of the Garter in 1539 and Earl of Bedford in 1550. The head of the great house of Russell still retains what had been a monastery, Woburn Abbey.[2]

A figure from the seventeenth century held up as a model to Bertrand was Lord William Russell, who was found guilty of high treason against Charles II and his brother James and was beheaded in 1683. He is regarded as a martyr of religious and political liberty. Young Bertrand was made vividly aware of the injustice of rulers through the *Life of William Lord Russell* (1819), written by Bertrand's grandfather, Lord John Russell.[3]

Lord John Russell, born in 1792 and educated at the University of Edinburgh, combined an eminent parliamentary career with literary efforts. His claim to fame rests on his leadership in the repeal of the Test Acts and in Roman Catholic emancipation. He introduced the reform bill that passed into law in 1832 and served Queen Victoria as liberal prime minister in 1846–52 and 1865–66. He sympathized with the northern cause in the American Civil War and with Garibaldi in the unification of Italy, and he continued the Whig belief in the eventual triumph everywhere of government by elected representatives.[4]

Bertrand Russell's parents, Viscount Amberley and his wife, Katherine, continued the tradition of independence from the establishment, both political and religious. They were ardent followers of John Stuart Mill, whom they chose as Bertrand's "godfather," professed utilitarian ethics, defended birth control, and in one extraordinary case practiced free love. Toward the end of his short life Viscount Amberley published *The Analysis of Religious Belief*. The full account of his persecution can be found in *The Amberley Papers*, two volumes edited by Russell with the help of Patricia Russell in 1937.[5] The story of his father's rebellion against orthodoxy was a secret that had been concealed from young Russell, and he wanted to reveal its full extent. It helps us to understand the psychology of the rebel. Paradoxically, then, Russell's rebellious nature is a family tradition.

Reflections on the Life of a Rebel

Beyond knowledge of the facts of Russell's career given in the Chronology lies the wisdom we may gain from rethinking the decisions of his life and reflecting upon them. When we say wisdom gained by examining a life, Socrates' definition of philosophizing, we mean, as did Russell himself, to recognize the folly of some choices. And when we present Russell as a hero of free thought, we cannot exclude the possibility that he is also a villain. Indeed, it is Russell himself who went to almost unmatched lengths to confess what society judges to be "vices" and to disclaim what are considered "virtues," especially by Christians. Those of us who are fascinated by his character see in him a paradigm of humanity: in intellect, how like a god; in passions, also like a beast.[6]

Bertrand Russell's life is best characterized by his search for wisdom, although he is most known for his extraordinary range of knowledge. This is evident from the essays in *Portraits from Memory*, especially "Knowledge and Wisdom."[7] "Wisdom" is what is most evidently lacking in our age, "a sense of proportion," and more than comprehensiveness, it is "an awareness of the ends of human life." It is the emancipation from "the tyranny of the here and now" and an achievement of impartiality. It is more than a hatred of evil for this is "a kind of bondage to evil." It is an avoidance of fanatical one-sidedness and itself a kind of knowledge that can be taught. The most profitable way to study the life of Russell is to reflect on his career and to join him in reflection on his life and its relation to our own lives.

Although we have many autobiographical accounts of Russell, the most important of family histories is *The Amberley Papers*. The two volumes conclude with a detailed account of the tragic end of Russell's parents, Lord and Lady Amberley. The story of the death of Kate Stanley Russell, nursing her daughter ill with diphtheria from which she also died, and the death of the heartbroken husband when Russell was three years old contradicts any view of the philosopher as heartless in the sense of lacking sympathy. Russell, in this and in other ways, makes an appeal that we understand the source of his faults as well as of his genius. [8]

"My Mental Development" (1943) [9] tells the story of his life from the age of three with the most distinguished liberal parliamentarian of Britain, Lord John Russell, eighty years older than his grandson, and Lady John, the very paradigm of Puritan virtues at the height of the Victorian age (1876). His young Victorian soul is troubled by the problem of "proving by metaphysics various things about the universe that religious feeling made me think important" (*PBR*, 11).

A much fuller account, beginning with Russell's attempt to find conclusive evidence for God, freedom, and immortality, his turn to philosophy at Cambridge, and the subsequent stages of success and failure comes in *My Philosophical Development* (1959). [10] This can be coupled with the analysis of Russell's intellectual friendships published earlier in *Portraits from Memory* (1956). The account of the deep personal concern of Alfred North Whitehead for his young protégé in Trinity College is a great tribute to kindness. [11] Toward the end of his long life Russell published his *Autobiography* in three volumes (1967, 1968, 1969). These are invaluable for understanding the reversal of his pacifist opposition to World War I to support of World War II as a "just war." [12]

Among biographies, the most generally satisfactory for Russell's life and thought down to his eightieth year is Alan Wood's *Bertrand Russell: The Passionate Sceptic*. [13] For a full account of Russell's four marriages and his notable alliances with Lady Ottoline Morrell and Lady Constance Malleson, with details of the later years devoted to preventing a nuclear holocaust, Ronald Clark's *Life of Bertrand Russell* is excellent. [14]

Women may well have the deepest insight into the character of Bertrand Russell. Beatrice Webb gives a vivid portrait of the young man. [15] She admired his detached intellect and his belief "only in

the 'order of thought' and 'the order of things,' " but felt he lacked
sympathy with "other people's emotions." Also, in his pride, he
was "a good hater" who was "almost cruel in his desire to see cruelty
revenged."

The two most poignant accounts of Russell are by his second
wife, Dora Russell, and by their daughter, Katharine Russell Tait.
Both *The Tamarisk Tree* and *My Father, Bertrand Russell* were published in 1975.[16] What one learns from them is that although
conventional people regarded the Russells' marriage, which allowed
other liaisons, as immoral, they entered into it to free love from
exclusive contractual restraints. From their perspective, this is a
higher morality and the acting out of principled theory.[17]

Russell, according to his daughter's fascinating account, took
children very seriously and treated them with respect. She, rereading
all his letters to her, was "overwhelmed by the love and concern
expressed in them." But she felt cheated of her "rightful due of
affection; yet, as far as [she] can observe, this feeling was mistaken.
If there was any failure, it was of communication, not of affection"
(*MFBR,* 196).

Katharine Tait became a devout Anglican and wife of a priest,
and for a time the two served as missionaries in Uganda. On her
last visit with her father she wanted to communicate that belief in
God is not "a lot of nonsense and prejudice [swallowed] for the sake
of a specious peace of mind." But conversation never broke through
into real talk. "There seemed no solution but to look at each other
with love as we drifted apart on our separate rafts of belief" (*MFBR,*
196).

Five Great Rebellions

In interpreting Russell's life it is necessary to recognize that his
decisions are rooted in five great rebellions.

First is his rebellion against obedience to parental authority; as
a child he was subject to his grandmother's Puritan will. It is
therefore understandable that Russell's educational theory is to max-
imize independence and freedom of the individual child.

Second is his rebellion against the identification of evil with
pleasure and sexual pleasure in particular. It is therefore comprehensible that children are to be liberated from feeling shame in their
nakedness and never forbidden to find pleasure in their genital

responses. Finally, since neither male nor female are naturally monogamous, marriage is not to entail exclusive faithfulness to the other person. Each partner in the union has the freedom to make love to others. Since neither is the property of the other, there is no trespassing or using of the other's property. Hence there is no such sin as "adultery," or more precisely, no "adulterous" breach of the marriage covenant, because the covenant has been reformulated without the clause "forsaking all others."

His third rebellion is against patriotic loyalty to the nation state, which carries with it the obligation to fight its enemies. The individual is to reason whether there is a just cause of war, whether there is not an alternative to violent conflict. It follows that good government must protect conscientious objectors to its war efforts.

Fourth is his rebellion against the artificial inequities of birth, particularly the inequality of inherited wealth and status. The alternative is to put wealth of ownership in the hands of the state, by nationalization of industry and business, and to allow equal educational opportunities to all to seek whatever level of accomplishment each is capable of achieving. It follows that socialist experiments must replace bourgeois capitalism with its pseudo-aristocratic basis.

These are four radical revisions of the institutions of child rearing and education, marriage, citizenship, and economic order. These four are united in a fifth, the rebellion against the tradition of basing child rearing and education in reverence for divinely appointed parents, marriage formulated in holy matrimony, loyalty to king and country as forms of loyalty to God, and property as the sacred trust binding the generations.

The modern rebellion is a rebellion against religious tradition, particularly against basing the ultimate justifiction on the command of God. If religious sentiment reinforces all the structures of life against which the modernist Russell is rebelling, and the religious institution of the church stands in the way, then religion becomes the great block to progress, the last of the great evils to be destroyed. This will be fully discussed in the last chapter.

Reflections on Russell's Rebellions

In a deep mood of reflection on his long life, Russell wrote on "Beliefs: Discarded and Retained" and "Hopes: Realized and Disappointed" (*PMem*, 40–49). We, too, can ask for his account of the results of his five rebellions. There is theory on which each is based; there are also now the results of practice. The value of making Russell central to our search for wisdom is that we can study the success and failure of modernity. To what extent has modernity been a mixture of successes and failures?

First, children cannot be granted complete freedom. Russell is very clear about the unwisdom of the new permissiveness. From the experience of running a school, he writes that "many . . . children were cruel and destructive. To let . . . children go free is to establish a reign of terror, in which the strong kept the weak trembling and miserable. A school is like the world: only government can prevent brutal violence" (*Aii*, 225). Russell supervised the three groups, bigs, middles, and smalls. "One of the middles was perpetually ill-treating the smalls, so I asked him why he did it. His answer was: 'The bigs hit me, so I hit the smalls; that's fair.' And he really thought it was" (*Aii*, 226). Russell goes on to give worse examples of hostility and discuss the necessity of discipline, especially where health and cleanliness are concerned. The conclusion is that children turn to destruction when they are bored, and there must be, for happiness, "a certain amount of order and routine" (*Aii*, 227).

Second, what of marriage without "complete fidelity"? Each of the three volumes of *Autobiography* deals with a marriage that ended in divorce (from Alys, *Ai*, 227–30; from Dora, *Aii*, 288; from "Peter" [Patricia], *Aiii*, 5). These relations that ended bitterly do not seem to have changed Russell's mind about marriage, although only the fourth brought what he considered "peace" (*Ai*, "To Edith").

Russell reflected on his second wife's bearing two children by another man. Dora Black quotes her ex-husband's analysis of the failure. According to Russell, "I had tried to preserve that respect for my wife's liberty which I thought my creed enjoined. I found, however, that my capacity for forgiveness and what may be called Christian love was not equal to the demands I was making on it. . . . Anybody else could have told me in advance, but I was blinded by theory" (*Aii*, 288). Russell still cared that his son should be legitimate so that he could inherit the family title; but this meant to Dora only the patriarchal possessiveness so antithetical to her matriarchal relation to children. The relationship is, according to her, earthy and no idealizing of "spiritual insight." And "Christian love and forgiveness had nothing whatever to do with our relations" (*TT*, 248).

Third, what of Russell's civil disobedience? Although Russell had believed early during World War I that opposition might lead to a negotiated peace, this belief faded, and after reflecting on the small minority of "civilized people [who] think it is wicked to kill other people, and . . . do not admit that a state of war puts an end to this ethical command," he decided they have little effect on any war (*Aiii*, 17, cf. 18–19, 28–29). Although pacifists are ineffective, Russell defends them, because "it is good for a community to contain some people who feel the dictates of humanity so strongly that even in wartime they still obey them." It is also "barbarous to compel a man to do acts he considers wicked" (*Aiii*, 17).

Russell confesses the passionate affection he feels for England and recognizes the difficulty of any national to go against his native land. "The judges of Nuremberg believed that the Germans should have committed civil disobedience in the name of decency and humanity. It is little likely to have been their view if they had been judging their own countrymen and not their enemies" (*Aiii*, 18).

Even more complex than Russell's positions on war are his relations to radical politics. Probably the best readable survey is Herbert Gottschalk's *Bertrand Russell: A Life*.[18] Just as clear as Russell's sympathies with moderate, that is, gradual socialism is his hostility to the communism of the Soviet Union. On the former the best is *German Social Democracy*,[19] on the latter, *Bolshevism*,[20] both the editions of 1920 and of 1949, and "Why I Am Not a Communist."[21]

Russell's pacifism of World War I was based on his prophecy that it would be a long war with disastrous consequences for freedom and democratic governments. No one now questions his great wisdom in urging a negotiated peace. Russell's anticommunism was based on a clear perception that the Bolsheviks were motivated by fanatical hatred of the aristocracy and bourgeoisie and by love of power for its own sake, and on their willingness, in the name of a new ideological religion, to suppress freedom. Gottschalk concludes that Russell "possesses an extraordinary prophetic faculty" because "all his prophecies had come true" by World War II, and "all his judgements had proved accurate" (*BRL*, 53, 52).

Russell, having lived decades with the Fabian hope for a gradual transition to socialism, expressed in the later years of his life, when Britain had become a welfare state, the ways in which the new organization had sacrificed freedom for security. The fullest argument came in his Reith Lectures, published as *Authority and the Individual*.[22]

The modern world has not solved the problem of balancing "the degree of social cohesion . . . necessary for survival" with "that degree of individual initiative which is necessary for progress" (*AI*, 1). With survival overemphasized, individual initiative is neglected and man is degraded by "this unswerving devotion to public duty." The argument takes a biological and a historical turn. First, he asserts that "ants and bees do not produce great works of art, or make scientific discoveries, or found religions teaching that all ants are sisters. Their social life, in fact, is mechanical, precise and static" (*AI*, 2). The historical argument is that to the degree that mankind becomes civilized, it must tolerate differences between one man and another, and thus prevent stagnation. The dissenter and nonconformist has the power "to introduce a totally new kind of organization, and to become throughout the world the symbol of a new order" (*AI*, 32). This is a development of the familiar "great man" theory of progress. Russell singles out a "Hebrew prophet, a poet, or a solitary philosopher such as Spinoza," and specifies "great religious and moral innovators [who] have done what lay in their power to make men less cruel towards each other, and less limited in their sympathies" (*AI*, 33, 32). Progress is not made solely through great scientists, which some would have expected Russell to claim, for progress also rests upon "creative emotions." Indeed part of the problem of modern life is to "know too much and feel too little" (*AI*, 35–36).

We have seen that Russell considered twentieth-century life over-organized, and although he cites totalitarian states, he criticizes both capitalistic and socialistic societies. How we could live again in the proud independence of city states of the medieval world and the Renaissance Russell does not tell us (*AI*, 34–35). The theory of good individuals at odds with mediocre society is qualified in two ways. First, there are bad individualists; these are not only criminals but politically ambitious rulers like Genghis Khan, Robespierre, Lenin, and Alexander (*AI*, 32–33). The second qualification is that individualism must not become anarchism. "Too much [liberty] brings chaos" (*AI*, 25).

With regard to the fifth rebellion of Bertrand Russell, against institutional Christianity, there is no final summing up. Probably the most revealing final reflections are contained in the selection of his letters written in response to inquiries during the last twenty years of his life, *Dear Bertrand Russell*.[23]

While many of the restatements of "Why I Am Not a Christian" show no change of position from agnosticism, which is "for all practical purposes" atheism (*DBR*, 6), and Russell is surprised by the old story that the infidel had had a change of heart, there are interesting shifts of emphasis. Russell accepts from Christians the tributes they pay to his virtues: one devout modernist admires his "gentleness and tolerance, and . . . desire for an impartial knowledge and expression of the truth, so utterly and profoundly Christian." Russell's response is that the organized creeds show little of these virtues, and if they show moral courage, they lack "intellectual courage," and these virtues are as much Hindu and Buddhist as Christian (*DBR*, 8–9).

What, then, might be the purpose of Russell's attacks? Probably, in the end, not to destroy but to "liberalize." Why? Because in his lifetime the powerful fanaticisms of the twentieth century have been the secular ideologies. "I have been saying for the last thirty years that the ultimate contest will be between the Vatican and the Kremlin and in that contest I shall side with the Vatican. My ground for preferring the Vatican is . . . that religions, like wines, mature with age." Because Buddhism is older than Christianity, Russell concludes that he should "prefer Buddhism" (*DBR*, 18). Of course, the principle would lead to Judaism over Christianity, and Greek over Latin Christianity, and to Hindu and Chinese traditions in the East, but Russell does not hint at these conclusions.

Although Russell does not agree that education should include religion, he would advise parents to teach children "to conform tacitly to whatever is generally practiced in the way of religion." Parents should be honest about what they do not believe, but they should not set out to make children unbelievers (*DBR*, 19). His reason comes from reflection on his own children. "I did not have my own children baptised and let them know my own attitude towards religion. The result was not exactly as I should have wished. Two of them have become earnest Anglicans" (*DBR*, 20). Although the church did not satisfy his needs, Russell has to grant that unlike the Nazis or Communists, it does "embod[y] the religious needs of populations" (*DBR*, 18).

Russell's Confession of Faith

In the year before his death, when Russell was ninety-six, he published the third volume of the *Autobiography*. We have surveyed his admission of many mistakes in his five great rebellions. Therefore his wisdom shows a humble reaffirmation of the purposes of a noble life.

But beneath all this load of failure I am still conscious of something that I feel to be victory. I may have conceived theoretical truth wrongly, but I was not wrong in thinking that there is such a thing, and that it deserves our allegiance. I may have thought the road to a world of free and happy human beings shorter than it is proving to be, but I was not wrong in thinking that such a world is possible, and that it is worth while to live with a view to bringing it nearer. I have lived in the pursuit of a vision, both personal and social. Personal: to care for what is noble, for what is beautiful, for what is gentle; to allow moments of insight to give wisdom at more mundane times. Social: to see in imagination the society that is to be created, where individuals grow freely, and where hate and greed and envy die because there is nothing to nourish them. These things I believe, and the world, for all its horrors, has left me unshaken. (*Aiii*, 330)

Chapter Two

The Quest for Certainty
in Belief, Knowledge, Truth

Except perhaps for Plato, is there is a more exciting philosophic adventure in history than that of Bertrand Russell? Russell's philosophic journey resembles Plato's in many striking ways: the basic search for excellence both in knowledge and in personal and civic virtues; the attraction to the mathematical represented by Pythagoras; the constant rejection of mere opinion when knowledge can be obtained, expressed as a devotion to truth; a confession of failure in the quest for perfect clarity; and the excruciating struggle with paradoxes. Both are aristocrats in their prophetic fear of vulgar corruption of the tradition in which they were born and bred. Both are intellectually religious, and if Plato represents for us the birth of philosophic theism, Russell represents the anguished failure to find evidence for God. Pythagoras was the philosophic model for applying theory to social and political practice. The harmony discerned in mathematics and astronomy, created in music, is also to be realized by people in community. Russell ends his chapter "Pythagoras" in *A History of Western Philosophy* with a tribute to the Platonic tradition: "an intimate blending of religion and reasoning, of moral aspiration with logical admiration of what is timeless, which comes from Pythagoras, and distinguishes the intellectualized theology of Europe from the more straightforward mysticism of Asia."[1]

We have touched upon the peculiar combination of motives in Russell's Platonic quest: "two very different human impulses, the one urging men towards mysticism, the other urging them towards science."[2] Some interpretations of Russell emphasize only the mathematical, logical, and scientific, and there is more than enough achievement here to count him of first importance, particularly as the author, with A. N. Whitehead, of *Principia Mathematica*. Many accounts of Russell call attention only to the rise of analytic method in the English-speaking philosophic community, but this is not

11

adequate to the origin and goal of his quest for certainty.[3] Almost every personal confession stresses the religious anxiety of the lonely teenager; he had failed to demonstrate human freedom and immortality and finally God.

The unforgettable central question of this philosophic journey dominates from the very first Russell's most successful solution to his quest for the synthesis of mysticism with logic, *Problems of Philosophy* (1912): "Is there any knowledge in the world which is so certain that no reasonable man could doubt it?"[4] Because of the quest for certainty we must consider the nature of belief, the kind of knowledge that is most satisfactory, and the ultimate standard of belief to which knowledge must conform—truth. Russell illustrates what he believes and knows and considers truths, and he reflects on all possible answers to the question: "what do we mean by 'belief,' by 'knowledge,' and by 'truth'?"

Russell's quest, as that of Pythagoras and Plato before him, is the quest of the good as well as of the true. The virtue of the human person is not only intellectual but moral, and as in Plato's *Republic,* the virtues of the perfect society are those of the individual on a large scale. During this longest of philosophic careers, eighty of ninety-seven years documented from the diaries of a teenager through sixty books and more than two thousand articles, we have an unparalleled record of philosophical journeying, often in different directions.

The journeys, Russell confesses, "have been . . . disappointing." Although in this chapter we develop Russell's Pythagorean Platonism, in a later chapter we take account of his "Retreat from Pythagoras" and the nominalistic revolt against the reality of forms. Should we not then say that his philosophic voyage ended in shipwreck? Certainly he stood in awe of "the starry heavens" and "impersonal truth," even if he could not permanently connect human values to a divine principle. Therefore he concludes that "although [his] intellect goes with the humanists, . . . [his] emotions violently rebel."[5]

We shall have to inquire into the exact kind of "emotion" not satisfied by a humanistic (or pragmatic) attitude, even though Russell is indeed a hero of humanists, in the sense of antitheists, and secularists who would make progress by freeing culture of what they regard as the central superstition, belief in God. What is it in what

Spinoza called the "intellectual love of God," in what Russell called "cosmic piety," that so commands his ultimate allegiance?

Four other paradoxes of Russell's quest for certainty lure people into joining this Odysseus on his long odyssey.

The first paradox of Russell's journey centers in the character of what he calls his "mental journey." Is it, as often alleged, analysis or movement from the concrete to the abstract understanding? Or is it the return from the abstract to the concrete? When he is most deeply reflective Russell assures us that his journey is both from the concrete to the abstract and back again. Analysis is abstraction by omitting.

Suppose you study population statistics, the people who make up the items are deprived of almost all the characteristics of real people before they are recorded in the census. But in this case, because the process of abstraction has not proceeded very far, we do not find it very difficult to undo it in imagination. But in the case of mathematical physics, the journey back from the abstract to the concrete is long and arduous, and out of sheer weariness, we are tempted to rest by the way and endow some semi-abstraction with a concrete reality which it cannot justly claim.[6]

Russell's journey is both toward the abstract elements and also *"back from the abstract to the concrete"* (*MPD*, 15, italics added). The youthful author planned two series of books, one going from the concrete to the abstract and the other from the abstract to the concrete.

The second paradox is that although he sought certainty, what fascinates him are the frontiers of knowledge, where all questions are "still open to serious doubt."[7] Had Russell sought certainty exclusively, he should have remained strictly within the sciences.[8] Philosophy is noted for liberating doubt and questions, but not for indubitable answers. To this there must be added a third paradox. What he wanted most to know, God, is what in the end he knows least.[9] In Russell's case, agnosticism, not knowing whether God exists, is a tragedy. And now a fourth paradox.

Along with the view of Russell as a heroic figure, larger than life, there is the view of Russell as a comic character.[10] The most famous characterization of Russell by another writer is "Mr. Appollinax" of T. S. Eliot:[11]

When Mr. Appollinax visited the United States
His laughter tinkled among the teacups.

. . . I heard the beat of centaur's hoofs over the hard turf
As his dry and passionate talk devoured the afternoon.
"He is a charming man"—"But after all what did he mean?"—
"His pointed ears" . . . "He must be unbalanced,"—
"There is something he said that I might have challenged. . . ."[12]

Russell's Theory of Belief

How did Russell's intellectual quest begin? There are two significant anecdotes, one based on grounding beliefs in sense, the
other on appeal to reason. As a boy, when he heard that the earth
was round, he doubted it because he "trust[ed] in the evidence of
the senses." When he sought to find out by digging a hole toward
the antipodes, it was in spite of clerical authority in the person of
Whitehead's father, vicar of the parish.[13] Later on, when, under his
brother Frank's tutelage, he began Euclid, he demanded that axioms
be proved. It seemed irrational merely to assume the truth of common notions, such as equals added to equals are equal, the whole
is greater than the part, and so on.[14] A further difficulty was that
in spite of "a strong bias towards empiricism," trusting in the
evidences of senses, he could not believe that $2 + 2 = 4$ "is an
inductive generalization from experience" (MPD, 11).

Russell personally then had asked the questions of the two parallel
movements of modern philosophy, empiricism and rationalism. Why
did these epistemological questions matter so deeply? He wanted
proof of human immortality and freedom and of God. If there is
order in nature and uniformity of law, how can there be chance?
And is not free will an infringement on divine omnipotence (MPD,
21, 27)?

We learn a very interesting lesson from Russell, which may not
be universal but is at least true of many persons: he does not cease
to believe something without replacing it with something else. A
little illustration is the fact that at Cambridge University Russell
did not simply reject all proofs for the existence of God. He may
have doubted the reasoning from the order of the cosmos to a divine
orderer—the cosmological proof—but he came to accept the ontological proof: God is the perfect being; perfection includes existence; therefore by definition God cannot fail to exist. "Great Scott,"
said Russell, returning from the tobacconist, "the ontological argument is valid!"[15] This turn of reasoning from God's essence, as
defined, to God's existence, shows a strong bias toward rationalism.

Although Russell is called a "passionate skeptic," he was also a "passionate believer." The romantics stirred his emotions, and he shared their love of nature; yet the believer is frustrated by doubt: the way Wordsworth, Carlyle, and Tennyson rested belief in God on feeling seemed to Russell a lack of "intellectual integrity" (*MPD*, 35).

Russell did not begin with a theory of belief: he had struggled with beliefs of many sorts, and we could illustrate the political and historical dogmas of his family's liberalism that were deeply shaken by World War I. He opposed that war with passionate conviction, sufficient to land him twice in court. World War II he could not oppose, for there was no way to reason with Hitler. His opposition to the nuclear armaments of the 1950s and 1960s landed him again in jail. The life of a believer and disbeliever who acts on his convictions is not one sheltered from conflict and danger.

But all this is merely preparation so that we may understand the question, the leading question that runs through all Russell's *Problems of Philosophy:* "Is there any knowledge in the world which is so certain that no reasonable man could doubt it?" (*PP*, 7).

Most ordinary beliefs can be denied without absurdity and do not satisfy the man who asks passionately for certainty. Perhaps the only things that can stand this fierce glare are such elements of knowledge as the certainty of feeling pained when one feels pained, and the self-evidence of knowing that a thing is what it is, *A* is *A* (the law of identity). Such a principle can be used to bind together the bits of knowledge. Between the stones of a structure there is mortar. Just so we go from "today is Tuesday, February 10" to "tomorrow is Wednesday, February 11." "The cement is the relation 'believing' " (*PP*, 128).

Belief contrasts to disbelief, just as knowing contrasts to ignorance and error. By believing we come to know when we discover evidence relative to the belief. When we do not know, we should not believe, and when there is contrary evidence or faulty reasoning, we should disbelieve. When what is believed, the judgment statable as a proposition, corresponds to fact, then the proposition is true. Otherwise, it is false. In more abstract terms, truth and falsehood are "properties of beliefs. . . . hence a world of mere matter, since it would contain no beliefs or statements, would also contain no truth or falsehood" (*PP*, 121). "The truth or falsehood of a belief always depends upon something which lies outside the belief itself" (*PP*, 121). "(1) it allows truth to have an opposite, namely falsehood, (2) makes truth a property of beliefs, but (3) makes it a property wholly dependent upon the relation of the beliefs to outside things" (*PP,* 123). "This may be made clear by examples. Othello believes falsely that Desdemona loves Cassio. We cannot say that this belief consists in a relation to a single object, 'Desdemona's love for Cassio,' for if there were such an object, the belief would be true. There is in fact no such object, and therefore Othello cannot have any relation to such an object. Hence his belief cannot consist in a relation to this object" (*PP,* 124). If the object is not simple or single, it is complex, as Desdemona, loving, and Cassio. "Desdemona and loving and Cassio must all be terms in the relation which subsists when Othello believes that Desdemona loves Cassio. . . . *Believing,* plainly, is not a relation which Othello has to *each* of the three terms concerned, but to *all* of them together: . . . 'believing' is knitting together into one complex whole the four terms Othello, Desdemona, loving, and Cassio" (*PP,* 125–26).

What is crucial to Russell's theory is that belief is mental, thus subjectivity is recognized, but the truth of belief is not mental, for it depends upon fact. Thus objectivity is guarded. We create beliefs and disbeliefs. We cannot create truth or falsehood (*PP,* 129–30).

How is correspondence possible between proposition and fact? In the mental order, "Desdemona" is the subject, expressed in the nominative case; "Cassio" is the object of the relation "loves," Cassio, expressed in the accusative case. In the factual order, there is no complex "Desdemona loving Cassio." It is a question of finding an arrangement between the terms of the complex fact that corresponds to the arrangement between the terms of the complex proposition. We may believe what we please, rearranging terms of discourse into believing that "Caesar murdered Brutus" or "Charles I died in bed." But if in fact Brutus murdered Caesar (*PP,* 126–27) and Charles I died on the scaffold (*OKEW,* 68), such beliefs fail to correspond and are therefore false.

Russell's theory is to account for beliefs that are true and beliefs that are false. But what of the "grades of certainty short of the highest"? There are varying degrees, says Russell, in science. Russell does not explain how the theory can explain these (*OKEW,* 75). How, further, does the theory account for what Russell calls "common beliefs" such as our belief in the external world? That is, we trust that "sensible objects in general persist when we are not perceiving them. Such also is the belief in other people's minds" (*OKEW*, 79). We must therefore ask whether it is adequate to say that beliefs are either true or false. Some are *not* either true or false—they are probably true, likely, or probably false, unlikely. Moreover, we cannot say from Russell's analysis of *Our Knowledge of the External World* how the *belief* corresponds to the *world*. The belief is sometimes acknowledged in the orderliness or regularity of events, but this is no matter of one simple relation or "sense" such as A "loving" B or A "murdered" B. In short, the model of "Othello believes Desdemona loves Cassio" is too simple.

Many other critical problems need to be answered before one can conclude that Russell has perfectly defended the Platonic distinction between knowledge and belief and never confused knowledge with mere true belief. We must proceed to a second great contribution of Plato, the theory of objective forms.

The tragic aspect of Russell's life of belief and disbelief is that he may have ended his passionate life of skepticism with dogmatic refusal to listen to the case for President Johnson when he was condemned by Russell as a war criminal.[16]

Knowledge of Universals

When we analyse such a statement as "Othello believes. . . ," called the "multiple-relation theory of belief," we are using different kinds of terms. "Othello" names a unique individual, but "believes" is general. We may refer to *this* horse, a particular individual in space and time with particular qualities. Or we may refer to *any* member of the general kind, the genus horse, referred to by Plato and Aristotle and many medieval followers as "horseness." We commonly say that the former, particulars, exist, but the latter is a matter of essence. Russell is true to the classical tradition in saying that everything we know is either a particular or a universal. The problem from Plato is whether the universal (general kind or form or essence) is real apart from the exemplifications. The problem from Aristotle is whether horseness, for example, is real only in the particulars, horses.

Sometimes Russell uses cats as examples and writes "CAT" to mean the real universal. The problem dominated medieval philosophy and, thanks to Russell more than to any other modern philosopher, has become again one of the liveliest issues. Although most great British philosophers in the succession of William of Occam, Hobbes, Locke, Berkeley, Hume, J. S. Mill, all rejected real universals, Russell, like Whitehead, sided with Plato and Aristotle. Russell's philosophy of universals, becoming explicit first in 1903, was an extreme Platonism, a realism completely at odds with the tradition of Occam and the whole great nominalist tradition. They are collectively known as nominalists because they say the universal is only in the *nomen,* or name, the word "cat" in contrast to cats or CAT.

The debate between extreme realists (or Platonists) and nominalists is marred by hostility, with each side considering the other foolish. It is common to find the arguments of the opponent regarded as a mere trick or expression of a misguided sense of reality. The enormous value of studying the succession of books and essays from Russell is that he is commonly used as the leading Platonist because of his chapters "The World of Universals" and "Our Knowledge of Universals" in *Problems of Philosophy* (1912) as well as the famous address "On the Relations of Universals and Particulars."[17] But he is also regarded as the triumphant hero of nominalism because, in outgrowing the most extreme Platonism, he devised techniques of substituting a description for a name, use of a propositional function for a proposition, and a theory of types. Particularly he set out to overcome the superstition that when we name a "golden mountain," even to say that "there is no golden mountain," that there must *be* something that isn't! (In the next chapter, on the logic of relations, we will examine what these techniques are.) Because Russell brought common sense to the debate, he is even regarded as having had a phase of moderate Aristotelian realism. Although this is most debatable, Russell may well have explored from the inside all the possible solutions.[18]

Although each of us is little likely to take the position that "only universals are real" or "only particulars are real" or "both universals and particulars are real," we can explore each of the possibilities through reading the contributions of Russell. The culmination is in an illuminating chapter "Universals and Particulars and Names" in *My Philosophic Development,* which begins with a fable full of irony (*MPD,* 116–17). Russell frequently argues realism against nominalism and nominalism against realism, and the way to enjoy this literature is as dialogues in which Russell, as Plato, takes each side successively. But, lest this suggest that Russell is merely playing alternate roles or, worse, insincerely mocking those who are over-serious, the issue is one on which the whole nature of knowledge hangs. Deep earnestness is no excuse for neglecting humor. Arguing for moderate realism against the linguistic analysts who followed Wittgenstein, Russell writes with charm: "It is not an altogether pleasant experience to find oneself regarded as antiquated after having been, for a time, in the fashion" (*MPD*, 159). Arguing against a more extreme realism than he could honestly continue, he writes: "My self of forty years is grateful for the doughty blows he [a defender of Russell's older position] strikes in defence of the poor ghost, but my self of the present day is compelled to undertake the parrying of those blows."[19]

If there is one most serious center holding together the internal dialogue of the Platonist and the nominalist, it is to discover the truth about reality, the world, or what there is. He summed it up: "The sole point . . . is that the question of 'universals' is not merely one of words, but one which arises through the attempt to state facts" (*MPD*, 117).

Russell had not always believed we must make a sharp distinction between particulars and universals. Part of the appeal of Hegel, to whose system Russell was more or less attached during the 1890s, was his overcoming this and every other dualism. Is there an "identity in difference"? "Socrates is particular"; mortal "is universal. Therefore . . . since Socrates is mortal, it follows that the particular is the universal." What is the fallacy? A stupid unintentional neglect of the difference between the "is" of predication with the "is" of identity has tricked us into the self-contradiction of saying "the particular is the universal."[20]

The revolt against idealism carried Russell to an extreme realism. In the tradition of mathematicians, God created the natural numbers; and so Platonic was Russell that he committed himself to the reality of classes and logical constants (such as "or" and "not"). "Whatever may be an object of thought, or may occur in any true or false proposition, or can be counted as *one,* I call a *term. . . .* A man, a moment, a number, a class, a relation, a chimaera, or anything else that can be mentioned, is sure to be a term; and to deny that such and such a thing is a term must always be false."[21]

The main thrust of the argument is that if mathematics is the truest science, and to be true means to correspond to reality, then there must be a realm of mathematicals. In the next section we shall examine Russell's steadfast devotion to truth. To consider numbers as all fictitious would then be self-betrayal. This is one way to interpret the emotional satisfaction he found in contemplation of the world of universals. The other motive is that the mathematician-metaphysician loves the perfection of order more than life and thereby gains "greatness of soul." These aspects of religious Platonism, best expressed in *Problems of Philosophy,* should not blind us to the step-by-step consideration of the nominalist alternative. Dialectically, by uncovering error after error in nominalism, Russell has confidently established the inescapable truth of Platonism, that there is a realm of forms to which intellect gives us access, a realm other than the world of particulars with which our senses acquaint us. This is, he assures us, the contrast between concepts and percepts, and the eternal against the temporal, a heaven against a world of things in space.

A great difficulty for Russell, as for Whitehead, in traditional realism is that it is largely moderate, or Aristotelian, realism. The ontology was linked with the logic of subject and predicate. That is, in the case of "Socrates is mortal," the subject "Socrates" refers to a substance, and the predicate "mortal" also requires a substance of higher order, MORTALITY. Socrates can be mortal because the attribute qualifies the substance. Plato would say that the individual participates in real MORTALITY. Now if the logic of relations is devised as it was by Whitehead and Russell to replace the old logic of subject and predicate, and also to reject the ontology of substance and attribute, how is it possible for them to be realists? There is a further difficulty, particularly for Russell, in that the whole argument, logic and ontology, may be linguistic only. Both may be based on the linguistic paradigm of a simple sentence made of a noun and adjective. Our grammar is Indo-European, and it sounds like a correct paradigm to say that "the horse is white." But there are many divergent grammars.

The same analysis of language that can be used to destroy the old metaphysics can however be used to re-create a new metaphysics. Do but examine language, Russell invites us, and it will quickly be observed that all the parts of speech are general except proper nouns and a few curious pronouns like "this" and "that," along with "here" and "now" used ambiguously to refer to some particulars. In philosophy of language Russell invented the problem of "minimum vocabularies," meaning by that "one in which no word can be defined in terms of another." Thereby all definitions are theoretically superfluous. The question is, can the vocabulary of arithmetic be reduced, as Peano claimed, to three terms?

Take, as one of the most important examples, the traditional problem of universals. It seems fairly certain that no vocabulary can dispense wholly with words that are more or less of the sort called "universals." These words, it is true, need never occur as nouns; they may occur only as adjectives or verbs. Probably we could be content with only one such word, the word "similar," and we should never need the word "similarity." But the fact that we need the word "similar" indicates some fact about the world, and not only about language. What fact it indicates about the world, I do not know. [22]

Just as relations are necessary to the solution of the problem of how a belief can be true to fact (the multiple relation theory in the last section), so relations become the prime example of universals, replacing substances and attributes. The new logic of relations corresponds to a grammar in which prepositions are as important as nouns and adjectives. Verbs and adverbs could just as well be selected from language to illustrate universals.

Given the expression of universals through verbs, adverbs, prepositions, adjectives, and common nouns, the linguistic argument for universals is given: "Every complete sentence must contain at least one word which stands for a universal" (*PP*, 52).

In what sense does such a preposition as "in" stand for a real relation IN? Unless this question can be satisfied, the demonstration fails. If relations were all mental and not real apart from our acts of comparison, the notion of a real relation would indeed be fantastic. One can easily mock the realist's position by asking whether, among things in his world, such as brown tables, he has also a large, brown IN? If the realist is a logician, said Russell himself, he might expect in the heaven which is rationality deserved, to encounter the real IN in good logical company with IF . . . THEN, AND, OR, NOT, SOME, and ALL!

If IN is real, is it mental or physical? Neither, answers Russell. It is an entity "which [does] not, properly speaking, *exist*."

Suppose, for instance, that I am in my room. I exist, and my room exists; but does "in" exist? Yet obviously the word "in" has a meaning, it denotes a relation which holds between me and my room. This relation is something, although we cannot say that it exists *in the same sense* in which I and my room exist. (*PP*, 90)

It cannot be that all relations are the work of the mind, over against a world totally without relations.

It seems plain that it is not thought which produces the truth of the proposition "I am in my room." It may be true [of the proposition] that an earwig [we should say "bug"] is in my room, even if neither I nor the earwig nor any one else is aware of this truth; for this truth concerns only the earwig and the room. . . . Thus relations . . . must be placed in a world which is neither mental nor physical. (*PP*, 90)

What else can be said of universals? Like Plato's forms, such as JUSTICE, they are apprehended by the mind. Therefore those philosophers who think that all knowledge must come through the senses cut themselves off from universals, unless from the world with which the senses acquaint us, we can somehow abstract universals. The mind leaving out the nonessential must know what is essential, and therefore acquaintance with universals themselves is presupposed. Russell has therefore a good reason for appealing to Plato rather than to Aristotle. Abstraction had failed in Locke and his empiricist successors to gain any real universals (*PP*, 95). The universal, says Russell, "not being particular, . . . cannot itself exist in the world of sense." It can be said to *subsist*. "Moreover it is not fleeting or changeable like the things of sense: it is eternally itself, immutable and indestructible" (*PP*, 92).

If universals are eternal, in contrast to particulars that are temporal, what is the relationship between the two worlds? Russell agrees with Plato on a surprising number of points. The particulars share in the universals, and "a *universal* will be anything which may be shared by many particulars" as just things share in JUSTICE (*PP*, 93). Though the conclusion passes into mystical illumination, and the Platonist says he *sees* the ideas in heaven, yet the theory is based on logical reasoning (*PP*, 92). Thus Russell's quest for the union of mysticism and logic appears satisfied.

The position survives encounter with the nominalist attempt to reduce all universals to particulars. The nominalist strategy is to select "some particular triangle, and to say that if that is called 'triangle,' then this word can be used of another particular." But which other can also be called by this name? One that resembles the first and has "the right sort of resemblance." But since there are many pairs of particular shapes, "it will be useless to say that there is a different resemblance for each pair." Then we should have to say that resemblances resemble each other! Then the nominalist is forced to admit one universal. If he has allowed one, he has no sound argument against others (*PP*, 96). Sometimes Russell added "all the others," but this is claim to more than can be demonstrated.

The results can be obtained from a correct analysis of complexes. Consider, Russell asks us, the relation between two places, say, "Atlanta is to the north of Tampa." That relation would be (in the sense of "subsist") even if we did not know it, because there is that fact. It was true before we came to it, and the universal "north of" is a relation between the places independent of our thinking (*PP*, 97–99). Sometimes we may apprehend the relation within a single datum of sense. In much the same way that we apprehended similar things, so we see on a page, one part above another, to the left of, and so on. In temporal experience as in spatial, these are relations. Corresponding to the spatial relations is the time relation of before and after as we remember events. Thus we are acquainted with universals and have immediate knowledge of them (*PP*, 101–3).

Russell's theory is important as a basis of exact knowledge and also serves to guide wisdom as to what is to be loved, perfection. Russell's world of universals is never the Good, the True, and the Beautiful, or a hierarchy from the mathematicals up to the Good, and emphatically not, as with Augustinians, the Mind of God. Yet perfection makes a claim upon the person who contemplates this world. No paraphrase can do justice to Russell's own words:

The world of universals, therefore, may also be described as the world of being. The world of being is unchangeable, rigid, exact, delightful to the mathematician, the logician, the builder of metaphysical systems, and all who love perfection more than life. The world of existence is fleeting, vague, without sharp boundaries, without any clear plan or arrangement, but it contains all thoughts and feelings, all the data of sense, and all physical objects, everything that can do either good or harm, everything that makes any difference to the value of life and the world. According to our temperaments, we shall prefer the contemplation of the one or of the other. The one we do not prefer will probably seem to us a pale shadow of the one we prefer, and hardly worthy to be regarded as in any sense real. But the truth is that both have the same claim on our impartial attention, both are real, and both are important to the metaphysician.

Indeed no sooner have we distinguished the two worlds than it becomes necessary to consider their relations. (*PP*, 100)

It is sometimes alleged that Russell rejected Platonic realism. Certainly, although he praised contemplation, there was never again, after 1912, quite the world of perfect forms. Wittgenstein's reduction of mathematics to tautology destroyed, to Russell's pain, part of the logical argument for the intellectual grasp of a priori truths. Among the relations of the structure of the world of universals there could not then be the purely "logical words . . . or . . . not . . . some . . . all" (*MPD*, 169). But much worse, it deprived him of real perfection worthy of worship.

There is a great difficulty with the dualism of two worlds. It is in this temporal world that "Alexander *preceded* Caesar," and the "other" eternal world has no such temporal relation. Russell grants that there is no such thing called "preceding." Yet the realism rests on the supposition that "a relation-word must point to something extralinguistic," but this must be a fact of this world (*MPD*, 174).

"What Is Truth?"

Important as are belief and knowledge of universals in Russell's quest for certainty, the purpose of the quest is to attain truth, and truth is the norm by which all beliefs and kinds of knowledge are judged and graded. Pilate's question, "What is truth?" (John 18:38) perplexed Russell and seemed to him "the fundamental question."[23] One thing is sure, and this is Russell's continuing devotion to truth. The very variety of differing theoretical interpretations, at least a dozen major chapters and articles over a sixty-year period, is evidence of the complexity and difficulty encountered in saying what truth means.

The first and important point about truth, which Russell himself neglects as too obvious and nearly all interpreters pass over as a truism, is that devotion to truth springs from ranking truthfulness as among the highest virtues, and certainly one that is necessary to be a good person. In the epilogue to *Wisdom of the West*, there is a reaffirmation of Pythagoras: "The pursuit of truth which is acknowledged as independent of the seeker . . . has been . . . the ethical driving force behind the scientific movement."[24] Even if a person is not a scientist, "the pursuit of truth is a good thing" and requires respect for others' opinions and their freedom. This conviction explains Russell's devotion to his friend G. E. Moore who swayed him away from idealism toward realism: "Moore was the most truthful man that I have ever known, and his obvious integrity was such that his lack of polite evasion gave no offence."[25]

In the earliest complete realism of Russell, according to which there are propositions, both true and false, the characteristics of being true or being false are inherent in the propositions. These attributes are indefinable, but we know them as surely and as directly as we know colors. "Some propositions are true and some propositions false just as some roses are red and some white."[26] Perhaps we can understand such a theory if we recall that Russell had recently written his first (and as it turned out only) study of another philosopher's system, that of Leibniz, and that the logical conception of truth is that a predicate is contained in a subject as 2 + 2 is contained in 4. Indeed, according to *Principles of Mathematics*, a true proposition contains its own truth as an element.[27] But it is, however simple, odd to extend this to the belief that "Caesar died" without resting the truth upon something external to, and independent of, the belief, namely Caesar's dying. Above, we examined the theory of 1912 that requires the fact to which the proposition must correspond. Although the move from monism to dualism means greater complexity, it responds to a distinction most of us care to make: it is one thing for a proposition to be asserted, and quite another for the proposition to be true. If " true" meant only "asserted," then no one could be in error because he or she asserted a proposition that is false to fact.

During the first decade of the present century the most central philosophic decision was whether to hold the coherence theory of truth with the idealists or the pragmatic theory with the pragmatists, or to revive the correspondence theory with the realists. Russell became the most outspoken polemicist against the idealist position to which he had subscribed in the 1890s; but he was even more vigorous particularly against the American pragmatists William James and John Dewey. One especially nasty slur, "Transatlantic 'Truth' " (1908), reprinted in 1910 in *Philosophical Essays,* was resented deeply by James who referred to Russell as an "ass"; American pragmatists still commonly feel that Russell was unfair as well as dogmatically blind to any alternative to his realism.

What was the attraction of coherence? The relationship to be judged was the logical one between judgments (or beliefs) so that we do not have the problem of knowing a fact as it is in itself. The idealist or monist deplores the fragmentation that leads to the paradox of a partial report that can be used to deceive. Each belief, "stated in all its fullness and without illegitimate abstraction, turns out to be the whole truth about the universe" (*MPD*, 130). Russell's objection is essentially simple; the consequence is that "all finite truth is only partially true." If there is a proposition, say, that "Russell murdered Whitehead," that is false; then whether it is partial is irrelevant (*MPD*, 131).

Russell took James's most popular characterization of truth as that which it pays to believe. Russell ignored the qualification that the decision whether to act could not be made with regard to a future fact, when the results of the act can occur in the future only if one acts.

More than fifty years after the 1908 attack on James, Russell was still aiming his big guns on the false theory of truth. James had written that the truth is what "pays." The nub of Russell's objection is this. If the pragmatist "paying" means the effects of a belief, then we must also judge the effects of these effects. Hence we can never know, because of this "endless regress," whether any belief is true (*MPD*, 131–32). Yet another consequence is relativism to the point of absurd contradiction. Therefore any proposition is both true and false. Pragmatists have, in his estimation, no comprehension that the either-or of the law of contradiction rests on factual reality. What Russell means is that either Bacon wrote *Hamlet* or Shakespeare wrote *Hamlet*. The meaning of the belief that Bacon was the author is whether it does or does not refer to fact (*MPD*, 134).

Pragmatism is then not only logically absurd, unrealistic, and undermining of a principle on which science is based but also immoral and irresponsible socially and politically. The unkindest cut of all is that, according to Russell, to follow American pragmatism would mean that a will to success would lead a pragmatic German just before World War II to be a Nazi. Belief would then be geared into government policy and police power (*MPD*, 132).

Although the strongest motive in James's pragmatic theory of truth was in defense of religious faith, and the predecessor here was Pascal's famous wager, Russell sides with the pope's condemnation. Why can Russell side with official Catholic teaching? Because he is, like the medievals such as St. Thomas Aquinas, a realist. Whether

God is or not depends upon whether there is a "being, outside space and time, who wisely orders the cosmos." Pragmatism is a way of trying to evade a metaphysical question (*MPD,* 134–35).

Truth is an absolute, argues Russell, and if relativized it spells the loss of human integrity, which rests upon securing something higher than man as an object of reverence. It would not be unfair to say that pragmatism for Russell, in theological terms, was a "damnable heresy." Russell is antipragmatist because he is of the opposite temperament to humanism: he is aware of "non-human limitations to human power" and does not "find Man an adequate object of . . . worship"; to one so minded, "the pragmatist's world will seem narrow and petty, robbing life of all that gives it value, and making Man himself smaller by depriving the universe which he contemplates of all its splendor" (*MPD,* 133, quoted from *PE*). When Russell rebuked Dewey, it was the same attack on humanism as in *Problems of Philosophy:* the lack of "cosmic piety."[28]

There are many technical changes in successive statements over 50 years, and a detailed account, such as A. J. Ayer's, shows that the relation between proposition and fact varies with the changes in the theory of belief and knowledge.[29] In the later Russell it is "sentences" rather than "propositions," and finally "beliefs" rather than "sentences." "True" comes to mean fulfilling the expectations of the believer, and this behaviorist interpretation gave comfort to some pragmatists that Russell had finally comprehended their point. There is, however, according to realism, always a fact, even though unknown, that is beyond the believer and whatever he does, and only by virtue of this can the belief be true (*IMT,* chap. 17, 236–46).

In the quarrel with the idealists over coherence, Russell did not deny that beliefs and propositions may be tested by coherence with other beliefs and propositions. But if the others are only coherent, then we might have only coherent falsehood. Somewhere the testing of beliefs must be anchored in fact, and this means a belief related somehow to what is.

Russell did not deny that consequences of acting are important tests. For example, the Ninth Commandment of his Liberal Decalogue says, "Be scrupulously truthful, even if the truth is inconvenient, for it is more inconvenient when you try to conceal it."[30] A technical definition of truth fails to do what the pragmatists did, that is, throw "light upon our preference for true beliefs rather than false ones."[31] "This preference is only explicable by taking account of the causal efficacy of beliefs, and the greater appropriateness of the responses resulting from true beliefs. But appropriateness depends upon purpose, and purpose thus becomes a vital part of theory of knowledge."[32]

The ultimate commitment to truth can be liberating as well as binding. Russell was free to reconsider his reading of James, and in *Sceptical Essays* he recognized that James's attention was to beliefs "which are incapable of being verified by any facts that come within our experience."[33] Yet in the same book Russell restates the very argument that James found so inapplicable to vital decisions: "that it is undesirable to believe a proposition when there is no ground whatever for supposing it true" (*SE*, 11).

Not only did Russell constantly alter his theories of truth; at any one period of development we can find him taking both sides to illuminate the problem in a dialectical way.

We have referred to Russell's quest for certainty as a quest for truth, and characterized this as quest for an absolute, to which he encouraged devotion. Yet he resisted the awe before Truth as though this were, as for Mohandas Gandhi, a way of approaching God. "There is," writes Russell sarcastically, "a tendency to use 'truth' with a big T in the grand sense, as something noble and splendid and worthy of adoration."[34] The truth about Truth is that it cannot be a substance or something independently real or even an essence of God. The collective noun means nothing more than a class of beliefs, sentences, and propositions to which in speech or writing we apply the adjective "true." Then, apart from so designating such beliefs, sentences, and propositions, there is nothing (*Ph*, 254–55).

Yet during the same year, 1926, in *Education and the Good Life*, Russell was preaching devotion to truth in the sense of truthfulness, as in G. E. Moore, his friend of unimpeachable integrity. "Untruthfulness, as a practice, is almost always a product of fear. The child brought up without fear will be truthful, not in virtue of a moral effort, but because it will never occur to him to be otherwise."[35] If Truth is humbug, so is deceit, and truthfulness is presented as not only intrinsically good but verifiably constructive of good relations between persons: "Rigid truthfulness in adults towards children is, of course, absolutely indispensable if children are not to learn lying. Parents who teach that lying is a sin, and who nevertheless are known by their children to lie, naturally lose all moral authority. The idea of speaking the truth to children is entirely novel; hardly anybody did it before the present generation. I greatly doubt whether Eve told Cain and Abel the truth about apples; I am convinced that she told them she had never eaten anything that wasn't good for her" (*EGL,* 160–61).

The quest for certainty is then in the end not divorced from moral belief. Whether there is moral knowledge and moral truth remains to be discussed in the chapter on social ethics, "Rational Man and Irrational Society" (chapter 7).

Chapter Three

The New Logic of Relations: The Order of Thought and the Order of Things

To Russell more than to any other philosopher we owe the new logic variously called symbolic logic, mathematical logic, but better, the logic of relations. There are many aspects of the new logic, but philosophically what Russell selects as important is the theory of order. "The theory of order is one of the most essential parts of Logic."[1] What must be done is to show how because of relation "order" can be defined. Order, the supreme belief of mankind since the myths of the gods bringing order out of chaos, becomes with the new logic a precisely defined term. Order is so basic to mathematics that mathematics itself is redefined as the "science of order." Because of innumerable applications of the order we think in our symbols to the real events of our environment, we have available a new way of comprehending nature. Cosmos or nature takes on new meaning when we can state in more subtle ways the various orders of space-time and inquire into the basis of our beliefs about the causal order. Can we know the regularities or laws of nature from observation of particular events? There is the new logic, as an organon (Greek for "tool," extended to method, as Aristotle's logic) to replace Bacon's *novum organum* of empirical observation, as Bacon had attempted to replace Aristotle's syllogistic logic. Yet the ways to comprehend nature as a causal order and to explain our knowledge of nature's laws remain two of the mysteries in Russell's philosophy.

The problem that challenges us is whether Russell fulfilled the dream of Leibniz, that there can be what he called a "universal characteristic." That is, can we so formulate the axioms and provide procedures that every problem can be so symbolized that never again need people fall into disagreement? They will, prophesied Leibniz, simply sit down together and say, "Let us calculate."[2] The deeper question, beyond Russell's advances, is can there be any such method?

Russell has provided several philosophic and literary guides to his achievement of the logic of relations. The pages and pages of notation in *Principia Mathematica,* including many pages designed finally to prove that $2 + 2 = 4$ is not likely to attract many readers.[3] Russell used to say that only six people had read the later parts of the book; three were Poles, subsequently liquidated by Hitler. The reader can go to the selections in *The Basic Writings* (145–74),[4] which include the preface, the introduction, the introduction to the second edition, and various summaries. There is also a set of lively chapters on "Logical Technique in Mathematics," along with both philosophic and mathematical aspects of *Principia Mathematica* in *My Philosophical Development.*[5] But the best plan is to read *Introduction to Mathematical Philosophy.*[6] The inspiration of the whole development comes in an article, which has unfortunately been neglected since its publication in *Mind* in 1901, that is central to this chapter, "On the Notion of Order."[7] Coming just after the book on Leibniz, who never achieved a systematic treatise stating his system, this essay shows how Russell at this period hoped to find a unifying principle of structure in the cosmos. This hope deserves to be pursued.

Is it possible that theory of order could be shown to be as exciting an adventure as the quest for certainty? Russell puts his mathematical philosophy in the same metaphorical context of a journey, and one "pursued in either of two opposite directions" (*IMP,* 1). This paradox of mathematics, moving by analysis toward "greater and greater abstractness" and also constructively toward "gradually increasing complexity," should not puzzle us. The motivation of two series of books, toward the furthermost abstraction and converging with the series toward the most concrete, is a parallel. The adventure of a philosophy of mathematics is to go in two directions at once, far from the middle in which we find ourselves. From the familiar we journey backward toward the logically simple, using, as it were, a microscope. But this opens up, as does a telescope, "fresh lines of advance" in whole new areas (*IMP,* 2).

How can we make sense of going forward by going backward? To comprehend this, Russell recalls the founder of philosophy and mathematics in our Hellenic tradition, Pythagoras. As he went back to numbers, so Russell goes even further back, to relations. This requires proof that from relations we can deduce numbers. To put the situation as stages of exploration, what was once called "ultimate" has not remained ultimate; it was ony the furthest a given philosopher in his circumstances could reach.

There are barriers to exploration, as there are ranges of mountains through which an adventurer cannot penetrate. Leibniz, for example, although he glimpsed the possibility of a philosophical calculus, was held back by certain Aristotelian presuppositions, such as the analysis of every proposition as the affirmation or denial of a predicate of a subject. The relational three-term proposition was ruled out. What could be more logical than this: if A is larger than B, and B is larger than C, then A is larger than C? From this perspective Kant's belief in the absoluteness of syllogistic logic was reactionary, even though relation became far more important in his categories than it had been in Aristotle's. Hegel's organic cosmos asserted that all events are interrelated, such that no aspect can be changed without altering the whole; his follower Bradley held that all relations are internal. They had constructed a barrier to the notion of independent events between which relations may be external. Indeed, many relations, because the terms in fact are diverse, must be real and external.[8]

Russell presents himself as a guide who can lead beyond the achievements of Pythagoras and Aristotle, Leibniz and Kant, Hegel and Bradley. Also Peano's postulate of three primitive ideas (zero, number, and successor) and five propositions (such as zero is the number that is not successor to any number), and his derivation of the natural numbers (1, 2, 3) does not satisfy Russell. "Number" itself must be defined, and if defined, it is not primitive, but derived from something else. Briefly, this can be similarity of classes, such as pairs of objects. If 2 is the number of the class of pairs, then generally *"A number is anything which is the number of some class"* (*IMP*, 19). Earlier, we recall, in considering the relation between particulars, that which could not be reduced to them was similarity, the primitive universal from which all the others can be derived.

Whitehead and Russell had made so much progress by journeying backward that they could well afford to grant later that others had progressed beyond *Principia Mathematica*. The introduction to the second edition (1925) cited such improvements that would require a complete rewriting (*BW*, 172–74).

Relations and Series

It was commonplace in medieval philosophy that if this is above that, then that is below this, or if this happened earlier than that, then that happened later than this. These are abstracted into the form aRb, symbolizing the terms by a and b, the relation by R, and the converse relation, a "below" in contrast to "above," or "later" in relation to "earlier," by $\breve{R}$. St. Thomas Aquinas had defined "order" by "relation" and used examples of what Russell called "asymmetry." In the case of symmetry, aRb implies bRa, when R is "similar to," or "equal to," or in the case of family relations "spouse of." The asymmetrical family relation, very common among Russell's examples, are "wife of" or "husband of." These require both R and $\breve{R}$, one the converse of the other. The asymmetrical relationship has *sense,* "it proceeds, so to speak, *from* one to the other" and is the source of series and order.[9]

We might begin with "spouse" and define "wife" as being "female spouse" and "husband" as "male spouse." Or we could begin "wife" and "husband," and combine them into "wife or husband" and derive "spouse." To put the matter more generally, should we begin with symmetry and derive asymmetry by specification, or begin with asymmetry and derive symmetry by combination? The traditional metaphysics of being began with the extreme symmetry of self-identity, where a single term is said to be itself, as in identity, where R stands for "is identical with," "being is, or has being," or in symbols aRa. There may be a deeper reason than Russell admits in *Principles of Mathematics,* and that is that process as temporal flow is asymmetrical, or has "sense," and that the logic of relations beginning with asymmetry corresponds in metaphysics to asserting the priority of becoming to being. Timeless constancy is scarcely the ground of change. *Introduction to Mathematical Philosophy* does not go so far, but is emphatic in saying that "asymmetrical relations are . . . the most characteristically relational of relations, and the most important to the philosopher who wishes to study the ultimate logical nature of relations" (*IMP*, 45). Given the priority of world order to language, this must mean that asymmetrical structure of the world, the time order of events, is more fundamental than the spatial orders. "We can of course obtain a symmetrical relation by adding together the given relation and its converse" as *"greater or less,"* symbolized $\gtrless$. This means "unequal," a symmetrical relation.

"But we cannot pass back from this symmetrical relation to the original asymmetrical relation except by the help of some asymmetrical relation" (*IMP*, 43–44).

Does asymmetry alone in an ancestor relation generate a series? From the emphasis on the successor relation, say, greater than by one, one might use as an example of series, 1, 2, 3, and so on, and answer yes. But although "greater than," the unqualified relation, holds both between 1 and 2 and between 2 and 3, there is yet another relation when there are three such terms. When between *a* and *b* and between *b* and *c* there is a relation holding also between *a* and *c,* we have the relation called "transitivity." Above we used the example of "greater than." It is indeed closely related to asymmetry when we consider only the relation of the natural numbers. But it is independent of asymmetry because, in the symmetrical relation of "equal to," when *a* = *b* and *b* = *c*, then *a* = *c*. Things equal to the same thing do equal each other. *a* = *b, b* = *c, a* = *c* is not a serial ordering because it is just as true that *a* = *c, c* = *b, ∴ a* = *b,* and indeed it has no "sense" because in the case of things equal to each other, they can be placed in all possible sequences. One is just as true as another and therefore logically equivalent.

There is yet another significant defining and essential factor in a series. This is stated: when we choose any two terms from the field ordered by *R,* calling them *x* and *y,* it must be that *xRy* or *yRx*. This is called "connexity." Connexity extends to all members of a set what obtains necessarily to *x, y, z,* related by asymmetry and transitivity, and it is anything but trivial. Because of this characteristic of a serial order, there must be one and only one place where a term can occur. This is true no matter how many terms there are in the series. Therefore, whether there are 15 million alphabetized cards, as in the Library of Congress now, or 15 billion, as there surely will be at some future time if acquisition and cataloguing continues, there is one and only one place where any given item (an index card) can occur. This may seem to be going from the definition of the concept to the application and use, and stressing the "advances into application" more than the "backwards journey." Indeed that is so, but the excitement of Russell's exposition of relations and series is the combination of movement back with movement forward.

Earlier we said that Russell went back behind "numbers," which were ultimate in Pythagoras's analysis, to "relations." How exactly does anyone deduce numbers from relations? This is a matter of logical technique, but the discovery, made by Russell in 1900 after meeting with Peano and reading his work, is retold in *My Philosophical Development* as the unique "logical honeymoon" of Russell's life (*MPD*, 75).

Number, Infinity, and Continuity

Russell's contribution to the logic of relations can be appreciated through his early philosophy of space. This is found in a dissertation, *An Essay on the Foundations of Geometry* (1897),[10] which he wrote to secure a fellowship at Trinity College. The problem may be stated: can space be external to us, that is, to our bodies, and can spatial relations be external to things, unless space itself, empty space, is real (*EFG*, 182)? The alternative to absolute space is relational space, and if relational, is not space subjective, internal to us, that is, what our minds supply? And how can we approach Euclidian space and analyze the three dimensions, or as the relativity theory has it, four, in terms of relations and order without concluding that the world, space, and time also are our constructions (*EFG*, 183)? The ground on which we must believe in the then incredible external relations is that in sense perception we are presented with a *This* that is "fragmentary and yet necessarily complex" (*EFG*, 183). By this he seems to mean that we can always compare the perception of *This* with another perception, which we might call a *That* (*EFG*, 185). And so also with regard to events in time, there is a continuity, and present can always be contrasted to past and future. How, then, can we establish "a multiplicity of real things"? A temporal diversity would be of succession, whereas a spatial diversity might be only "simultaneously existing things." The complexity must be "a reference beyond itself" (*EFG*, 186). The conclusion is that "space is given only as spatial order; that spatial relations, being given, appear as more than mere relations." Empty space, as more than "logical possibility of space-relations" is then unnecessary (*EFG*, 194). Therefore, there can be real relations without absolute space (and time). This "spatial order" is not "unbounded extension and infinite divisibility," and the antinomies of the infinite, which we need to examine, are avoided (*EFG*, 195). "Empty space is [merely] a name for the logical possibilities of spatial relations" (*EFG,* 197). The theory allows for both unity and diversity; hence there is reference of the terms to each other, a ground for interaction that Leibniz's theory lacked (*EFG,* 198). Space is not merely quantitative; hence we are not led to assimilate geometry to arithmetic or to attempt to deduce geometry from algebra (*EFG,* 199–200). Further room is allowed, on empirical grounds, to allow non-Euclidian space. As far as our observations are concerned, "two straight lines can never enclose a space" (the axiom of three dimensions); parallel lines never meet (the axiom of parallels); and we have a basis for "a knowledge of diverse but interrelated things, the cornerstone of all experience" (externality principle) (*EFG,* 201).

Russell took very seriously the problems of whether nature is discrete, that is, atomic, or continuous, one whole. He is concerned, as we saw above, with the nature of time and space, and the mathematical logic he devised was to deal with the foundations of the modern scientific worldview. Traditional theory had considered mathematics to be the science of quantity (and indeed still does). One of the grounds of Russell's dissatisfaction is the easy way in which we think that if we can add up units of anything, then we are thinking scientifically. One example, crucial to ethics, is utilitarianism. J. S. Mill, along with his predecessors and successors, talks of units and sums of pleasure, as though pleasure is like money, and we can get an answer to "how many?" as of dollars. In "On the Relations of Number and Quantity" (1897), although later repudiated by the author, there is one conclusion that put hedonism beyond consideration.[11] Pleasure may have "intensive quantity that is subject to judgment of more or less, but not extensive quantity."

A measure of pleasures, as Hedonists have to acknowledge, is unattainable. A sum of pleasures, as their opponents have urged, is not itself a pleasure. Similarly a difference of pleasures is not a pleasure, and a "balance of pleasures over pains" is unmeaning. All these are properties of intensive quantities generally, and reveal the fundamental impossibility of a Calculus of intensive quantities. For a strict Hedonist, the problem of weighing two small pleasures against one big one ought to be meaningless, since an aggregate of two pleasures does not form a single quantity of pleasure. (*RNQ,* 335)

It is then important to ask the question "what is a number?" If we assume that numbers are merely 1, 2, 3, . . . and that everything can be treated quantitatively, then we can be easily hoaxed into thinking that pleasures can be summed, as 2 pleasures + 3 pleasures = 5 pleasures. Russell concluded that traditional metaphysics was not better than the hoax of utilitarianism because tradition teaches, since Aristotle, that quantity is an attribute of substance. Then the prime example of number is unity, one, and we say solemnly that "one" basically refers to "being," as in the old principle "to be many is to be one" (*MPD*, 69). Since arithmetic advanced beyond Roman numerals by the use of zero, null, "0" in the Arabic system, which originally was Hindu, the answer Russell considers must be on the basis of 0, 1, 2, 3. . . .

The new way to answer "what is a number?" is not to think of number as a characteristic of things. If not a property of things, could it be of "propositional functions," which sounds very obscure, or of "classes," which sounds more familiar? Russell finally concluded that either would do, and they are not really different. What they share is thinking relationally of similarity and one-one relations. Russell admits modestly that what he proposed had been formulated sixteen years earlier, and he was rediscovering the definition. His own exposition is matchless:

I defined 2 as the class of all couples, 3 as the class of all trios, etc. A couple is defined as a class of which there are members x and y, x is not identical with y, and, if z is a member of the class, then z is identical with x or with y. A number, in general, is a set of classes having the property which is called "similarity." This is defined as follows: two classes are similar if there is a way of coupling the terms one to one. For example, in a monogamous country, you can know that the number of married men is the same as the number of married women, without having to know how many there are of either (I am excluding widows and widowers). Again, if a man has not lost a leg, you may be pretty sure that the number of his right hand shoes is the same as the number of his left hand shoes. If every member of a company has a chair to sit on and there are no empty chairs, the number of chairs must be the same as the number of people sitting on them. In all these cases there is what is called a one-one relation between the terms of one class and the terms of another, and it is the existence of such a one-one relation which is defined as similarity. The number of any class is defined as all the classes that are similar to it. (*MPD*, 70)

But does this definition of number have the advantage of answering the question, "is zero or null a number?" The answer is

obvious. "0 is the class of those classes that have no members—
i.e., it is the class whose only member is a class having no members.
1 is the class of those classes that have the property of consisting
of whatever is identical with some term x" (MPD, 70). Another
advantage is that this definition "gets over difficulties concerning
the one and the many. Since the terms counted are counted as
instances of a propositional function, the unity involved is only that
of the propositional function, which in no way conflicts with the
plurality of instances." Finally, the theory "get[s] rid of numbers
as metaphysical entities." Here is an illustration of what Russell
called "the retreat from Pythagoras," and it is the turn from Plato's
realism to Occam's nominalism. Numbers "become, in fact, merely
linguistic conveniences with no more substantiality than belongs to
'etc.' or 'i.e.' ". Not even the integers, believed once by mathematicians to have been created by God, have independent being.
All of them are thus derived by mathematicians from pure logic.
"This," confesses Russell, "was my first experience of the usefulness
of Occam's razor in diminishing the number of undefined terms
and unproved propositions required in a given body of knowledge."
    The final advantage of Russell's definition is that it eliminates a
difficulty with regard to infinite numbers, and this will carry us on
to the next questions "what is infinity?" and "what is continuity?"
(MPD, 71). "Definition of Number" (IMP, chap. 2) also ends with
the distinction between finite and infinite collections. If numbers
were derived from counting, or taking terms one by one, we could,
given our human finitude, have only finite collections. Would not
an infinite collection require an infinite time? Counting applies only
to such a limited class as the number of dollar bills we may possess.
But suppose no limit, as with units of space or time, with always
another beyond. Such a number is beyond counting, or as mathematicians say, "innumerably many." But this presupposes that the
infinite is a collection that could be enumerated if the mind counting
had infinite time.
    Although the question "What is infinity?" was asked by ancient
Greeks, and Russell studies their paradoxes with unusual seriousness, he is convinced that we must be freed from their prejudices.
Leibniz was still in bondage because he was stunned by the paradox
that there are as many numbers are there are odd (or even) numbers.
Although we generally accept as axiomatic that "a part has fewer
terms than the [whole] of which it is a part," as there are fewer

Americans than all members of the human race, this is true only of finite numbers.

This breakdown of the maxim gives us the precise definition of infinity. A collection of terms is infinite when it contains as parts other collections which have just as many terms as it has. If you can take away some of the terms of a collection, without diminishing the number of terms, then there are an infinite number of terms in the collection. . . . There are just as many even numbers as there are numbers altogether, since every number can be doubled. This may be seen by putting odd and even numbers together in one row, and even numbers alone in a row below:—

$$1, 2, 3, 4, 5, \textit{ad infinitum}$$
$$2, 4, 6, 8, 10, \textit{ad infinitum}.$$

There are obviously just as many members in the row below as in the row above. [12]

What had been an absurdity is here taken to be the definition. Although Russell often appeals to common sense, he often points out that "critical common sense" can perceive the limits that must be transcended. One of Russell's important conclusions is that "there is no longer any reason to struggle after a finitist explanation of the world."[13] There are two remarkably thorough chapters devoted to "The Problem of Infinity Considered Historically" and "The Positive Theory of Infinity." The point is the same as that in answering "what is number?" The tradition could not think in the concepts provided us by the logic of relations and theory of order. The way of liberation was taken by Galileo toward Cantor's conclusion of "an infinite number of different infinite numbers, and that the conception of *greater* and *less* can be perfectly well applied to them" (*OKEW*, 199).

The third question "what is continuity?" is a more modern question than the other two. But just as "what is number?" and "what is infinity?" so continuity gives rise to paradoxes. One of the earliest essays, "Mathematics and the Metaphysicians" (1901) gives a non-technical, and indeed very eloquent account of the solution (*ML*, 91–92). The historical background is found in *Our Knowledge of the External World*, chapter 5, "The Theory of Continuity," with particular attention to motion. If motion is complex, then it seems to be made of parts, and change seems to be "by small finite jumps" (*OKEW*, 155). But if there are gaps between these parts, which must be infinitesimal, how do we account for continuous motion and the perception of continuity of change (*OKEW*, 154)? Zeno's paradoxes were framed to show that motion and change are absurd. Russell is realistic and his robust common sense resists a conclusion that can be suggested by the same pattern of argument that space and time are unreal (*OKEW*, 135).

Once again, as with infinity, so with continuity; there is no precise definition. One meaning is a compact series, one in which "between any two terms of the series there are others. But this would be an inadequate definition, because of the existence of 'gaps' in series such as the series of ratios" (*IMP*, 100).

Russell, in the end, admits that the mathematical solution is so technical that only mathematicians can understand it. It is based upon the concept of a "limit," which is the ideal infinitesimal, not the "term to which the terms of some series approximate as nearly as we please," but "the series which it limits may not approximate to it at all." The solution is as paradoxical as that of the problem of the infinite: "the smallest of the infinite integers is the limit of the finite integers, though all finite integers are at an infinite distance from it" (*ML*, 92).

What is clear is Russell's confidence that "the notion of continuity depends upon that of *order*, since continuity is merely a particular type of order." Once again the logic of relations has banished quantity "except from one little corner of Geometry." The logic of relations is so powerful that from relation Russell predicts the deduction of "all types of series" (*ML*, 91).

The theory of the infinite and the continuum involves a tradition claiming, particularly in Zeno's paradoxes, Leibniz's contradiction, and Kant's antinomies, that these are absurd notions. We cannot go into the details of each famous formulation, but we can recommend Russell's expositions of Zeno and Kant because these show the most serious study of the historical background: in no other instance is there a historical chapter carefully documented before there is analytic construction (*OKEW*, Lecture 6 and Lecture 7). Historians of philosophy have not, however, approved of Russell's approach because it offers to demonstrate that all past metaphysicians were in error and it is the new method of mathematical logic that can give a complete explanation. [14]

Order

It is a distinct relief to read Russell on order, rather than on number, infinity, and continuity, because the definition of "order" is lucid. Number, infinity, and continuity, particularly the latter, are obscure. Happily, the more obscure these philosophic concepts are, the more Russell places them in the context of the lucid theory of order. In this section we shall go beyond the earlier section "Relations and Series" to use the exact definition of "order," and to ask the extent to which the logical and mathematical notion can be used in solving philosophical problems. This leads directly into the last section of this chapter on similarity of structure.

In many essays Russell stresses the centrality of order in arithmetic, geometry, and other fields of mathematics. The best statement is in "The Definition of Order" in *Introduction to Mathematical Philosophy:*

The notion of order is one which has enormous importance in mathematics. Not only the integers, but also rational fractions and all real numbers have an order of magnitude, and this is essential to most of their mathematical properties. The order of points on a line is essential to geometry; so is the slightly more complicated order of lines through a point in a plane, or of planes through a line. Dimensions, in geometry, are a development of order. The conception of a *limit,* which underlies all higher mathematics, is a serial conception. There are parts of mathematics which do not depend upon the notion of order, but they are very few in comparison with the parts in which this notion is involved. (*IMP, 29*)

Order or series is a relation between members of a class that is asymmetrical, transitive, and connected. This definition has become standard in the theory of order, which has been considered of central philosophic importance by philosophers other than Russell, such as Josiah Royce and Alfred North Whitehead.[15] Since we introduced the three defining characteristics in the section "Relations and Series," we are ready for a formal definition:

(1)   If x precedes y, y must not also precede x. . . . A relation having this first property is called *asymmetrical.*

The illustrations show the philosophic importance:

This is an obvious characteristic of the kind of relations that lead to series. If *x* is less than *y*, *y* is not also less than *x*. If *x* is earlier in time than *y*, *y* is not also earlier than *x*. If *x* is to the left of *y*, *y* is not to the left of *x*. On the other hand, relations which do not give rise to series often do not have this property. If *x* is a brother or sister of *y*, *y* is a brother or sister of *x*. If *x* is of the same height as *y*, *y* is of the same height as *x*. If *x* is of a different height from *y*, *y* is of a different height from *x*. In all these cases, when the relation holds between *x* and *y*, it also holds between *y* and *x*. But with serial relations such a thing cannot happen.

(2)   If *x* precedes *y* and *y* precedes *z*, *x* must precede *z*. . . . A relation having our second property is called *transitive*.

The illustrations again show the philosophic importance:

This may be illustrated by the same instances as before: *less, earlier, left of*. But as instances of relations which do not have this property only two of our previous three instances will serve. If *x* is brother or sister of *y*, and *y* of *z*, *x* may not be brother or sister of *z*, since *x* and *z* may be the same person. The same applies to difference of height, but not to sameness of height, which has our second property but not our first. The relation "father," on the other hand, has our first property but not our second.

(3)   Given any two terms of the class which is to be ordered, there must be one which precedes and the other which follows. [To parallel the statements of (1) and (2): Given *x* and *y*, any two members of a well-ordered series, either *x* precedes *y*, or *y* precedes *x*.] . . . A relation having this property is called *connected*.

The illustrations show the philosophic importance:

For example, of any two integers, or fractions, or real numbers, one is smaller and the other greater; but of any two complex numbers this is not true. Of any two moments in time, one must be earlier than the other; but of events, which may be simultaneous, this cannot be said. Of two points on a line, one must be to the left of the other. (*IMP*, 31–32)

The illustrations above show not only the central convictions about nature as cosmos but many of the orders found in human society. In the midst of technical discussions of the formal properties of relations that are serial, Russell points out "the vital importance for the understanding of continuity, space, time and motion" (*IMP*,

38). The political order of England is used as another more concrete illustration. "The series of the Kings of England, for example, is generated by relations of each to his successor. This is probably the easiest way, where it is applicable, of conceiving the generation of a series" (*IMP*, 35).

The first important philosophic position about order is that order here means real order, that is, an arrangement that we discover between events rather than one we impose upon them. That is, Russell's position is order-realism as opposed to the most common view, order-subjectivism.

People are apt to suppose that the order of a set of terms is more or less arbitrary, that we can arrange them as we will, and that there is no intrinsic order among terms. Now it is true that, when a finite number of terms have no intrinsic order, it is possible for us to give them any order we please. But this possibility depends entirely upon the fact that there are sets of terms having intrinsic order, with which any other set of terms can be correlated. A casual collection of terms may be ordered by counting, in which case they are correlated by the integers; by speech, in which case they are correlated with a series of times; or by writing, in which case they are correlated with a series of places. But the order arises, in each case, from the intrinsic order of the integers, the times, or the places respectively. These have an order independent of our caprice—they form what I shall call *independent* or *self-sufficient* series. . . . All orders by correlation are logically dependent upon intrinsic orders. (*ONO*, 30–31)

Objectivity of the basic orders does not negate relativity. Any given set of events has a number of orders. We may, that is, order the integers in a variety of different ways other than the order of magnitude. It is a mistake to call magnitude *the* order of the integers: we might as well order the odd numbers first, and then the even numbers. This is so, runs the argument, because any "one set of terms has many orders" (*IMP*, 30). How can this relativity accompany objectivity?

We can no more "arrange" the natural numbers than we can the starry heavens; but just as we may notice among the fixed stars either their order of brightness or their distribution in the sky, so there are various relations among numbers which may be observed, and which give rise to various different orders among numbers all equally legitimate. And what is true of numbers is equally true of points on a line or of the moments of time: one order is more familiar, but others are equally valid. (*IMP*, 30)

Eighteen years separate the publication of these two defenses. One rests objective order with the magnitude of the integers, points of space, moments of time, as intrinsic; the other account affirms the givenness of various orders of any set of things and events.

In several ways Russell's theory of order, attractive because boldly stated and with a precisely defined serial order, is left unguarded against negative criticism. Some of these were discovered by Russell in the course of writing "On the Notion of Order." Some remained for him to discover much later. Some he appears never to have discovered. We shall single out one of each kind, along with the constructive suggestion to be developed in the next section of this chapter and in succeeding chapters that each is a difficulty that can be overcome, and indeed that a more general theory of order was the framework within which Russell worked and that this remains a viable philosophic alternative.

There are many definitely arranged complexes that we commonly call "ordered" that do not satisfy the definition. A relation that is asymmetrical, transitive, and connected is exemplified by a series of points on a line, and we say a linear order is serial. But there is also cyclical order, as the rhythm of seasons, tides, animal bodies. There is a linear order of spring, summer, autumn, and winter that satisfies the definition, but when winter is followed by spring, the repeated presence or recurrence means that a successor of winter is also a successor of itself, and each season is also a predecessor of itself. There is symmetry as well as asymmetry because of the cycle that repeats, and therefore there can be no connexity.

At the very end of the chapter "The Definition of Order" in *Introduction to Mathematical Philosophy*, Russell takes note of another anomaly. Although the three terms may be a series when satisfying the definition of ordering relation, this may also be specified by the relation "between." "Cyclical order," such as that of the points on a circle, cannot be generated by the three-term relation of "between." We need a relation of four terms, which may be called "separation of couples." The illustration makes the abstractions imaginable: "One may go from England to New Zealand by way of Suez or by way of San Francisco; we cannot say definitely that either of these places is 'between' England and New Zealand." The term "separation of couples" is neat because given a and b, x and y, to go from a to b is through either x or y, and the converse (*IMP*, 40–41).

Even more obviously symmetry, the balance of one side against the other, is illustrated throughout the natural world. It needs only two terms, whereas a series requires three. Are we to refuse to call symmetry or balance or equilibrium an "order" because it fails to satisfy the technical definition? Russell himself noted the oddity of saying that the relation of equality was not an order, even though x = y = z has transitivity, as we noted above under "Relations and Series."

Another oddity is that "the logical order" is not strictly an order. The reason is the same as mentioned for cyclical order, the order of balance, and of equality: there is sometimes symmetry between theorems rather than strict asymmetry. Russell's example is from the very model of order, geometry. The logical order of Euclid's propositions "depends upon the relation of implication, but is rendered peculiar by the fact that implication is sometimes symmetrical and sometimes asymmetrical" (*ONO*, 35). That is, an earlier proposition may imply a later without necessarily excluding the fact that the later also implies the earlier. Sometimes the relation is asymmetrical, sometimes symmetrical, and sometimes transitive, sometimes intransitive. The logical order is not therefore necessarily connected. Russell concludes that "logical order is a very obscure notion" (*ONO*, 35–36).

Given a theory of order based on the logic of relations, Russell might have concluded that series is only one type of order, and that the definition he is working with is therefore too narrow.

The second difficulty with Russell's theory of order concerns the phenomena and events in which we discover order. The model above uses "the starry heavens" and the heaven of mathematical forms (*IMP*, 30). Order may well be, according to Pope's *Essay on Man,* "heaven's first law," but equally traditional is the observation that the material earth is basically disorderly, if not chaotic. "Order" has meaning in contrast to its opposite "disorder." The only anomalies Russell notes are, as above, on the formal level when certain kinds of order do not fit a strict definition. But what of chance in conjunctions of sequences of events, accidents that cannot be predicted? Surely a philosophy using scientific method that makes so much of theory of order should allow for random sequences. Not until later did Russell confront disorder as a problem, as we shall see in the chapter on metaphysics. Particularly for a philosophy of order-realism, the reality of disorder makes Russell himself question the objectivity. Perhaps science itself, with its tradition of the "reign of law," has been based on wishful thinking of an intelligible and manageable world, a "rage for order." Particularly after the achievement of C. S. Peirce, one of the founders of the logic of relations, Russell seems to have failed to profit from Peirce's paradoxical doctrine that "disorder is a mode of order."[16] Only at the end of his systematic work in *Human Knowledge* did Russell explore theory of probability. When we give a statistical statement we are showing order in disorder.

The third oddity, given Russell's attention to the spatial and temporal orders, is his neglect of the causal order. Russell's contemplative bias in epistemology may be at fault here. The human observer is almost solely the passive recipient of the orders he discovers. What place is there for the human agent as motivated by interest to produce certain orders? The "generation" of orders meant in Russell almost never the biologically productive, almost always mathematical specifications of formal conditions. We shall see below in the chapter on metaphysics that here, too, Russell came to recognize a fundamental neglect.

Does Russell develop a broader theory of order than that using series as the only model? We proceed immediately to argue that this is the theory of structure. The broader conception is similarity of relations, which includes correlation, based upon two sets of relations, and therefore including such symmetrical orders as balance or equilibrium. The model of correlation is the mapping of a country. The model requires agency of the mapmaker, whose interests control the terms and scale and perspective. We proceed to contrast similarity of relations or structure as a broad theory of order to the narrow theory of serial order.

Similarity of Relations and Structure

The concept of order that seemed the unifying idea of philosophy became, when precisely defined as series, the central concept of mathematics. Russell never denied the claims he had made for the importance of order either in logic or generally in philosophy. But there was another concept of similarity or likeness. Similarity of qualities, such as whiteness, is one basis of Russell's Platonism. What we have just examined is similarity of classes, the basis of

Russell's definition of number. What we have to examine, as a concept rivaling order, is similarity of relations or structure. [17]

What is the relation between the general idea of order and the general idea of structure? Because similarity had different contexts, those of universals and numbers, it developed in Russell's philosophy without explicit relation. Because similarity is less precisely defined, it can be more widely used. Its story of eclipsing order can be traced from "Similarity of Relations" in *Introduction to Mathematical Philosophy* (1919) through "Importance of Structure in Scientific Inference" in *The Analysis of Matter* (1927) to the sequence of chapters in *Human Knowledge* (1948): "Structure," "Structure and Minimum Vocabularies," "Structure and Causal Laws," "Analogy," and "Summary of Postulates." What happened to the theory of order, which in the early essay of 1901 had such promise that all philosophical problems seemed soluble? It becomes a submerged part of the general study of relations, and this is most evident in what should be called "theory of structure." In the last section we encountered certain grave difficulties in Russell's theory of order. Are these difficulties overcome in *Human Knowledge* because of the totally fresh section "Probability" and the chain of chapters on structure?

The definition of "similarity" in Russell is sometimes said to be "having the same number of members." [18] What are similar are then two classes. This is a particular version of similarity devised to give the definition of number as the class of similar classes, as two is the class of pairs, three is the class of trios, and so on. How do we get to the class "having the same number of members"? Obviously by using a one-one relationship, and Russell's oft-repeated example is perfect monogamy. The logic of monogamy is that for every male x, husband of y, there is only one y, and for every female y, wife of an x, there is only one x. Similarity contrasts to order. Order is a relation that is asymmetrical, but similarity is symmetrical. Order is asymmetrical, as husband of/wife of, in contrast to spouse-spouse, and such a symmetry is as one-one (monogamy is symmetrical only as to number, but asymmetrical as to sex).

Russell formalizes symmetry: "If class α is similar to β, then β is similar to α." Also reflexivity: "every class is similar to itself." What relationally is the same? This is transitivity: "if α is similar to β and β to γ, then α is similar to γ" (*IMP*, 16). We have already recognized a familiar relationship that is symmetrical, reflexive, and transitive: this is equality.

This is a broadening of the earlier theory of order, which limited the concept to the strictly ordering relation, which is necessarily *asymmetrical*. Not that Russell could reduce ordering relations to a subset of structural relations. That could not be because asymmetry cannot be derived from symmetry. But there is a common sense meaning of "order" that includes balance and harmony in which it makes no difference whether one says that "α balances β, or β balances α" or "α harmonizes with β, or β harmonizes with α." These are symmetrical rather than asymmetrical. Moreover, not all logical relations are strictly and exclusively asymmetrical. The series of theorems in Euclid, Russell showed, were sometimes such that an earlier implied a later theorem, but also there can be coimplication. That is, not only does E (earlier) imply L (later), but L (later) implies E (earlier). Allowing for "structure" as well as "order" is required by the example of geometrical deduction. It is very odd to have a logical definition of order that rules out logical order.

Not only is structure not restricted to asymmetry, as is order, in the sense of series but there is a different relation to number. Whereas "order has more and more predominated over quantity (*ONO*, 30), similarity is the relation that defines number and generates all numbers.

Another contrast is that order was interpreted by Russell so as to emphasize intrinsic order, the order of the starry heavens, that we cannot change but need only to acknowledge. Russell's realism was intended as "an investigation into the very heart and immutable essence of all things actual and possible" (*ML*, 68). Theory of order is Platonic or an example of extreme realism. Theory of structure, like correspondence between the knower's belief and proposition and the arrangement of what is known, includes subjectivity as well as objectivity. "Like Leibniz's monads, we mirror the universe, though very partially and very inaccurately; in my momentary mirroring there is a mirror-space and a mirror-time, which have a correspondence, though not an exact one, with the impersonal space and time of physics and history."[19]

How can we understand the extreme realism of Russell's theory of order? Clearly he was opposing Bradley's theory that all relations are based in the mind and are, therefore, subjective. This accounts also for the overemphasis of asymmetry.[20] Theory of structure, by contrast, is critical because it is defending moderate realism in the face of the serious problem of the degree to which the human mind invents and imposes patterns on the phenomena. Much is now written of interpretation. Russell does not deny that we give meaning to what we observe and that science is not free from interpretation. So that knowledge and truth be preserved, Russell's kind of interpretation "means that *structure* must be preserved" (*LA*, 378).

I do not believe, for instance, that those who disbelieve in the reality of relations (in some such sense as that explained above) can possibly interpret those numerous parts of science which employ asymmetrical relations. Even if I could see no way of answering the objections to relations raised (for example) by Mr. Bradley, I should still think it more likely than not that some answer was possible, because I should think an error in a very subtle and abstract argument more probable than so fundamental a falsehood in science. Admitting that everything we believe ourselves to know is doubtful, it seems, nevertheless, that what we believe ourselves to know in philosophy is more doubtful than its most sweeping generalizations.

The question of interpretation is of importance for almost every philosophy, and I am not at all inclined to deny that many scientific results require interpretation before they can be fitted into a coherent philosophy. The maxim of "constructions *versus* inferences" is itself a maxim of interpretation. But I think that any valid kind of interpretation ought to leave the denial unchanged, though it may give a new meaning to fundamental ideas. In practice, this means that *structure* must be preserved. And a test of this is that all the propositions of a science should remain, though new meanings may be found for their terms. A case in point, on a non-philosophical level, is the relation of the physical theory of light to our perceptions of colour. This provides different physical occurrences corresponding to different seen colours, and thus makes the structure of the physical spectrum the same as that of what we see when we look at a rainbow. Unless structure is preserved, we cannot validly speak of an interpretation. And structure is just what is destroyed by a monistic logic.

I do not mean, of course, to suggest that, in any region of science, the structure revealed at present by observation is exactly that which actually exists. On the contrary, it is in the highest degree probable that the actual structure is more fine-grained than the observed structure. This applies just as much to psychological as to physical material. It rests upon the fact that, where we perceive a difference (e.g., between two shades of colour), there is a difference, but where we do not perceive a difference it does not follow that there is not a difference. We have therefore a right, in all interpretation, to demand the preservation of observed differences, and the provision of room for hitherto unobserved differences, although we cannot say in advance what they will be, except when they can be inferentially connected with observed differences.

In science, structure is the main study. A large part of the importance of relativity comes from the fact that it has substituted a single four-dimensional manifold (space-time) for the two manifolds, three-dimensional space and one-dimensional time. This is a change of structure, and therefore has far-reaching consequences, but any change which does not involve a change of structure does not make much difference. (*LA*, 378–79)

Although defined mathematically, Russell generally uses the concept of structure in the context of knowledge. What, he often asks, is the relation between our perception of the world and the physicists' formulation of events? In contrast to the realism of Russell's theory of order is the critical approach to our knowledge of physical events (*P*, 155).

On more than one occasion Russell complained that his readers overlooked the importance of structure in his philosophy. The "knowledge of the physical world is only a knowledge of structure" (Schilpp, 716). For those who have not the training to read volume 2 of *Principia Mathematica* (*PM*, vol. 2, pt. 4, section 150ff), Russell supplies a summary in *The Analysis of Matter* chapter 24, "Importance of Structure in Scientific Inference." Structure is not of classes but of "relations or systems of relations"; although broader than series, and indeed inclusive of them, it is "fully defined." "It is not merely one-one, but may be [one-many or] many-one."[21] Whereas order was almost strictly mathematical, structure is generally epistemological. It is also metaphysical and, as we shall shortly see, artistic and because causal, applicable to practical life.

The most important problem of interpretation is that of the relation between the structure of language and the structure of the world. For most of his career Russell denounced inferences from language to the world as fallacious (*LA*, 377). Because a word is a noun grammatically does not imply that that to which it refers is a substance. As we shall see in the next chapter on Russell's analysis, metaphysics hinges on inferences from the structure of language to the structure of the world (*IMT*, 341ff). How could this be valid? Only if the structure of the world is reduplicated in the structure of language. Russell's structural approach evidently gave him greater confidence that, however the human perspective distorts, it succeeds in making some reliable maps of the world.

Order, in Russell's philosophy, is almost never illustrated from the arts. Structure is more flexible and generally suggests examples from music. Although Russell is not commonly thought to have contributed to aesthetics, it is easy to discern that what he considers important is the form of the work of art. It is structure that is common to different performances of the Symphony in C Minor. "Two different performances are not exactly identical in structure, and it is the minute differences which make the difference between a good performance and a bad one. But they are all very nearly identical in structure, not only with each other, but with the score. The reader will remark that 'structure' is a very abstract concept, so abstract that a musical score, a gramophone record, and the actual performance may all have the very same structure. There is thus an actual identity of structure, though not in every minute particular" (*HK*, 479–80).

Order, in Russell's theory, is spatiotemporal, but never causal. This is one of the grave neglects. It is made good in "Structure and Causal Laws" (*HK*, book 6, chap. 6). The new context is dynamic: an actor performs in order to produce an effect in those who are present responding to the play.

Many critics have noted in Russell that the person tends to be a spectator, and not an agent, and that he tends to reduce the cause-effect relation to spatial contiguity and temporal succession. Could it be that "causal efficacy," a term Russell invented, but used by Whitehead to refute the reduction of causal order to spatiotemporal order, contains the solution? In 1944 Russell writes that dynamic causal efficacy also solves the long-standing problem of induction. The illustration is pertinent to the question, how do I know that that shape is my shadow? "If you walk in the evening with the sun behind you, a shadow marches in front of you and you do not for a moment doubt that it has a causal connection with your own body" (*BW*, 154). We would normally say that the association of my body and the shadow is that of cause and effect. How do we know that? "Sometimes, especially at sunset, or when you are standing with others on the edge of a deep narrow valley and your shadow appears on the hill opposite, you may have difficulty in deciding to which person a given shadow belongs, but if you wave your arms and see the shadow wave its arms you conclude that the shadow is yours; that is to say, you assume a certain kind of causal connection between it and yourself. This causal connection you infer from identity of structure in a series of events" (*HK,* 482).

This example is fascinating because it combines order, in the sense of "series of events," with "identity of structure." Russell enlivens the abstract theory of order and structure by using it to show the solution to the detection of Mr. Smith as the culprit in "brides-in-the-bath murders": he "was duly hanged" (*HK,* 482).

The causal order then takes a central place, which it had never previously had, in Russell's concept of nature. (See especially the postulates of "separable causal lines," "spatio-temporal continuity in causal lines," and "common causal origin of similar structures" (*HK,* 506ff).

Russell published *Human Knowledge* when he was seventy-five years old and was enriching his concept of order in yet another valuable way. A whole important part was on theory of probability. In many cases, all we know are events from which we have made a "random selection" (*HK,* 397). We may not know the causes of any phenomenon, but find a significant structure through some statistical correlation. Later in the chapter on metaphysics, we shall see that Russell struggled with the idea that the real world is disorderly. What structure has a world of sheer chance?

One might have expected some extended account of chance, since Russell, in his historical accounts, frequently ascribes to "chance" what cannot be expected and predicted.[22] "What do I mean by a 'chance' event? I mean one of which the causation is unknown. 'Chance' decides whether an expected child turns out to be a boy or a girl, and 'chance' decides which of the hereditary possibilities that Mendelian principles allow will be realized." Russell thereby switches the subject from the unknown in history to those events that are predictable by use of probability on a statistical basis for large numbers. "But when we deal with large groups, 'chance' no longer decides: there will be about twenty-one boys to twenty girls" (*PBR,* 738). The conclusion should be that even disorder is a mode of order.

The logic of relations was furthered more by Russell than by any other philosopher, and the richness of application sustains the hope that it is the category of categories. It plays a role comparable to that of substance in traditional Aristotelian philosophies. We have examined the claims to have solved the problems of number, infinity, and continuity, and seen how order, narrowly defined, can be made less restricted by subsumption into a general theory of structure. We are ready to proceed to two explorations, of the method of analysis and of the relation of thought to reality, metaphysics.

Chapter Four

Words and the World: Shall Philosophy Be No More Than Analysis of the Order of Language?

Retreat from Pythagoras: The Journey Down

So far we have traced Russell's journey into Platonism with the Pythagorean confidence that the logic of relations is the fundamental science of sciences. To use the ancient Greek metaphor, common from Heraclitus to Plotinus, it is a "way upwards." We have hinted that Russell turned from Platonism, and indeed one phase of his intellectual adventure was this opposite turn. One of the most revealing chapters in *My Philosophical Development* is "Retreat from Pythagoras." In the most famous account of this development, the introduction to the second edition of *The Principles of Mathematics* (1937), he gives a succinct ten-page outline of the "way downwards." The "up" is to the universal, and the "down" is to the particular. It is reason that exalts the contemplative mind to the height of the heavenly forms, but the senses recall us to the basis of knowledge of existence in the particulars. For some metaphysicians the "way down," or empiricism, is a decline in the sense of a loss. But Russell himself, more than any other philosopher, took the steps of logical and linguistic analysis that led to the dominance in English-speaking lands of analytic philosophy. The great Oxford Franciscan of the late Middle Ages, William of Occam, had once used his razor to cut away what he thought unnecessary, Plato's real universals. The really real things of Occam's world are particulars, known through the senses. The common statement of Occam's razor is "things are not to be multiplied beyond necessity" *(entia non sunt multiplicanda praeter necessitatem)*. The problem of this chapter is set by Russell's conclusion to the empiricist declaration of 1937: "How far it is possible to go in the direction of nominalism remains, to my mind, an unsolved question, but one which, whether completely soluble or not, can only be adequately investigated by means of mathematical logic."[1]

Russell is the greatest seminal influence of Anglo-American philosophy of the twentieth century. All the seeds of the analytic movement are found in him, and the problem suggested by the title "The Journey Down" is that the story of philosophy in Britain and America, and indeed wherever philosophic English is read, has been the move from systematic metaphysics to piecemeal analysis. For those who are convinced that the idealists of the turn of the century, Bradley and Bosanquet in Britain, Royce in the United States, represent viable continuity with the great tradition, it was only a short step from the kind of realism represented by Russell to taking language as the subject matter of inquiry. If the way of the pragmatists, the tradition of C. S. Peirce, with the scope of studies of James and Dewey, represents something great, then the narrowness of the analysts is a decline into something petty. But we must not without much further study beg the issue, because the advances in logic made philosophers dissatisfied with the broad style of systematic philosophy and the vagueness of pragmatism. Philosophers demanded greater rigor of argument.

In this chapter we must face the various paradoxes made famous by Russell and consider whether the solutions he argued were required. The problem is far more difficult than that of dividing the field and deciding whether one is for or against metaphysics, especially when this division is taken to be tantamount to that against or for analysis. The complication is that it is not at all evident that Russell's analysis is antimetaphysical. We must distinguish kinds of analysis; and when we face Russell's critique of his analytic followers, chiefly Wittgenstein and A. J. Ayer, we must ask again the questions he posed to them: if language is made clear, what does this language tell us of the world? It may become evident that twentieth-century philosophy is the only way that could have been followed, given the circumstances of change in social and political problems, as well as in logical and scientific techniques. But one result of the revolutions in philosophy is that there may shortly be no commonly accepted philosophy.

What Is Analysis?

The twentieth century in Anglo-American philosophy has already been named the Age of Analysis. More than any other philosopher, it was Bertrand Russell who set the style.[2]

Perhaps Russell's earliest use of what he later called analysis is in an account of a philosophy of complexes (1904).[3] There are all sorts of complexes, such as in perception. If an empiricist refers to a "simple," something without parts, one can reply, "Have you ever seen one?" Perception itself is the act of perceiving, the object perceived, and the content, which Russell later calls the sense-data. The most interesting example is a melody, which he analyzes, as we are all taught in music, into notes. Just any assemblage of notes is not a melody unless there is the right relation. A melody has duration, and our perceiving of the notes is after the sounds have ceased to exist. This Russell calls internal perception. Just as there is a past, so we anticipate a future of the melody (EA, 28–32).

"Analysis" is commonly defined as "resolution or breaking up of anything complex into its various simple elements, the opposite process to synthesis."[4] Although the method sounds familiar to us because of the chemical methods of finding the elements of compounds, a historical dictionary (OED) teaches us that the word was earlier philosophic, referring, for example, to the definition of a word. Only in the seventeenth century did it come to mean the physical or mechanical separation of objects or parts. Such a traditional logic as that of the hymn writer Isaac Watts (1724) distinguishes three of four kinds of analysis. We are still familiar with grammatical analysis (finding in a sentence the particles of speech such as noun and verb), logical analysis (distinguishing subject and predicate), metaphysical analysis (resolution of knowledge into principles, particularly the general principles "underlying concrete phenomena"). Also "analysis finds out causes by their effects." This is a most helpful way to proceed. Is Russell's analysis grammatical, logical, and also metaphysical? Are more distinctions among kinds required? We shall answer yes to the first, and also to the second.

Analysis falls under the categories whole and part; there is a type of philosophy that prefers the whole to the part, and therefore to break up wholes into parts is bad. To what extent had Russell himself held this opinion in his Hegelian period (1893–98)? We know that he thought it still important in 1903, when he considered "the doctrine that analysis is falsification." "Whatever can be analyzed is a whole, and we have already seen that analysis of wholes is in some measure falsification. But it is important to realize the very narrow limits of this doctrine. We cannot conclude that the parts of a whole are not really its parts, nor that the parts are not presupposed in the whole in a sense in which the whole is not presupposed in the parts, nor yet that the logically prior is not usually simpler than the logically subsequent."[5]

Clearly, Russell's analysis is logical. He neatly takes Bradley's warning against falsification into his defense: "Though analysis gives us the truth, and nothing but the truth, yet it never gives us the whole truth. This is the only sense in which the doctrine is to be accepted. In any wider sense, it becomes merely a cloak for laziness, by giving an excuse to those who dislike the labour of analysis." Russell, as we shall see, was contemptuous of easy philosophizing, or "philosophy without tears."

Later in *The Principles of Mathematics*, he considers the metaphysical argument against analysis: wherever there are organic unities, to divide them into parts is to treat them as mere mechanical assemblages and to kill them. One defense against the poet Wordsworth's contempt for the botanist who analyzes a flower (plucked from his mother's grave, the dissected flower is murdered) is that a philosopher uses *"conceptual analysis* [rather than] real division into parts." Since the idealists meant by "conceptual" that what was being analyzed (the analysandum) would not have these distinctions without a mind analyzing, Russell stresses real relations discovered in every case of analysis:

A distinction is made, in support of organic unities, between conceptual analysis and real division into parts. What is really indivisible, we are told, may be conceptually analyzable. This distinction, if the conceptual analysis be regarded as subjective, seems to me wholly inadmissible. All complexity is conceptual in the sense that it is due to a whole capable of logical analysis, but is real in the sense that it has no dependence upon the mind, but only upon the nature of the object. Where the mind can distinguish elements, there must *be* different elements to distinguish; though, alas! there are often different elements which the mind does not distinguish. The analysis of a finite space into points is no more objective than the analysis (say) of causality into time-sequence + ground and consequent, or of equality into sameness of relation to a given magnitude. In every case of analysis, there is a whole consisting of parts with relations;

it is only the nature of the parts and the relations which distinguishes different cases. Thus the notion of an organic whole in the above sense must be attributed to defective analysis, and cannot be used to explain things. (*PMath,* 466)

When Russell defended analysis according to his doctrine of real and external relations, he knew that the philosophic community was dividing "friends of analysis from its enemies." What is the issue of Hegel's philosophy and idealism, and what was called "holism" by General Smuts? The holist, according to Russell, is dissatisfied with such a statement as "John is the father of James" and replies, "Before you can understand this statement you must know who John and James are. Now to know who John is, is to know all his characteristics, for apart from them he would not be distinguishable from any one else. But all his characteristics involve other people or things. He is characterized by his relations to his parents, his wife, and his children, etc."[6] Russell's defense is that holism implies that the knower must take "account of the whole universe." Indeed, Bradley does say that the true interpretation of any given proposition is "reality is such that John is the father of James." But then one can never know anything without knowing everything. Therefore, the alternative to analysis is absurd.

If analysis is the reduction of complexes to simples, then it is atomism. The only name Russell ever accepted for his own philosophy was "logical atomism." The charge of opponents of atomism againt Russell is that we can never by any method reach the completely simple, which would mean something without attributes or relations. And if we set out by analysis to move toward the simple, we do so by ignoring relations or structure, which are supposedly what his philosophy of relations is to lead us to recognize clearly. Since the completely simple could not be expressed in propositions that are complex and rest upon a recognition of the complex facts of the world, analysis, if it succeeded, would be beyond empirical tests and indeed beyond rational statement. Therefore, if analysis were to succeed, it would lead to complete mysticism. If the world were only of simples in the last analysis, then the only possible position would be mysticism. Our philosophy would be mute: it could only point to the inscrutable and the incommunicable. This may have been the way Russell's student Wittgenstein was led to conclude his *Tractatus:* "Whereof one cannot speak, thereof one must be silent."[7]

Is Russell's analysis reduced to absurdity by this sequence of objections, which have been here compounded into a succinct refutation? By taking each one in turn, we can become more clear about what he thinks his analysis is and what it is not.

Can we know simples, and does analysis require that we know simples? Russell is regularly skeptical as to whether we can know simples. The reason is that "it is not clear that there must be terms which are *incapable* of definition: it is possible that, however far back we go in defining, we always *might* go further still. On the other hand, it is also possible that, when analysis has been pushed far enough, we can reach terms that really are simple, and therefore logically incapable of the sort of definition that consists in analysing." Russell concludes that the undefined, or simple, is "undefined for the moment, though perhaps not permanently" (*IMP,* 4). In several careful definitions of analysis, it is proceeding "towards the simple and abstract."

What is a simple? Is there a simple in the same sense that there are complexes? Russell's most careful statement from "Logical Atomism" follows:

When I speak of "simples" I ought to explain that I am speaking of something not experienced as such, but known only inferentially as the limit of analysis. It is quite possible that, by greater logical skill, the need for assuming them could be avoided. A logical language will not lead to error if its simple symbols (i.e. those not having any parts that are symbols, or any significant structure) all stand for objects of some one type, even if these objects are not simple. The only drawback to such a language is that it is incapable of dealing with anything simpler than the objects which it representt by simple symbols. But I confess it seems obvious to me (as it did to Leibniz) that what is complex must be composed of simples, though the number of constituents may be infinite. It is also obvious that the logical uses of the old notion of substance (i.e. those uses which do not imply temporal duration) can only be applied, if at all, to simples; objects of other types do not have that kind of being which one associates with substances. The essence of a substance, from the symbolic point of view, is that it can only be named—in old-fashioned language, it never occurs in a proposition except as the subject or as one of the terms of a relation. If what we take to be simple is really complex, we may get into trouble by naming it, when what we ought to do is to assert it. For example, if Plato loves Socrates, there is not an entity "Plato's love for Socrates," but only the fact that Plato loves Socrates. And in speaking of this as "a fact," we are already making it more substantial and more of a unity than we have any right to do.[8]

Is analysis solely the discovery of simples, whatever they are? Russell is most clear in the chapter "Analysis" that there is the discovery of a part of a whole, but that there are "wholes composed of interrelated parts."[9] Russell's analysis is not reductive, eliminating the relations between the parts. Sometimes "atomism" in philosophy has meant that there is *"nothing but* atoms and the void." In his clearest argument, he appeals to what everyone knows:

A child who is being taught . . . to read the word "CAT," learns to make, in succession, the sounds "k," "a," "t." (I mean the sounds these letters stand for, not the names of the letters.) At first, the interval between the sounds is too long for the child to be conscious of their succession as forming a whole, but at last, as the rapidity increases, there comes a moment when the child is aware of having said the word "cat." In that moment, the child is aware of the word as a whole composed of parts. Before that, he was not aware of the whole; when he can read fluently, he ceases to be aware of the parts; but in the first moment of understanding, whole and part are equally present in consciousness. (*IMT,* 335–36)

"What is given [in perception] is a pattern, and [judgment of perception is] the realization that it consists of interrelated objects" and parts in relation.

Because the word "analysis" by itself suggests reductive atomism, the belief in "nothing but atoms," it is wise to call Russell's method relational analysis. Since we only approach simples, but know the relations between the parts, what is important is the discovery of form, which psychologists call Gestalt and Russell called structure. We cannot then reject Russell's analysis as merely corrective of error or trivial because the subject is the cosmos, and "analysis with reflection" is the discovery of categories.[10] A common error is to ignore the continuity of Russell's philosophy with the great tradition.

When we say that Russell's analysis is relational analysis and even categoreal analysis, what we are stressing is the order-realism and the structural realism. There are other forms of analysis that lack realistic ontological commitments, and unless we understand this, it becomes a mystery why Russell, as we shall see at the end of this chapter, becomes the harshest critic of what is known as "linguistic analysis." Russell's main objection to "holism" is that it makes the world out to be one "block universe." William James objected that this is bad because it denies freedom to human individuals. Russell's objection is ontological rather than moral. There are many individuals. If this were not true, scientific knowledge would be impossible. "We must therefore suppose that natural processes have the characteristics attributed to them by the analyst, rather than the holistic character which the enemies of analysis take for granted. I do not contend that the holistic world is logically impossible, but I do contend that it could not give rise to science or to any empirical knowledge."[11]

It follows then that since Russell's analysis is realistic, it cannot be, like the analysis of A. J. Ayer, the complete rejection of all metaphysics. Sometimes Russell sounds positivistic, but we shall devote a section to show that this is an exaggeration that was short-lived. Russell's analysis is not, as with many British analysts, the extreme version of empiricism.[12]

One way in which Russell's realistic analysis is stated is in close relation to the methods of the sciences.[13] Russell stresses the discovery of spatiotemporal and even causal relations. The best statement of this scientific characteristic of analysis is: "It is generally assumed by men of science, at any rate as a working hypothesis, that any concrete occurrence is the resultant of a number of causes, each of which, acting separately, might produce some different result from that which actually occurs; and that the resultant can be calculated when the effects of separate causes are known."[14] The obvious examples are calculating the movements of the moon's orbit, attracted both by earth and by the sun, and the calculation of the resistance of air to falling bodies, affecting the rate of fall in a vacuum.

Sometimes Russell contrasts the analytic method of philosophy, moving from the complex toward the simple, to the special sciences, moving from the abstract toward the complex. But this is an exaggerated contrast, because the larger point is the continuity of philosophic with scientific method. It is not only the sciences but philosophy also that eliminates particularity and focuses attention on "the logical *form* of the facts."[15] Both the sciences and philosophy are constructive. Russell is talking generally and including both when he says: "The logical analysis of a deductive system is not such a definite and limited undertaking as it appears at first sight. This is due to the circumstance just mentioned—namely, that what we took at first as primitive entities may be replaced by complicated logical structures."[16] What Russell probably means is the method he learned from Whitehead, who "invented a method of constructing points, instants, and particles as sets of events, each of finite extent." Here is a method of logic eliminating real points, an aspect, Russell says, of using Occam's razor.[17]

We are now prepared for the summary of philosophic method by which Russell should be best known. Toward the end of "Logical Atomism," the philosophic self-portrayal of 1924, Russell writes: *"The business of philosophy . . . is essentially that of logical analysis, followed by logical synthesis."*[18]

Paradoxes and Their Solution

In the history of Western philosophy there have been four philosophers famous for their paradoxes: Zeno's to prove that motion is impossible, Abelard's *Sic et Non* (Yes and No) to show that authorities contradict one another, Kant's antinomies such as that there is just as good an argument to believe past time infinite as finite, and finally Russell's paradoxes of the liar, paradox of the class of all classes not members of themselves, and the paradoxes of naming and describing.

Russell explains autobiographically how and why he became engaged in solving paradox. He admits that it is very unpleasant to deduce a contradiction, especially from what all logicians accept. The value of such a deduction is that it shows "that *something* [is] amiss." The challenge is to find "how matters [are] to be put right" (*MPD,* 75).

What is Russell's paradox of the class of all classes not members of themselves? The best account to begin with is autobiographical:

I was led to this contradiction by considering Cantor's proof that there is no greatest cardinal number. I thought, in my innocence, that the number of all the things there are in the world must be the greatest possible number, and I applied his proof to this number to see what would happen. This process led me to the consideration of a very peculiar class. Thinking along the lines which had hitherto seemed adequate, it seemed to me that a class sometimes is, and sometimes is not, a member of itself. The class of teaspoons, for example, is not another teaspoon, but the class of things that are not teaspoons, is one of the things that are not teaspoons. There seemed to be instances which are not negative: for example, the class of all classes is a class. The application of Cantor's argument led me to consider the classes that are not members of themselves; and these, it seemed, must form a class. I asked myself whether this class is a member of itself or not. If it is a member of itself, it must possess the defining property of the class, which is to be not a member of itself. If it is not a member of itself, it must not possess the defining property of the class, and therefore must be a member of itself. Thus each alternative leads to its opposite and there is a contradiction. (*MPD*, 75–76)

The irony of discovering a paradox in mathematics is that mathematicians had brushed aside the ancient paradox of the liar as something "that had nothing to do with their subject" (*MPD*, 77).[19] "The best known of [the Greek paradoxes] was the one about Epimenides, the Cretan, who said that all Cretans are liars, and caused people to ask whether he was lying when he said so. The paradox is seen in its simplest form if a man says 'I am lying.' If he is lying, it is a lie that he is lying, and therefore he is speaking the truth; but if he is speaking the truth, he is lying, for that is what he says he is doing. Contradiction is thus inevitable. This contradiction is mentioned by St. Paul (Titus i. 10–13), who, however, is not interested in its logical aspects but only in its demonstration that the heathen are wicked" (*MPD*, 77).

In line with the realistic metaphysical analysis we established in the last section, the context of Russell's analysis is the persistent questioning of the nature of things: What kinds of things are there in the world? How many things are there?[20]

What kinds of things are there in the world? We saw earlier that Russell concluded that there must be both particulars and universals. Analogously, his early mathematical philosophy recognized both individuals and classes. There is another question, quantitative rather than qualitative, how many things are there? In his easiest example he asks us to "suppose there were exactly nine individuals in the world." Russell, like most philosophers, defers the question of what an individual is. Then what of 9 + 1 or 10? There is a class of cardinals, 0 to 9, but "9 + 1 is a class consisting of no classes, i.e. it is the null-class" (*IMP*, 132).

One of the most attractive traits of Russell as a writer, even on the admittedly obscure problem of types, is that if something is presented confusedly in one book, it is clarified in some other book.

For example, the matter of the number of classes in relation to the number of individuals. This is obscure in *Introduction to Mathematical Philosophy* but lucidly explained in *My Philosophical Development*. One may be baffled as to what is meant by "a class of n terms has 2^n subclasses." But consider, says Russell, "at the end of dinner, your host offers you a choice of three different sweets, urging you to have any one or two or all three, as you may wish. How many courses of conduct are open to you? You may refuse all of them. That is one choice. You may take one of them. This is possible in three different ways and therefore gives you three more choices. You may choose two of them. This again is possible in three ways. Or you may choose all three, which gives you one final possibility. The total number then is eight, i.e. 2^3." When this is generalized, 2^n is greater than n. "Applying this, as I did, to all the things in the universe, one arrives at the conclusion that there are more classes of things than there are things" (*MPD*, 80).

The interesting conclusion is that there are more classes than individuals. If there are 9 individuals, then 2^9 number of classes, or 512. Classes of classes number 2^{512}, and classes of classes of classes, numbers "2 raised to a power which has about 153 digits." Russell is writing in prison during World War I, and he patriotically refrains, because of the paper shortage, from writing out the number. This is an example of an important type of order, hierarchy. In this case we can always "travel . . . further along the logical hierarchy" (*IMP*, 133). The most interesting question then emerges: from a finite number of individuals, do we arrive at an infinite number of classes (*IMP*, 135)?

Is there in this argument some hocus-pocus? Russell is reminded of the magician who pulls things out of the hat. The person with a *"robust sense of reality"* knows there was no rabbit in it before the conjurer took it in hand. How can the finite hat contain an infinite number (*IMP*, 135)? The italicized phrase "robust sense of reality" became famous.

Some doctrine of types is needed to protect us against fallacy. In answer to the question of the greatest cardinal, there are two arguments with contradictory conclusions. On one hand, there can't be more members than members of a class, and there is no greatest cardinal. Further, whatever number n is proposed, there is always $n + 1$. On the other hand, we can count classes, classes of classes, etc. and so on, and there is a greatest cardinal. The axiom of infinity, "if *n* be any inductive cardinal number, there is at least one class of individuals having *n* terms," and *n* is not equal to $n + 1$.

The best concise statement of the way in which thinking of classes generates paradox is the following:

The comprehensive class we are considering, which is to embrace everything, must embrace itself as one of its members. In other words, if there is such a thing as "everything," then "everything" is something, and is a member of the class "everything." But normally a class is not a member of itself. Mankind, for example, is not a man. Form now the assemblage of all classes which are not members of themselves. This is a class; is it a member of itself or not? If it is, it is one of those classes that are not members of themselves, i.e. it is not a member of itself. If it is not, it is not one of those classes that are not members of themselves, i.e. it is a member of itself. Thus of the two hypotheses—that it is, and that it is not, a member of itself—each implies its contradictory. This is a contradiction. (*IMP*, 136)

Russell had already put his finger on the fallacy: including the class as though it were a member, ignoring the difference of type between mankind, the species man, and individual human beings. We can now add that if one attended the General Assembly of the United Nations and asked, where is the representative of the UN? the appropriate reply would be: the United Nations is not itself a nation![21]

Russell's reputation as an original philosophic logician rests more on theory of types than on any other contribution. The theory appeared first as the second appendix to *The Principles of Mathematics* (1903). It was clarified and refined and forms an important part of *Principia Mathematica,* and is frequently the subject of technical articles.

Paradoxes may be solved by nominalism when they have been produced by realism. That is, when a contradiction is produced by such an entity as a class, analyze it and discover whether it is not merely a mental entity. Russell the nominalist concludes that "classes are not 'things' " (*MPD*, 81). Another way of expressing this is that a class is like a propositional function, such as "if *x* is human, *x* is mortal," and "the propositional function itself is only an expression" (*MPD*, 82). Philosophically we have then another example of the difficulty with extreme Platonism. It overpopulates the world, and Occam's razor, nominalism, is to reduce the population. As one of Russell's followers once quipped: "Occam's razor shaves off Plato's beard."

When we make a transition from the paradox of universal classes to the paradox of denoting, what is the relation between one paradox and the other? Russell clearly thought them related, as philosophic problems that demand corrective analysis. Something has gone wrong in the grammar of language, but are the antecedent errors sufficiently similar to that of the paradoxes so that their solutions are analogous? Both involve the question of whether we are referring to real entities in the world. One is the question of individuals, the other the question of naming: these are the two sides of semantics. A class is not an individual solves the problem of the class of all classes. "The author of *Waverley*" is not the name of an author, as Scott is. Both the class and a description are our constructions, functions of our thought (*MPD*, 83–85).

What is Russell's theory of descriptions about? It is about what certain sentences are about: "A phrase may be denoting, and yet not denote anything; e.g., 'the present King of France.' " For a philosopher to talk about the present king of France is obviously absurd, since the monarchy was terminated. Historically the phrase must seem silly, and put us on guard against hocus-pocus. Why, therefore, was Russell so deeply concerned that it took him years to arrive at the essay "On Denoting" (1905)?[22]

A paradox occurred to Russell in the writing of *The Principles of Mathematics*. It must be quoted, because paraphrase loses both the deathly humor and the deadly seriousness:

People often assert that man is mortal; but what is mortal will die, and yet we should be surprised to find in the *Times* such a notice as the following: "Died at his residence at Camelot, Gladstone Road, Upper Tooting, on the 18th July, 19—, Man, eldest son of Death and Sin." *Man,* in fact, does not die; hence if "man is mortal" were, as it appears to be, a proposition about *man,* it would be simply false. The fact is, the proposition is about men, and here again, it is not about the concept *men,* but about what this concept denotes. (*PMath,* 53–54)

What is denotation? We should certainly say that "Louis XVI" denotes the Bourbon unfortunate whose head was severed by the Paris mob in 1793. We seem to refer to the same hapless monarch by saying "the husband of Marie Antoinette, the queen who would give cake in case the populace ran out of bread." "Louis XVI" is a proper name and "the husband of Marie Antoinette" is a denoting phrase (but nonproper rather than improper). In all ordinary history examinations, they mean the same, but historians are not as concerned by what they mean as are philosophers (or not concerned in the same way). If only proper names denote, then the phrase does more than point to an individual, that is, it says something about it, him in this case, and therefore deals in such a general meaning as "husband of," a relation that is virtually universal among males past puberty.

Therefore a solution must occur to the reader. "The present king of France" is like "the husband of Marie Antoinette." It is not a name; it does not refer to an individual. It may have some sort of connotation, but no necessary denotation. Meaning must therefore be of at least two sorts. The proof of this parallels Russell's analysis of the question "is Scott the author of *Waverley?*" If the denoting name means the same as the denoting phrase, then the question could be restated "is Scott Scott?" But the questioner, supposedly King George IV of England, knew that without asking. Therefore, a denoting phrase is not a name, and if only names denote existing individuals, the denoting phrase does not necessarily refer. We may say things about "the present King of France," such as "the present King of France is bald."

Russell as a Platonist had accepted the argument (of Meinong) that "if you say that the golden mountain does not exist, it is obvious that there is something that you are saying does not exist—namely, the golden mountain, therefore the golden mountain must subsist in some shadowy Platonic world of being, for otherwise your statement that the golden mountain does not exist would have no meaning" (*MPD,* 84).

The attraction of linguistic analysis is to solve the puzzles that are produced when we do not attend to language and use "bad grammar."

Russell's Analysis: A Method of Metaphysics

Those who consider the analytical methods of Bertrand Russell to be wholly antithetical to metaphysics have read him superficially. In this section we shall consider one book, *An Inquiry into Meaning and Truth,* which shows the kind of analysis Russell practiced and advocated in 1940. This is not at all the dissolution of all past metaphysics, as was A. J. Ayer's *Language, Truth and Logic*, then at halfway between the first and second editions (1936, 1946). Superficial readers are misled by the connotations of "analysis," and by the overt declaration of the author's preface: "As will be evident to the reader, I am, as regards method, more in sympathy with the logical positivists than with any other existing school" (*IMT*, 7). In the last chapter Russell declines to be classed with "the Nominalists and some of the Logical Positivists" because they maintain that "knowledge is only of words." Russell's argument leads him to side with those who believe that the world and its facts are not wholly unknowable; Russell's profession is "that, with sufficient caution, the properties of language may help us to understand the structure of the world." Therefore he sides with "a very distinguished party; they include Parmenides, Plato, Spinoza, Leibniz, Hegel, and Bradley" (*IMT*, 341).

To reason from the structure of language to the structure of the world was in Russell's nominalistic phase the very model of fallacious reasoning. We might have thought Russell a positivist antimetaphysician who had finally dissolved all past philosophy. There are many arguments that unite him with Ayer. All these are ways in which Russell's direction was "retreat from Pythagoras": these arguments are very clear.

One semantical difficulty with going from the order of words to the order of the world is that grammatical order is manmade and varies considerably from language to language (*IMT*, 38). There are many ambiguities of language that can refer to either of two unambiguous facts. For example, to what does the title "The Great Sioux Massacre" refer? To the fact that General Custer slaughtered Sioux? To the fact that Sioux slaughtered General Custer? Language is full of such ambiguous failures to communicate the factual asymmetry. There are many such difficulties, but the most original difficulty in *An Inquiry into Meaning and Truth* is heterogeneity of the world represented by the homogeneity of words.

"Day precedes night" and "night precedes day" are both true. There is thus, in such cases, an absence of logical homogeneity between the symbol and its meaning: the symbol is universal while the meaning is particular. This kind of logical heterogeneity is very liable to lead to confusions. All symbols are of the same logical type: they are classes of similar utterances, or similar noises, or similar shapes, but their meaning may be of any type, or of ambiguous type, like the meaning of "type" itself. The relation of a symbol to its meaning necessarily varies according to the type of the meaning, and this fact is important in the theory of symbolism. (*IMT*, 38)

The conclusion from this might be that we can't know the structure of the world without knowing the structure of the world that language suggests ambiguously.

The theory of types breaks down in language because some words do not clearly refer to objects, other than themselves, or to themselves self-referentially. "Word" may refer to noises and therefore be secondarily referring to objects in the primary language, or it may refer as meanings to themselves. " 'Word' is, itself, of ambiguous order, and therefore has no definite meaning; if this is forgotten, contradictions are apt to result. Take, e.g., the contradiction about 'heterological.' A predicate is 'heterological' when it cannot be predicated of itself, thus 'long' is heterological because it is not a long word, but 'short' is homological. We now ask is 'heterological' heterological? Either answer leads to a contradiction. To avoid such antinomies, the hierarchy of languages is essential" (*IMT*, 79).

Apart from such semantic difficulties, which should put us on guard against metaphysics, are three other considerations that are typical of logical positivism. The first of these is such general skepticism that all typical metaphysical terms become suspect. What is "substance"? "An unknowable something in which predicates inhere" (*IMT*, 97). This is an unwanted mystery of naive common sense. Therefore honest philosophy should "substitute articulate hesitancy for inarticulate certainty" (*IMT*, 11).

What then can we trust? Only two things: basic propositions and science based on them. The example of the first is "when we see a shooting star and say 'look'." Then the theory of gravitation applies to paths of comets (*IMT*, 18). The conclusion with regard to knowledge? "Everything that we know, or think we know, belongs to some special science; what then is left over for theory of knowledge?" (*IMT*, 12). What is here demonstrated is that analysis can be turned against the antimetaphysician. The very proposition "everything known belongs to some special science" is either in a special science or it is not. If it is not, then it cannot be known. If it is, then there is another science that is about special sciences. This is a contradiction.

Logical analysis can work in construction of metaphysics, not merely in its destruction. It can, for example, lead to the discovery of categories (*IMT*, 21). It may even support the belief in "natural kinds." Experience, common sense, and science, in many cases, support traditional metaphysics. "Fortunately many occurrences fit into natural kinds." There is constancy of things in time because our world is solid as well as gaseous, and things do resemble one another (*IMT*, 76). Animals produce similar offspring; for example, cats have kittens and dogs have pups (*IMT*, 80).

Russell constantly subjects what he had written earlier to skeptical scrutiny. The theory of real universals, Platonism, is exposed to nominalism, the theory that there are no real universals. The result is reassuring. One such, capitalized, as CAT was earlier, is DOG. Somehow, along with BLACK and so on, they are, as Plato said, "laid up in heaven," but less mythically they always remain immutably there (*IMT*, 25). In the older language, applied especially to relations, they "subsist" (*IMT*, 48).

It would be wrong to suggest that Russell's metaphysics is only the survival of ancient principles as restated in Russell's early commitments. Russell's metaphysics is making progress in restatement of first principles.

No longer does Russell search for absolute certainty; he now contends that it is not the mathematical but the empirical model that is uppermost. Since our language must be vague, when dealing with matter of fact, we must be satisfied with high probabilities (*IMT*, 105, 117). The standard of truth cannot be correspondence to fact alone; we must test for coherence (*IMT*, 123). Because we are not exclusively spectators, but agents, we must consider history an important kind of knowledge. We produce changes in our environment, and we can as agents learn the consequences of our actions (*IMT*, 84, 102). All these shifts are those taken by the pragmatists and lessen considerably the distance between realism and pragmatism.

Have we any precise knowledge of a rather more fluid cosmos? There is metaphysical knowledge that is a grasp of principles and of structure. These are neither empty, as logical or mathematical truths, nor empirical. This is Kant's solution of synthetic a priori truths. Among them is the principle of temporal asymmetry: "If x precedes y, y does not precede x" (*IMT*, 40). There is also reflexive knowledge: "I know that I know" (*IMT*, 49).

In some cases metaphysical knowledge has certainty: "We certainly know that two different colors cannot coexist in the same place in one visual field" (*IMT*, 82). How do we know this? There is a kind of intuitive or direct knowing: "We *see* the incompatibility" (*IMT*, 82).

Such knowledge is capable of exact statement: there is an order of events such that "(1) x does not precede y; (2) if x precedes y and y precedes z, then x precedes z; (3) if x and y are different, either x precedes y or y precedes x (*IMT*, 101).

Russell's Attack on Linguistic Analysis

In Russell's own account, after World War I, which drew him into public affairs, the main influences on philosophy, British first, then American, were Wittgenstein and positivism: Wittgenstein's *Tractatus*, then the logical positivists (Ayer the chief in Britain), with both of whom Russell was sympathetic, and then Wittgenstein's *Philosophic Investigations*. It was the latter that disgusted Russell and provoked a series of attacks. Although early Wittgenstein was doing hard work, convincing Russell that mathematics and "logic consists wholly of tautologies" (*MPL*, 119), later Wittgenstein encouraged philosophy to take only ordinary language seriously. Russell's scorn exceeds even that which he had for the American pragmatists: "We are now told that it is not the world that we are to try to understand but only sentences, and it is assumed that all sentences can count as true except those uttered by philosophers" (*MPD*, 217).[23]

Russell was perfectly aware that the central problem of the *Tractatus* was the relation of the structure of a sentence to the structure of fact.[24] The problem of order is prominent in the *Investigations*.[25] To comprehend the complexity of the relation between Russell and his former student, one should read the chapters in *My Philosophical Development*, "The Impact of Wittgenstein" (110–27) and "Some Replies to Criticism" (214–54), which concerns his controversies with followers more strongly attached to Wittgenstein and therefore hostile to Russell. For those who dislike lengthy controversy and do not relish nastiness, there are two short masterpieces of wit: "The Cult of 'Common Usage' "[26] and the introduction to Ernest Gellner's *Words and Things*.[27]

The attack on Wittgenstein is that he was a man of "bogus humility" who appealed to common usage or ordinary language rather than to scientific thought or even to the language of the educated (*MPD*, 214). Russell's argument is that unless we have studied mathematics we use the word "speed" in a vague and imprecise way, and we can expect muddles like this: The motorist claims "I was at rest," while a friend says "You were moving at 20 miles an hour," and the police say "He was traveling at 60 miles an hour" (*PMem*, 156). In ordinary life we cannot settle the problem, and therefore, although it is easy to listen to such speech, if we want to *know* we must turn to scientists. The argument is elaborated: Wittgenstein "debased himself before common sense" (*MPD*, 214). Russell himself often appealed to common sense, but the controversy forced him to show that it is common sense as refined when necessary by scientific knowledge.

The cult of common usage is based, according to Russell, on "the *mystique* of the 'common man.' " The ignorant may well resent the technical language of the learned, but why should philosophers erect this prejudice into a norm? Here again, Russell becomes a critic of common sense. Ignorant common sense once taught "that there could not be people at the antipodes, because they would fall off" (*PMem*, 156). Those who make such a criticism are often resented as "elitist" who "sin against democracy" (*PMem*, 154). But so what? Common sense is often false.[28]

The defense of linguistic analysis is that it is necessary to clarify the meanings of what is said. To refute the argument about clarity Russell often told a story. Once he was cycling to Winchester and stopped to ask a shopkeeper the shortest way.

> He called to a man in the back premises:
> "Gentleman wants to know the shortest way to Winchester."
> "Winchester?" an unseen voice replied.
> "Aye."
> "Way to Winchester?"
> "Aye."
> "Shortest way?"
> "Aye."
> "Dunno." (*PMem*, 157)

The point of the story is that clarification of meaning is worthless unless it occurs in the context of a search for truth. What Russell argues is put in the title: "Clarity Is Not Enough."[29]

To get truth, as we have seen in Russell's analysis, requires something other than language, namely facts. What makes our propositions true is what is or is not the case in the world. The positivists had prepared for linguistic analysis by rejecting the concept of correspondence between what we say and what is. Reality was supposedly too metaphysical. Again a story that Russell told:

> At a certain period, when [Hempel's] finances were not very flourishing . . . he entered a cheap restaurant in Paris. He asked for the menu. He read it, and he ordered beef. All this since entering the restaurant was language. The food came and he took a mouthful. This was confrontation with facts [which Hempel had denied in theory as possible or necessary]. He summoned the restaurateur and said "this is horse-flesh, not beef." The restaurateur replied, "Pardon me, but the scientists of my culture-circle include the sentence 'this is beef' among those that they accept" [the only test of truth, Hempel maintained]. Hempel on his own showing would be obliged to accept this with equanimity. This is absurd. (*MPD*, 218)

Linguistic analysis is, according to Russell, even more absurd. "The desire to understand the world is, they think, an outdated folly" (*MPD*, 219). Russell's denunciation of Wittgenstein's analysis as degenerate springs from his contempt for the refusal of the hard work of genuine philosophy and his charge that linguistic analysis alone is sterile. "The later Wittgenstein . . . seems to have grown tired of serious thinking and to have invented a doctrine which would make such an activity unnecessary. I do not for one moment believe that the doctrine which has these lazy consequences is true. I realize, however, that I have an overpoweringly strong bias against it, for, if it is true, philosophy is, at best, a slight help to lexicographers, and at worst, an ideal tea-table amusement" (*MPD*, 216–17). The final charge against linguistic analysis is that its results are trivial. The problem then might end with the March Hare's solution: "I'm tired of this. Let's change the subject."

Whether Russell's polemics against Wittgenstein and practitioners of linguistic analysis are unfair we have not time to explore. We have admitted that the whole affair, largely in the late 1950s, was nasty. Russell was in his late eighties and undoubtedly was expressing a bitter and resentful side of his nature. The most charming remark, full of pathos: "It is not an altogether pleasant experience to find oneself regarded as antiquated after having been, for a time, in the fashion. It is difficult to accept this experience gracefully" (*MPD*, 214).

The value of Russell's attack, apart from the superb literary style, is the reinforcement of the view that we are studying a metaphysical realist and a moralist. Analysis, in Russell's sense, is full of fun, wit, satire, jokes, but in the end it is as deadly serious as Plato's politics and religion.

Chapter Five

Metaphysics: Knowledge of the Real Order?

Death and Rebirth of Metaphysics

The significance of Russell's relation to metaphysics is often said to be wholly negative. That is, his career is taken to show the demise of all metaphysics, particularly those types characterized by a doctrine of God, or the unity of the whole in the Absolute, or the reality of universals in a world transcending the world of sensed particulars. These are three of the successive metaphysical commitments he made between 1885 and 1912. That Russell abandoned these positions means for some interpreters that they are untenable. Russell's powerful logical objections to metaphysics make him seem one of the positivists, that is, one who says that knowledge comes only by the ways familiar in the empirical sciences and that all claims to know a more comprehensive reality are bogus. No one disagrees with Russell himself that he failed to establish a metaphysical system. Far from it; his career shows a succession of metaphysical trials, most of which he felt obliged to abandon because he detected errors. Nevertheless, there are positive achievements, and there are significant constancies as well as what appear to be erratic changes.

Russell was not only the critic of all previous metaphysics; he became the critic of antimetaphysics. Although metaphysical arguments were all logically and linguistically faulty, nevertheless the intention to say something about the world and its structure remains legitimate. Can we go so far as to find in Russell not only the death but also the rebirth of metaphysics? Beyond the positivist attack is the counterattack that natural science itself, not theology only, rests upon presuppositions beyond what can be empirically verified. Seen in this double way, Russell and metaphysics have a double significance, and the very complexity, when seen as a whole, makes this not merely the longest but also the most significant career in the history of philosophy.

Is such a dialectical approach required? The objection to the yes-and-no approach is that Russell himself was a Hegelian who used the method of thesis and antithesis for only a short period, 1894–98, according to his own account, and came to regard his idealistic writings as "unmitigated rubbish."[1] He became famous, not for the zigzagging method, but rather for a strictly linear argumentation that because of its directness is esteemed as "clear," even when nondialecticians miss profundity and adequacy. If, in Russell's conception of metaphysics, this is "the union and conflict of two very different impulses," then only dialectic is adequate.[2] But if there is nothing in common between mysticism, "the attempt to conceive the world as a whole," and science, then we have only conflict. The impulses of the contemplative and the scientist are so diverse that it seems impossible to find a common language; and Russell, after making a study of Pythagoras (whom he coupled with Jesus and Buddha) and Hegel (who also tried to fuse mysticism and logic) decided that both had failed.[3] Hegel's logic was bad, and his mysticism was turned to glorifying the Prussian state.

Russell conceptualized scientific method and the religious impulse in a way to reconcile what institutionally he found opposed. What characterizes "a truly scientific philosophy" is that it is "more humble, more piecemeal, more arduous, offering less glitter of outward mirage to flatter fallacious hopes, . . . more indifferent to fate, and more capable of accepting the world without the tyrannous imposition of our human and temporary demands" (ML, 32). Although epistemologically science is valued for its devotion to truth and production of knowledge, these characteristics are also those of "religion and . . . every deeply serious view of the world and human destiny [namely] an element of submission, a realization of the limits of human power" (ML, 31). Is "cosmic piety" the essential motive of both science and religion or merely an insufficient effort to unite impulses by conceptualizing them in similar terms?

Does it produce a viable metaphysics to conceptualize the content of science and religion in the same terms? If science is based upon the presupposition that the world is cosmos, an ordered whole, and religion is the conviction that there is a universal orderer, then science and religion require each other. When Russell tells of the earliest study of the axioms of Euclid, it is in the context of natural laws stated mathematically and resting on a divine First Cause.[4]

Earlier we had to take account of Russell's childhood belief in God as First Cause, and this form of ultimate metaphysical explanation commonly is of a lawful and therefore intelligible world. The metaphysical aspect of Newtonian physics is that gravitation holds because the Lord so created nature. Russell affirmed

the belief that nature operates according to mathematical laws, and that human actions, like planetary motions, could be calculated if we had sufficient skill. By the time I was fifteen, I had arrived at a theory very similar to that of the Cartesians. The movements of living bodies, I felt convinced, were wholly regulated by the laws of dynamics; therefore free will must be an illusion. But, since I accepted consciousness as an indubitable datum, I could not accept materialism, though I had a certain hankering after it on account of its intellectual simplicity and its rejection of "nonsense." (*PBR,* 7)

Russell continues to refer to the cosmic order in the Victorian phrase, "reign of law," and records the changes required by scientific progress. All of these have fundamental metaphysical implications. The first of these is that physics "no longer assumes matter as permanent substance."

The theory of relativity, by merging time into space-time, has damaged the traditional notion of substance more than all the arguments of philosophers. Matter, for common sense, is something which persists in time and moves in space. But for modern relativity-physics this view is no longer tenable. A piece of matter has become, not a persistent thing with varying states, but a system of inter-related events. The old solidity is gone, and with it the characteristics that made matter seem more real than fleeting thoughts. Nothing is permanent, nothing endures; the prejudice that the real is the persistent must be abandoned.[5]

The full confidence of scientific faith was once in a *"universal* reign of law," that is, that there were "no exceptions, not even human volitions" (*BW,* 243, 241, emphasis added). The stress on universality is psychologically a function of the human "passion for safety," whereas the stress on freedom expresses the "passion for power" (*BW,* 243). The problem is whether laws of physics can apply to all levels, or whether the laws of chemistry and biology presuppose physical order but require greater complexity. Russell inclines to the latter (*BW*, 242). The oversimple physical order that had been dogmatically asserted to explain everything makes a likely target for the skeptic (*BW*, 244).

Sometimes Russell's reaction against deterministic order carries him to the skeptical extreme of thinking all order the imposition of human patterns. Although modern philosophy has tended to regard order as produced by human perception and interest, and this has been a common position shaped by Kant and such American philosophers as William James, Russell defends the classical view and combines in his defense of objective order an appeal to emotion and to science. He continually reaffirms that his concern is the cosmos. There are

very obvious things, such as the starry heavens and a stormy sea on a rocky coast; in part the vastness of the scientific universe, both in space and time, as compared to the life of mankind; in part of the edifice of impersonal truth, especially truth which, like that of mathematics, does not merely describe the world that happens to exist. (*PBR*, 19)

Had Russell been content to express his cosmic vision as a poet, perhaps claiming for it to be no more than "a likely tale," as in Plato's *Timaeus*, the search for reality as a cosmic whole might have been the happy evolution of a cosmology, as in the case of White-head. But Russell sought certainty. If there is an "edifice" of necessary, not merely hypothetical, truths, then we should know these truths and be able to demonstrate the fundamental science of being and becoming. Russell, like many twentieth-century philosophers, was hesitant to name his position and once said that he had only accepted one position as his own, "logical atomism," which, although a "realism," was "characterized rather by [its] logic than by [its] metaphysic."[6]

Russell's "Logical Atomism" ends with "an outline of a *possible* structure of the world," a world of events in space-time relations (*LK*, 341–42). In this structure there are "discoverable laws" and since "a mind and a brain are not really distinct," there is no break between the physical and the mental orders (*LK*, 242–43). Although events are many and independent, there are "compresent events . . . taken as wholes." Russell maintained that this position had never been refuted. That is, although not like other metaphysics, presented by their proponents with "certainty of its own exclusive truth," his view is to be "refined in order to fit in *completely with scientific fact*" (*LK*, 343).

Russell's metaphysics remains ever problematic: if such a position as logical atomism fits scientific knowledge of the cosmos, must it fail to give the emotional satisfaction of mysticism?

The first volume of Russell's *Autobiography*, which covers the years 1872–1914, tells of his finding the Hegelian system inspiring.[7] Although there was deep cultural malaise before World War I, university philosophers were expected to give utterance to a vision of a high destiny of mankind. Although Russell's Hegelian period had ended more than a decade earlier, he still could communicate the vision of the whole in 1912 as "something sublime, something to which we could wish to yield assent."[8] True, he had indeed expressed the despair of "A Free Man's Worship," but he was still working within the framework of a vision. His life plan was to achieve the synthesis beyond the thesis of the abstract and the antithesis of the concrete.

I resolved not to adopt a profession, but to devote myself to writing. I . . . made projects for future work. I thought I would write one series of books on the philosophy of the sciences from pure mathematics to physiology, and another series of books on social questions. I hoped that the two series might ultimately meet in a synthesis at once scientific and practical. My scheme was largely inspired by Hegelian ideas. (*Ai*, 184–85)

Russell had already experienced disillusionment and despair, but surely the bitterness and cynicism of World War I intensified his well-developed skill of debunking what is fraudulent. We must therefore proceed to examine his critical rejection of all previous systems, a rejection rooted in personal frustration.

The Frustrated Metaphysician and Critic of All Previous Metaphysics

Immanuel Kant's Copernican revolution in philosophy was expressed as the subjective study of the mind's own categories. Without our forms of intuition, including space and time, there could be no order in what comes from the external world. Although Russell's realism was a rejection of the idealism of Kant and post-

Kantian philosophers who made mind prior to nature, there are
expressions in Russell of a rejection of what we have traced to the
ancient Greeks, that man can comprehend the cosmos in mathematical laws. The skeptical Russell doubted that the world is a
unity.

The most fundamental of my intellectual beliefs is that this is rubbish. I
think the universe is all spots and jumps, without unity, without continuity, without coherence or orderliness or any of the other properties that
governesses love. Indeed, there is little but prejudice and habit to be said
for the view that there is a world at all.[9]

How much of this is the serious scientist-metaphysican telling
of the oddity of the new physics of quanta replacing with "a world
of unreal and fantastic dreams . . . the Newtonian order and solidity" (SO, 97)? What has got in the way is Russell's attacks on
various reconciliations of science and theology. He attacks the phy-
sicist Millikan for using the formula "God works through law" (SO,
96 note). This type of religious apology continues the deist eighteenth-century welcoming of "the reign of law, since they thought
that laws implied a Lawgiver" (SO, 96). "In metaphysics my creed
is short and simple. I think that the external world may be an
illusion, but if it exists, it consists of events, short, small and
haphazard. Order, unity, and continuity are human inventions just
as truly as are catalogues and encyclopaedias" (SO, 98).

Russell has put his finger on the great change in scientific thought,
from a necessary order of an all-determining nature or God, in which
laws exclude any chance or unpredictable consequence, to a conception of laws that are statistical probabilities. In the former, law
is universal in the sense of excluding any exception; in the latter,
exceptions are merely statistically unlikely, but not impossible.
What is ironic is that Russell characterizes the world of the new
physics "a more higgledy-piggledy and haphazard affair" from the
perspective of the old physics (SO, 94). It was the old physics as
well as the old theology of omnipotence that had made human
freedom, and therefore moral responsibility, impossible. By refusing
to see the advantage of the shift to a new conception of order-
disorder, Russell's criticism of all previous metaphysics is neither
as careful nor as profound as Whitehead's.

When Russell's writings on the logic and language of past meta-physicians are considered, beginning with *A Critical Exposition of the Philosophy of Leibniz,* first published in 1900, down to *An Inquiry into Meaning and Truth,* 1940, we find a sequence of powerful objections to all previous metaphysics. Just as in the quote above, he denounces the belief in order, as traditionally conceived, as "rubbish," so he denounces metaphysics generally as the imposition of our thought on the world. Our thought is formulated in language and logic according to human convention, which is arbitrary and relative to time, and incurably dependent on human interest. The illusion is that the world is and must be as we think it should be. As we have seen above this is both unscientific and irreligious. Metaphysics is shot through with arrogance and pride. Russell is ever the puritan who would smash idols.

In the middle of this period comes *The Philosophy of Logical Atomism,* 1918, in which there is the most general summary: *"Practically* all traditional metaphysics is filled with mistakes due to bad grammar, and . . . all the traditional problems of metaphysics and traditional results—supposed results—of metaphysics are due to failure to make the kind of distinctions in what we may call philosophical grammar."[10]

The mistakes are all aspects of the subject-predicate form of the proposition used in Aristotelian logic. The common model used by everyone is "Socrates is mortal." The subject term names a substance, and substance is the primary category. All other categories are predicates which may be affirmed in a true proposition because they are attributes of the substance. For centuries this has been taught as the natural way in which to state truths and to deduce truths validly from major and minor premises to a conclusion. The logic of relations, as we have examined it, disproved that the syllogism is the only validating form of inference. What we need now to examine are the metaphysical assumptions on which the logic was based and the metaphysical implications drawn from the logic.

As we have seen in considering the logic of relations, there is the "is" of predication (ϕx)); the "is" of definition ($=$ df); the "is" of equivalence ($=$); the "is" of existence ($\exists$(x)); the "is" of class membership ($x, y \in u$); the "is" of class inclusion ($x \subset y$). If at least these six are made as required, and traditional metaphysics does not make them, then, since metaphysics is the science of being, the "science" is based on failure of distinction and confusion. It is often alleged that the ontological argument for God's existence is drawn from defining God as perfect, and then characterizing perfection as lacking nothing. Therefore God cannot fail to exist. So stated, the argument is a simple fallacy to the new logician equipped with distinctions between meanings of the verb "to be." The argument slips from meaning to meaning, and illegitimately leaps from definition, solely within the conceptual order, to the existential order (from = df to $\exists(x)$). Russell's arguments often so rest upon dichotomy of orders. One interesting example that makes the point more concrete is from *An Inquiry into Meaning and Truth:* "Suppose, for example, I say 'similarity exists.' If 'exists' means what it does when I say 'the President of the United States exists,' my statement is nonsense. What I can mean may, to begin with, be expressed in the statement: there are occurrences which require for their verbal description sentences of the form *'a* is similar to *b'* " (*IMT,* 347). Russell does not here say that similarity as a universal *subsists,* nor does he ever provide a symbol for saying that a universal subsists, say $S_{(x)}$ in contrast to $\exists_{(x)}$. But we may not doubt that the similarity of similar things is included in the "non-linguistic fact" of "pairs of similar things" (*IMT,* 347).

The next aspect of "bad metaphysics" indicated by subject-predicate logic is substance-attribute ontology. Russell's understanding of Aristotle is that substance is what is not predicable, but attributes are predicable when "present in a subject." According to Russell, Aristotle is giving us a mere "linguistic convenience" or a piece of "grammatical knowledge" of Greek and similar Indo-European languages. "A substance in the above primary sense is an individual thing or person or animal. But in a secondary sense a species or a genus—e.g., 'man' or 'animal'—may be called a substance. This secondary sense seems indefensible, and opened the door, in later writers, to much bad metaphysics" (*HWP,* 200).

Russell's *History of Western Philosophy* is a story with a villain. To make Aristotle the bad guy is nothing new: this was a commonplace among humanists of the Renaissance who were out to break up scholasticism based on considering Aristotle *"the* Philosopher."[11] Humanists were bent on replacing syllogistic reasoning with language based on studying such rhetorical models as Cicero. What is new in Russell is the charge that the long dark shadow of Aristotle's logic had prevented Leibniz from publishing his new "universal characteristic," and only by the middle of the nineteenth century did a new logic, one stating the foundations of mathematics, come to finally replace syllogistic reasoning. Thus the European mind was unshackled. The liberation from restrictive syllogism is also justified by the metaphysical failure and exhaustion of modern philosophy. The supposed liberator, Kant, was, as Russell seldom fails to tell us, addicted to Aristotelian syllogistic logic, as he was to Euclidian geometery and to Newtonian science.

Does the logical pattern of the proposition dominate metaphysical systems? Russell's theory of logic as the essence of philosophy has often been challenged as an exaggeration. The most detailed defense is in Russell's *Philosophy of Leibniz.*[12] The most sweeping claim is made with regard not only to Leibniz's metaphysical pluralism, called monadism because each substance is called a monad, but also to various theories of two or three substances, which in the case of Descartes are matter, mind (and God), or the elimination of all but matter, materialistic monism, or of all but mind, idealistic monism. In Spinoza's case there can be nothing but God or nature. Modern metaphysics had seemed to have exhausted the possibilities open to it and to have deadlocked itself in insoluble problems.

Has a simple logical dogma, that every proposition consisted of a subject and predicate, had such vast consequences? Russell's analysis is that traditional logic is drawn from manipulating nouns and adjectives, as in "Socrates is mortal," and overlooking verbs and prepositions. "This omission has had a very great effect upon philosophy; it is hardly too much to say that most metaphysics, since Spinoza, has been largely determined by it" (*PP*, 94). Because an adjective attributes a quality to a single thing, expressed by a noun, the belief is supported that every proposition can be regarded as attributing a property to a single thing.

Relations between two or more things are overlooked. Hence it was supposed that, ultimately, there can be no such entities as relations between things. Hence either there can be only one thing in the universe, or, if there are many things, they cannot possibly interact in any way, since any interaction would be a relation, and relations are impossible. (*PP*, 95)

Russell's linguistic criticism, which liberated many philosophers from the presupposition that philosophy must build such monadistic or monistic systems, has been carried much further. One next step is to question the logic of relations. Is it not just as restrictive as the subject-predicate logic? Observe that although symbolic logic substitutes half a dozen symbols for "is," they are all still timeless or untensed verbs like the copula "is" in "Socrates is mortal." (A "copula" is so called because it links subject and predicate.) One might say that Russell's whole concern with eternal universals is produced by overlooking actions finished, in process, and yet to come, as in "Russell thought," "Russell thinks," "Russell will think." And similarly we miss "can," "cannot," "must," "may," "ought," and so on. These are also overlooked in his logic. The logic of relations is just as much a calculus of propositions. Russell came to appreciate natural language in the context of Vico's new science, an understanding of how language grows with societies. [13]

The logical criticism of all previous metaphysics was expressed classically in a series of papers from "Mathematics and the Metaphysicians," 1901 (*ML,* chap. 5), "The Study of Mathematics," 1902 (*ML,* chap. 4), "On Scientific Method in Philosophy," 1914 (*ML,* chap. 6), and particularly "Logic as the Essence of Philosophy," 1914 (*OKEW,* chap. 11), and other essays in *Our Knowledge of the External World as a Field for Scientific Method in Philosophy* on continuity and infinity. [14] Even in *Principia Mathematica* we are dealing with logic as an instrument for talking about what is real. The problems are most frequently metaphysical: must there be a subsisting "Platonic world of being"? What light can be thrown on "what is meant by 'existence' " (*MPD,* 84)?

Although Russell rejected traditional logic as trivial nonsense and a training in those habits of solemn humbug which are so great a help in later life, his intention was thoroughly Aristotelian in the sense of providing an instrument for reasoning about reality and in defending common sense. For example, what of the speculations about the whole? Russell is skeptical about the Hegelian inspiration, as Aristotle had been of his predecessors.

There are no propositions of which the "universe" is the subject; in other words, that there is no such thing as the "universe." What I do maintain is that there are general propositions which may be asserted of each individual thing, such as the propositions of logic. This does not involve that all the things there are form a whole which could be regarded as another thing and be made the subject of predicates. It involves only the assertion that there are properties which belong to each separate thing, not that there are properties belonging to the whole of things collectively. (*ML,* 110–11)

There may be, in other words, many things without there being "a whole composed of those things." It goes back to the problem of individuals and classes of individuals, and the common sense metaphysics is that the class of objects, such as bananas, is not another banana. There must be a critique of ordinary language as well as the language of metaphysicians because "grammatical structure does not represent uniquely the relations between the ideas involved. Thus 'a whale is big' and 'one is a number' both look alike, so that the eye gives no help to the imagination." This is from the introduction to *Principia Mathematica* (*BW*, 162).[15]

Just as Russell is deeply Aristotelian even though debunking the Aristotelian logic and metaphysics, so also he is deeply Kantian even when debunking the Kantian tradition. One passage, also dealing with the universe or the world as whole, is intended to continue Kant's Copernican revolution.

> The oneness of the world is an almost undiscussed postulate of most metaphysics. "Reality is not merely one and self-consistent, but a system of reciprocally determinate parts" [Bosanquet, Logic II, 211]—such a statement would pass almost unnoticed as a mere truism. Yet I believe that it embodies a failure to effect thoroughly the "Copernican revolution," and that the apparent oneness of the world is merely the oneness of what is seen by a single spectator or apprehended by a single mind. The Critical Philosophy, although it intended to emphasise the subjective element in many apparent characteristics of the world, yet, by regarding the world in itself as unknowable, so concentrated attention upon the subjective representation that its subjectivity was soon forgotten. (*ML*, 99–100)

The metaphysical systems of German idealism grew out of the Kantian criticism of the categories. The despair of not knowing the world was exchanged for a metaphysical dogmatism. After the Russellian Copernican revolution, is any kind of nondogmatic metaphysics possible?

The Metaphysician in Spite of His Criticism of Metaphysics

Insofar as the criticism of past metaphysics rested upon the lack of "a correct symbolism," that lack had been made good in *Principia Mathematica*. Therefore, with a new organon designed to analyze the formal characteristics of relations, do we find a new metaphysics emerging? The necessary step between his critique and any positive construction of the world order is the rejection of the antimetaphysics of positivism and linguistic analysis. In this section we take that step, toward metaphysics, and in the next section we attempt a reconstruction of a metaphysics of order.

The crucial book is *An Inquiry into Meaning and Truth,* the William James lectures for 1940 at Harvard University. Many of his audience expected from Russell a debunking of any metaphysics, not only of idealism and of pragmatism, but of Russell's own early realism.

The new style in philosophy was logical positivism coming from the Vienna circle by way of A. J. Ayer. In 1935 Ayer published *Language, Truth, and Logic* and it came with the highest praise of Bertrand Russell: had he been young again, this is the book he would have wished to have written. [16] Then did Russell himself reject all metaphysics as nonsense? In the preface of *An Inquiry into Meaning and Truth* we read that it is "evident that I am, as regards method, more in sympathy with the logical positivists than with any other existing school" (*IMT,* 7). Ayer's charge of nonsense attacked any sentence that could not be verified. The key question of meaning could be answered only by empirical evidence (*IMT,* 7).

Was there a positivist Russell who renounced his Platonism and mysticism in the name of clear empirical language and strict verification of every sentence? The surprise is that he expressly rejects the "Nominalists and some of the Logical Positivists" because they held that knowledge is only of words. In contrast, Russell sided with "Parmenides, Plato, Spinoza, Leibniz" and in spite of some aspects of mysticism, "Hegel and Bradley" (*IMT,* 341). Exactly what, we must ask, is the argument that leads Russell to oppose antimetaphysics and to come to the defense of the metaphysical tradition, including Leibniz, Hegel, and Bradley, all of whose systems Russell had, as we have seen, exposed as based on bad logic?

The metaphysical principle is that we can *"infer properties of the world from properties of language"* (*IMT,* 341, italics added). The distinguished metaphysicians, in their varied ways, are giving affirmative answers to the question: "What [if anything] can be inferred from the *structure* of language as to the *structure* of the world?" (*IMT,* 342, italics added). The simplest example given is that if "W is a complete group of qualities," such that our judgments of perception are "W is red," "W is round," "W is bright," then there is something making it true to say that there is something, and this subject has compresent (i.e., present together) qualities: red, round, bright. This is close to agreeing with the rejected Aristotelian theory of subject and predicate, and we might surmise that Russell almost named Aristotle among the distinguished metaphysicians. But the subject is not an Aristotelian substance, but closer to what empiricists, such as Hume, would call a "bundle of compresent qualities" (*IMT*, 342). Even if the subject is an "occurrence" or an "event," which has no necessary permanence, still in "this is red," "this" is particular, and "red" is universal. Earlier Russell had used the Platonic formula that particulars share in universals. Here his analysis is that in the case of "that is red," he replies that "this" and "that," and any other thing, *"all have a common part, which is what the predicate designates"* (*IMT*, 343, italics added).

Earlier the case for real universals used relations, expressed by prepositions as the chief examples. The realism of 1912 takes the same form in 1940. Sentences "require words other than names." This restates the formula that no complete sentence can be composed of nouns only; references to particulars are meaningful only when at least one word is general. Among the relation words are predicates, such as we examined in the previous paragraph as qualities, and these are monadic relations, that is, relations to one thing only rather than between two or more things. The concluding inference, since a " 'universal' may be defined as the meaning (if any) of a relation-word," is that at least as related to things, there must be universals (*IMT*, 343).

The nominalist objection to real universals in 1940 took a behaviorist form. What are words but sets of similar noises called for by a set of stimuli?

A defender of universals, if attacked, might begin in this way: "You say that two cats, because they are similar, stimulate the utterance of two similar noises which are both instances of the word 'cat.' But the cats must be *really* similar to each other, and so must the noises. And if they are *really* similar, it is impossible that 'similarity' should be just a word. It is a word which you utter on certain occasions, namely, when there *is* similarity. Your tricks and devices," he will say, "may seem to dispose of other universals, but only by putting all the work on to this one remaining universal, similarity; of that you cannot get rid, and therefore you might as well admit all the rest." (*IMT*, 344)

What are some of the structural similarities shared by events, for which we have evidence in the structure of language? Russell reiterates the importance of temporal and spatial relations. We perceive in a complex "A-before-B," and also "A-above-B," and there are innumerable other such relations of temporal priority and vertical order which we call the asymmetrical relations. The importance of order or structure of our world is that it is illustrated both in what we perceive (as the noise A preceding the noise B) and in what we produce as in writing A before we write B. The "structure of the world" reaffirmed in 1940 is that of 1912, even in what Russell's world order most commonly lacked, a principle of causality.

As we saw when studying the dialectic of the nominalist attack on the realist, the objection to real universals is that although cats may be similar, there is no such thing as CAT, or SIMILARITY either. "Suppose, for example, I say 'similarity' exists? If 'exists' means what it does when I say 'the President of the United States exists,' my statement is nonsense." The realist, according to the nominalist, needs only the word "similar." But why "similarity"? The point is that when one says "A is similar to B," a person means the fact that A is similar to B. The realist means not a fact about language, but that in the world there are pairs of similar things, such as yellow things (*IMT*, 347).

The argument concludes:

We have arrived . . . at a result which has been . . . the goal of all our discussions. The result I have in mind is this: that complete metaphysical agnosticism is not compatible with the maintenance of linguistic propositions. Some modern philosophers hold that we know much about language, but nothing about anything else. This view forgets that language is an empirical phenomenon like another, and that a man who is metaphysically agnostic must deny that he knows when he uses a word. For my part, I believe that, partly by means of the study of syntax, we can arrive at considerable knowledge concerning the structure of the world. (*IMT*, 347)

Russell's Metaphysics of Cosmic Order

Russell met the positivistic linguistic analyst on analytic ground, and by using his opponent's techniques he reaffirms the realistic position. *Inquiry into Meaning and Truth* seems a success in coming to a definite conclusion about our knowledge of the structure of the world. It is not, however, complete. Why, then, after 1940 did he not finally proceed to finish his metaphysical system? The war and its aftermath preoccupied him, but not to the exclusion of two large and important contributions, *A History of Western Philosophy,* 1945, and *Human Knowledge: Its Scope and Limits,* 1948, and a somewhat smaller project, *Human Society in Ethics and Politics,* 1954, which comprised the chapters on ethics originally intended for *Human Knowledge.*[17] They were not included in the latter volume because he was "uncertain as to the sense in which ethics can be regarded as 'knowledge.' "

Russell often makes sharp distinctions, and having distinguished, fails to unite. Therefore, having dichotomized reason from emotion, and knowledge of fact from evaluative preference, there can be no synthesis of them (*HSEP,* 7–11). If a metaphysical system sets out to find connections, as Russell intends, between particulars and universals, but they cannot be found because of ultimate chasms and discontinuities, then no such system can be produced. To any technical difficulty of dichotomy or dualism, the predominant insoluble problem of Cartesians, finding a connection between mind and body, Russell devoted *The Analysis of Mind* and *The Analysis of Matter,* and defended neutral monism. There are no such Cartesian substances, thinking substances and extended substances, but events that can be interpreted as mental events or physical events, and it is we who chose the categories. The events are neither; only our categories introduce both.

Probably there were many factors that together blocked Russell's achievement of a metaphysics of cosmic order. How could there be metaphysical knowledge in addition to scientific knowledge?[18] The inferences from the new physics, as inferences from the structure of language to the structure of the world, hardly seem to give us any certainty, and alternative worldviews satisfy neither the requirement of science nor that of emotion.[19] If there is an emotive aspect of metaphysics, which Russell calls "mysticism," should it be satisfied if it brings superstitions?[20] By 1925 Russell's friend and senior colleague, Whitehead, developing his metaphysics in *Science and the Modern World,* had found it necessary to introduce God. Russell's famous review had the title "Is Science Superstitious?"[21] Below we will consider this, but in context of another and virtually unnoticed appreciative review.

Russell was blocked in his metaphysical quest by a characteristic of Anglo-American habits of mind. Albert Einstein, who owed to Russell's writing "innumerable happy hours," nevertheless has to count the heroic endeavor to formulate a system "fruitless" (*PBR*, 279).

Why does a philosopher, namely Russell, have a "bad intellectual conscience" about doing metaphysics (*PBR*, 291)? Einstein reads through the lines of Russell's writing and senses in him "a fateful fear of metaphysics." We may cite the German original because the kind of fear is "Angst," the characteristic of human existence in face of death or nothingness: *"eine verhängnisvolle 'Angst vor der Metaphysik' "* (*PBR*, 288–89). How does Einstein understand the guilty feeling of a philosopher? The historical reason is that philosophers originally trusted reflection to give them knowledge. But now science is the model of knowledge, and reflection is ersatz, a cheap substitute for observation and experiment. What the philosopher does, to make his enterprise seem honest, is to put his words into quotation marks, as "world," "things," and so on (*PBR*, 281). Beyond anxiety and guilt, Einstein also senses the "sickness" produced in philosophers by empiricism. This is, says Einstein, a by-product of Hume's skeptical criticism.

Einstein does not say that the metaphysician should not be anxious, guilty, or sick. Plato, Spinoza, and Hegel trusted reflection, and this gave life to their pictures of reality. Maybe they were victims of prejudice or illusion, admits Einstein. Evidently Russell was not offended by something close to psychoanalysis. "When he says," replied Russell, "that fear of metaphysics is the contemporary malady, I am inclined to agree." Rather than "probe questions to the bottom," the contemporary thinker goes along with empiricism because it is fashionable (*PBR*, 696–97).

Did Russell make efforts to do speculative and systematic philosophy? A very interesting series of reviews and articles comes from the 1920s, the decade during which Whitehead was developing his system. There is "Science and Metaphysics" (1923). In 1926, when Whitehead published *Science and the Modern World,* Russell published his well-known "Is Science Superstitious?" But there is also "Relativity and Religion."[22] This was followed by "Physics and Metaphysics" (1928).[23] When Russell is discussed, the relation to Whitehead often takes the form of contrasting Russell's failure to Whitehead's success in metaphysics, or in exalting the success of

Russell in analysis and pouring contempt on Whitehead's confusion and vagueness.[24]

The contrast between Whitehead and Russell is stated in metaphor. Said Whitehead to Russell, "You think the world is what it looks like in fine weather at noon-day. I think it is what it seems like in the early morning when one first awakes from deep sleep." A reader writes: "This statement so captured my imagination that I have been at last constrained to write to you to ask please could you tell me exactly what he meant by it." Replied Russell: "Another way of expressing the difference between Whitehead and me is that he thought the world was like jelly and I thought it was like a heap of shot. In neither case was this a deliberate opinion, but only an imaginative picture."[25]

By contrast we might say that the root metaphors of the "world . . . at noon-day" and "like a heap of shot" convey an atomism against an organism, or things clear and distinct related externally rather than things interrelated and not sharply cut off from each other because internally related.

It cannot be denied that Whitehead identified his metaphysics as "the philosophy of organism," while the only philosophy with which Russell identified himself was "logical atomism." Nevertheless, in these articles during the mid-1920s, 1923–28, Russell was close to Whitehead's speculation.

We have already called attention to several crucial doctrines on which Russell agrees with Whitehead. One such doctrine is a relational theory of space and time, now expressed as four-dimensional space-time. What is actual is events or occasions replacing substances. Another doctrine is that there are universals, which Whitehead called "eternal objects." There are structures or relational patterns, the orders constituted by universals in particular events, and these are statable as laws, which are sometimes no more than statistical regularities. Given these four cardinal points of agreement of the Russell of 1923–28, it would not be wrong to call him a process philosopher. What Whitehead was then writing, *Process and Reality,* has the subtitle "An Essay in Cosmology," and this was what Russell also was proposing.

But does Russell agree that the sciences do not give us a complete picture of what there is? His statement is that "the more [science] has taught us how to handle nature the less it has professed to tell us about the metaphysical reality displayed in nature. The knowledge embodied in science has gradually been found to be more and more abstract. We know certain very general features of the structure of the physical world, but we know nothing of the ingredients of the structure" (*S&M,* 716). But does Russell, to get the "meanings" of the words of the new map, turn to all aspects of culture, such as poetry and theology? Here comes a difference: the latter is "pious illusion."

Russell characterized *Science and the Modern World* as an effort to supply "an intellectually satisfying basis for future science, which is to be at the same time emotionally satisfying to extra-scientific aspirations of mankind" (*SS,* 38). But does Russell agree that when we know an event by concrete apprehension we know its value as the fulfillment of a possibility? Here is another difference: Russell cannot bridge the gulf between fact and value.

Russell agrees that the scientific movement, as characterized in chapter 1 of *Science and the Modern World,* rests upon a prescientific faith that the Creator has made an intelligible creation. Russell quotes: "There can be no living science unless there is a widespread instinctive conviction in the existence of an *Order of Things,* and, in particular, of an *Order of Nature.*" A basic duality between universals and particulars in Russell supports this conviction that there are two orders. We have already seen that the youthful Russell had connected the reign of law in nature with a First Cause who imposed laws. But does Russell make the transition from a transcendent omnipotence, "the Lord," to an immanent creative purpose in nature? Whitehead's reconception of God struck Russell as a reconciliation with "superstition." The deep difference here is that Whitehead ceased to think of cause as unknowable because unobserved. We as agents know when we have effected our aim. Russell hesitatingly and very late agreed on causal efficacy (*BW,* 154–55) but not early enough to revise his theology (or rather antitheology) as had Whitehead. Russell's view, like Hume's, had a duality of strict determinism or absolute chance. Whitehead's efficacious agency includes for all agents an element of self-determination, to a degree free, but to a degree conforming to conditions.

From the Whiteheadian perspective, Russell was in the grip of prejudices about fact-value dichotomy, also bound by the prejudice that the divine is absolute power or nothing, and the belief that causality is determination or pure chance. From the Whiteheadian perspective, Russell was obstinately continuing parts of the Newtonian metaphysics when he renounced Newtonian physics. Could there then have been in the 1920s a collaboration between White-head and Russell in producing a metaphysics, as between 1900 and 1913 there had been the collaboration that produced *Principia Mathematica?* "Physics and Metaphysics" gives us a taste of what we have missed of the combination of Russell's lucidity with Whitehead's profundity.

The impermanent world of events has for Russell, as it did for Whitehead, replaced the world of matter. A new grammar is now needed to express the fluidity of nature. Russell turns to poetry to express the vision of physics: "We are such stuff as dreams are made." As Buddhism reconstructed the concepts of soul and things, so, argues Russell, must we. What identity is there from moment to moment? Russell grants that the older claim to exactness is gone, and all we say even in physics is "probably not quite true." In this new situation, metaphysics also must speak analogically and in metaphor. Russell becomes more poet than logician:

Suppose that on a dark night you see the beam from a searchlight, or a lighthouse, moving about the sky, or sweeping over the sea; the beam in some sense preserves its identity and yet you do not think of its being a "thing." Or again, suppose you hear "the Star Spangled Banner" sung; it is one tune, but you would not think of it as a "thing": it is a series of notes, and the notes themselves are essentially brief. When I say that there are no "things" I mean that tables and chairs and loaves of bread and so on are really just like the beam of light and the song. They are a series of more or less similar phenomena, connected, not by substantial identity, but by certain causal connections. (*P&M*, 910)

There is here no trace of what Einstein called "anxiety before metaphysics" or "bad intellectual conscience." Nor is there the atomistic picture of the world "like a heap of shot" imposed upon the interrelations of organic wholes. There is a phase of Russell's work that could have issued, like Whitehead's *Process and Reality,* in a new system of categories.[26]

Chapter Six
Manifest Evils: Imperatives of the Moral Order

Many books on Bertrand Russell as a philosopher end after considering his contributions to mathematical logic, to theory of knowledge and philosophy of science, to analytic philosophy, and to an aspect of his worldview called ontology. What is there to say of his practical philosophy?[1] The purist does not regard ordinary reflections on morality, society and politics, and religion as properly parts of philosophy. And indeed it is Russell who, holding that "logic is the essence of philosophy," ruled out such beliefs because they were extralogical. Furthermore, all normative questions are judged extrascientific and beyond the realm of knowing. But this is only one phase of his complex philosophy. In other phases he did formal ethics and considered from the beginning to the end that criticism of society, state, and church and other institutions cannot be ignored by anyone seriously concerned with human values. Russell's *History of Western Philosophy* relates all the great philosophers of ancient, medieval, and modern times to their societies and political states. And sometimes he remarked that the greatest philosophers had a concern, as had Spinoza, not only with the cosmos but with ultimate human happiness, that is, with religious salvation.

Russell is important as a moralist, a social critic, and a philosopher of religion. The exact connections with epistemology, science, and metaphysics are not easy to comprehend, and in many ways he set out to break the ties. Most philosophers now would share Russell's opinion that values are extrascientific. In spite of his opposition to philosophic systems in which every sphere is organically linked to every other, the theoretical Russell cannot be understood without the practical Russell, for as we found when examining his motivation, the two series of books on the abstract and the concrete were finally to coalesce. What is there always behind the search for truth in logic, theory of knowledge, and the value-free sciences? The presupposition is the high place of veracity, and the motivation is trying to hold only true beliefs. Can there be knowledge of the good and any moral truth? This is the crucial question of the coherence of Russell's philosophy.

Russell is remarkable for his lifelong concern with morality and ethics. Morality refers to persons, their acts, rules, judgments, and institutions. Ethics refers to the theory of what persons ought and ought not to do, what is right and wrong, and what is good and evil. Generally philosophers work at theory, limiting themselves to ethics, but leave the practical problems of morality to others. Except for John Dewey, there is in modern philosophy no other philosopher who has so continuously worked in both morality and ethics. Like Dewey, Russell turned his back on no practical problem, yet unlike him, in ethical theory, he opted for each of the common alternatives, generally to abandon one for yet another. There seems to be no unity between Russell the moralist and Russell the "ethicist." One most profitable way to read his writing on moral practice and ethical theory is to ponder how they might be made coherent.

Many readers know Russell the moralist and then come to recognize that he is also a philosopher who worked in ethical theory. One needs no logical symbols to read *The Conquest of Happiness* or even to understand "The Elements of Ethics." It is only the simplest theory of knowledge that is involved: on what facts do the truths of moral propositions depend? Because we would not suspect any relation to technical intricacies of arguments, it is perhaps best to enjoy Russell's analyses of human virtues and vices, to ask the extent to which he is offering us wisdom, and then later to ask him to satisfy the high standards that, according to Russell, no previous moral philosopher, practical or theoretical, succeeded in satisfying.

Beyond the details of his morality and ethics is the significant role Russell has played as the most outspoken opponent of traditional Christian ethics and therefore the leading Anglo-American secularist philosopher.[2] Whatever personal faults he has had, therefore, add up, in the eyes of the theologians in self-defense, to demonstrate the inadequacy of the whole gamut of nontheological ethical theories that Russell has defended at one time or another. Since Russell has also been one of the sources of the sexual revolution, his personal life has often been used polemically to demonstrate that he was himself a most immoral person. In this the theologians have been joined by the feminists, who privately regret that, although he led the battle for equality between the sexes, toward women individually he was sometimes unfeeling and even cruel. Throughout this chapter on morality, and the next chapters on politics and religion, we will only suggest many judgments about Russell that are as partisan as the positions he took. These have added to the interest in his philosophy, but must be deferred because they are more germane to his critics than to Russell.

Has the Anti-Puritan Philosopher
Fully Escaped Puritanism?

When we think of his life, is it to be wondered at that Russell was extraordinarily sensitive to human evils? He was orphaned at four and taken by ancient grandparents through legal action. The regime of their household was severe: each act had to be justified as fulfillment of duty, with the end that private obligation was to produce public good. Pleasure was frowned upon as temptation to sin. In "The Recrudescence of Puritanism" he commented bitterly that the old, in the name of morality, always wish to rob the young of innocent pleasures.[3] In Russell's moral experience, one of the worst evils is customary and institutional morality, especially that of commandments and prohibitions justified as God's law for mankind. One of the most important set of arguments to understand is why he concluded that his childhood and youth had been lived in a false morality. How can we understand his moral revolution?

Russell described himself as "a highly virtuous child" who "acquired a conscience which has kept [him] working hard."[4] Among the virtues was that which we now characterize as the Puritan work ethic. The religious basis given by Bertrand Russell's grandparents was "Satan finds some mischief still for idle hands to do." In the Puritan moral consciousness there is ever present the fear of evil that ultimately is damnation. Although once Russell, like practically all children, "believed all that [he] was told," his philosophy was a deliberate effort to free morality from the theology of divine command and prohibition, such as "thou shalt's" and the "thou shalt not's" of the Ten Commandments. In morality we can understand the developing revolt against the traditional dependence of ethics on Christian theology. Yet in demoting work from the major unqualified virtue to a minor one qualified by conditions such as "not too much," and so on, he recognized that there are other kinds of Christianity, such as that of Italy, that did not take the

Calvinistic turn so characteristic of northern European peoples of the Industrial Revolution. The thread of continuity that runs through Russell's practical morality and theoretical ethics is that there are certain habits that are proposed as indubitably good and others that are condemned as certainly bad. The pattern of sharp discrimination of virtues and vices remains, even when on questions of pleasure, particularly sexual pleasures, Russell became famous (or, we might write, notorious) for denying, in practice as well as in theory, "thou shalt not commit adultery."

What is so perverse in the Puritan is the demand that what he regards as sinful must be painfully punished even though it has "no visible bad effects upon others than the agent" (*SE*, 121). Rather than true virtues of tolerance and sympathy, the Puritan shows "moral fervor" or what some have called shouting morality (*SE*, 123). The Puritan is a moral fanatic who singles out certain evils to be suppressed at all cost and produces far greater evil than he opposes. Russell's illustration is obscene literature, which although mildly bad, yet when destroyed by the post office, is suppression and denial of freedom and justice (*SE*, 123–24). The ethical error of the Puritan is to imagine that "his moral standard is *the* moral standard." The correction is education in the variety of moralities. Russell has been the antiPuritan attempting in countless popular essays to "weaken the ardor of our too virtuous masters" (*SE*, 128).

We make an error, according to students of the Puritan movement, if we fail to recognize that the leaders were often humanists and enlightened opponents of authoritarians whose control the liberal Puritan discredited.[5] John Milton is a splendid example of this type of person, one of whose finest studies was *The Doctrine and Discipline of Divorce* (1644), an enlightened study hardly matched for centuries and never equaled.

Often linked historically to Puritanism is liberalism. This aspect of the heritage of the Russell family was continued in his practical decisions. The manifest evils fought by Bertrand's ancestors sprang from the authority of king over representatives of the people in Parliament: in any controversy, it is the people who are right. The principle of evil here is the power to suppress opinion and oppress opposition to tyranny. Freedom is the great moral good of liberal thought.

There is much evidence for the thesis of George Santayana that Bertrand Russell's morality and ethics must be understood to be an

outcome of his Puritan temperament.[6] Santayana knew Russell well
and became famous for his memoir in the form of a novel, *The Last
Puritan*. Among the kinds of evidence cited from Santayana in the
next section, there is Russell's troubled conscience, his defense of
the conscientious objector to evil, and his constant awareness of evil
which spurs just people to struggle to replace evil by good.

The Puritan seeks a personal relation to God and regards himself
as responsible for carrying out God's commandments. To what does
the anti-Puritan remain responsible? To truth, and out of respect
for truth, Russell examines his conscience:

When will people learn the robustness of truth? I do not know who my
biographer may be, but I should like him to report "with what flourish
his nature will" something like this: "I was not a solemn stained glass
saint, existing only for purposes of edification; I existed from my own
centre, many things that I did were regrettable, I did not respect respect-
able people, and when I pretended to do so it was humbug. I lied and
practised hypocrisy, because if I had not I should not have been allowed
to do my work; but there is no need to continue the hypocrisy after my
death. I hated hypocrisy and lies: I loved life and real people, and wished
to get rid of the shams that prevent us from loving real people as they
really are. I believed in laughter and spontaneity, and trusted to nature
to bring out the genuine good in people, if once genuineness could come
to be tolerated."[7]

Puritans historically were opponents of civil and ecclesiastical
institutions imposed by rulers, especially when they seemed contrary
to Scripture. The English and American revolutions were led by
men who chose to "serve God rather than kings." Russell cannot
appeal to God, but conscience remains with all the divine authority
to countermand society's law. In *Authority and the Individual*, Russell
gives an effective expression of the Puritan tradition:

Respect for law is an indispensable condition for the existence of any
tolerable social order. When a man considers a certain law to be bad, he
has a right, and may have a duty, to try to get it changed, but it is only
in rare cases that he does right to break it. I do not deny that there are
situations in which law-breaking becomes a duty: it is a duty when a man
profoundly believes that it would be a sin to obey. That covers the case
of the conscientious objector. Even if you are quite convinced that he is
mistaken, you cannot say that he ought not to act as his conscience dictates.
When legislators are wise, they avoid, as far as possible, framing laws in

such a way as to compel conscientious men to choose between sin and what is legally a crime.[8]

The most significant way in which the personal conscience and protesting social policy remains Russell's Puritan philosophy is his preoccupation with evils. Russell was close to his friend G. E. Moore and with him argued for the study of evils as essential to understanding the good. Russell, responding in 1904 to Moore's *Principia Ethica,* discovers that his "power of judging is at once more subtle and more certain than [he] had supposed."[9]

The great evils are to admire what "is evil or ugly, to hate what is good" (cf. Isaiah 5:20). The judgment is based on the existence of objective evil and objective good, and it is especially bad if we know the evil to be evil and yet admire it, or to hate the good when we know it to be good. But what of pain? Consciousness of great pain is indeed among preeminent evils, but in itself "does not make a whole much worse, and may even make it better, as in the case of sympathy for suffering." Further, "a whole formed of two evils may, *as a whole,* be good; hence, when one evil exists, it is sometimes good to create another." It is not "the *existence* of evil [that] is essential to the ideal," but "its mere apprehension *is* essential, as may be seen by the excellence of Tragedy" (*MG,* 332–33).

Russell's moral philosophy has the fascinating duality of good and evil, virtue and vice, and part of the logic of ethics is to set one opposite against the other. The Puritan mind has the virtue of making clear what it is *against* as well as what it is *for.* The beauty of Russell's moral clarity is in no small measure to be attributed to his Puritan upbringing and temper. Many have wondered also whether he ever fully escaped its fanaticism.

Is There Truth in Moral Judgments and Are These Parts of a Science?

The alliance between Russell and Moore, best known as the initial stage of British realism and analysis, was committed in ethics to appeal only to "ethical facts," exercising "care in the analysis," and was devoted solely to "the discovery of truth" (*MG,* 328). It may come as a shock that Russell's "The Elements of Ethics" (1910) aims at the discovery of "true propositions about virtuous and vicious conduct and that these are just as much a part of truth as true propositions about oxygen or the multiplication table."[10] The aim of ethics then is not conduct, but theory about conduct.

Can the quest for certainty be satisfied in ethics as it is in logic? Just as in logic we discover self-evident truths (A is A, not both A and − A, either A or − A) so in ethics there are principles that are immediately known to be true. "We judge, for example, that happiness is more desirable than misery, knowledge than ignorance, goodwill than hatred, and so on." These fundamental propositions concern not what *is,* but what *ought* to be. Therefore they cannot be proved by experience. We cannot deduce what *ought* to be from facts of the world, which we gain a posteriori. "It is only important to realize that knowledge as to what is intrinsically of value is *a priori* in the same sense in which logic is *a priori,* namely the sense that the truth of such knowledge can be neither proved nor disproved by experience" (*PP,* 76). Often we appeal to "moral principle." We mean by this something true under all circumstances and not subject to change. Rules may be altered when we observe them to fail. Russell's first ethics affirmed the certainty of changeless truths.

Ethics, as Russell and Moore conceived the science, is not concerned only with human conduct or with the goods we can attain. "Ethics is the general inquiry into what is good, and into what *good* is. . . . *Good* itself is indefinable: an ultimate, simple notion, like yellow. Not that it is impossible to define *the good,* i.e., the things which are good; but that what we mean when we say that a thing is good, cannot be explained in any other terms" (*MG,* 328–29).

The proof that good is indefinable, and that all forms of ethics that define good as "according to the will of God" or "the will of the most powerful" or "conducive to maximum pleasure" or "more evolved in evolution" are fallacious, is exceedingly simple. "This is established by observing that, however we may propose to define *good,* it is always significant to say that 'pleasure is good,' we then say something different from: 'pleasure is pleasure'; thus *good* cannot mean the same as pleasure" (*MG,* 329). Earlier we saw Russell's demonstration of the absurdity of hedonism.

All definitions of good are, if correct, merely tautologies. Hence there is yet another objection that Russell regards as fatal. A "barren tautology can be no basis for action." Russell seeks an answer to the questions "why should I prefer this to that?" and "what ought we to do?"

The whole of Russell's philosophy, and this is essential to ethics, is based on the search for truth. Why "ought we to speak the truth"? Why shouldn't we communicate error or deceit? The reason

will always be concerned, not only with the actions themselves, but also with the goodness or badness of the consequences likely to follow from such actions. We shall be told that truth-speaking generates mutual confidence, cements friendships, facilitates the dispatch of business, and hence increases the wealth of society which practices it, and so on. If we ask why we should aim at increasing mutual confidence, or cementing friendships, we may be told that obviously these things are good, or that they lead to happiness, and happiness is good. (*EE,* 2)

Why the irritation if one asks for a further reason, as "why be happy"? Somewhere the demand for a further reason must stop. Something must be good on its own account, and when we have found it we have the only solution to what we ought and ought not to do, and know why some habits, such as veracity, are virtues, and others, such as mendacity, are vices.

Good, good on its own account, ought to exist, and *Bad,* bad on its own account, ought not to exist. The moral imperative, based on recognition of good and bad is that "if it seems to be in our power to cause a thing to exist or not to exist, we ought to try to make it exist if it is good, and not exist if it is bad" (*EE,* 4).

But what of saying that good is what we desire, and bad is what we abhor? This, according to Russell's science of ethics, makes the impersonal depend on the personal, the good in itself on the human good, and this is backward thinking. "When a thing is good, it is fitting that we should feel pleasure in its existence; when it is bad it is fitting that we should feel pain in its existence" (*EE,* 4).

Russell, like Moore, believed that he had discovered an "important truth," that he could refute the moral error that made ethical principles subjective. Just as Russell's logic had laws of things, based on identity, so in the science of ethics there are laws of contradiction and excluded middle. "Everything is in itself either good or not good, and cannot be at once good for me and bad for you. This could only mean that its effects on me were good and on you bad; but here good and bad are again impersonal" (*EE,* 5).

Russell is a severe critic of the ethics of self-interest, as in the maxim "honesty in the best policy." In a conflict between private interest and what is good, "the general good," there is no question of the implication Russell validly draws: "self-interest ought to give way" (EE, 27). This strict and high moral teaching may seem fantastic idealism, but the illustration brings us to consider whether cynical worldly wisdom is really wise. The cynic may be the fool and the saint the wise man. In international politics it is thought that it is "right for an English statesman to pursue exclusively the good of England, and a German the good of Germany, even if that good is to be attained by greater injury to the other" (EE, 26–27). We might not notice Russell's attack on the logical absurdity of trying to justify acts otherwise unjustifiable, except for the fact that this is the theoretical basis for Russell's condemnation of World War I. Only four years after he had written "The Elements of Ethics" (1910) came the war of 1914–18 produced by German rivalry of England's naval and imperial strength.

Is it a virtue to be honest, no matter what? Few philosophers have so struggled with this problem as did Russell. The problem is that certain kinds of acts are judged good, such as telling the truth, but these habits must be good, not in themselves, but because of the probable consequences of conducing to what is good in itself. The contradiction is that virtues seem to be both good in themselves and also good in their consequences. But we heard that this could not be. It must be one or the other. Yet in either "virtue is its own reward" (Stoic) or "virtue conduces to happiness" (Aristotle) there is inadequacy (EE, 28–29).

Much of the persuasiveness of Russell's argument lies in illustrations of virtues and vices. Moore held up friendship as intrinsically good and commended the enjoyment of works of art. Russell tends to expose to our moral horror hatred, envy, and cruelty.[11] There is no argument and such ethical discourse almost discourages argument. To question the viciousness of hatred, envy, and cruelty makes the questioner appear an evildoer or, worse, a defender of evildoers (EE, 8).

Russell the ethicist is Russell the moralist. The conclusion also shows that he had regained a measured faith in free will. The argument is simple. Morality is a choice between possible acts. If it were not, it would make no sense to praise one person for his virtuous act, and to blame another person for his vicious act. Since morality depends on freedom, determinism cannot be wholly true (EE, 32).

Santayana's Naturalistic Critique and Russell's Switch to Ethical Subjectivism

In 1912 Santayana published a critique of Russell's view of the indefinable good and the moral truths claimed to be a priori. In *Winds of Doctrine* Santayana called the analysis of good "hypostatic ethics" because good was claimed by Russell and Moore to be real independently of human life. Can good be an objective quality unrelated to the needs and interests of persons? The criticism is in line with Russell's own relational thinking that had already freed his philosophy from substantial matter and mind, space and time, and if good is a quality, must it not have a ground in some desire?

We must examine Santayana's argument in a bit more detail, because Russell immediately and ever after abandoned intuitionism, rejecting Moore's position and affirming what Santayana said is the truth about good and bad: they *"are derivative from desire."*[12] Later Russell added cryptically: *"whatever objectivity the concept may possess is political rather than logical"* (*EE,* 1, footnote by Russell). If good and bad are relative to desires, even then, if desires are fairly standard in a society, then these discriminations are the standards of that society. Relativism may be psychological or sociological, and Santayana influenced Russell to abandon the logical view that the same thing cannot be both good and bad. My good may be your bad, and my society's good may be your society's bad. There is then no necessary a priori reason for saying that either is in error or false. Good, says Santayana, is not like a color quality yellow or red, but more like relations "to the right of" and "to the left of." Thus he reduces Russell's statement to absurdity. "If a man here and another man at the antipodes call opposite directions up, only one of them can be right, though it may be very hard to know which is right!"[13] Russell had to abandon his axiom that when persons disagree about good or bad, only one can be right.

Russell had granted, to use his typical illustration, that I may like raw oysters, but they may not be to your taste. Why, asks Santayana, is a judgment of character any different? Are moral judgments of virtue and vice any different from attitudes of admiration and revulsion? Santayana, as a Catholic, had been long chafing under disapproval of Protestant contempt and made an issue of the basis of Russell's dogmatism in his Protestantism.

The most effective ad hominem argument is that Santayana can explain such appeal as Russell's theory has on grounds that the "Calvinist rigidity" of Russell's character expresses itself with "courage and sincerity." The theory of Russell and Moore has "purity and dogmatic sincerity" but this merit is also the human defect that it tends "to grow narrow, strident, and fanatical." Santayana opposes to Russell's asceticism a "sympathy with what is animal" in human life. Santayana misses in Russell normal patriotism with its loves and hates. Is it true that all Puritans lack a "pious reverence for the nature of things"?

The problem of Russell's naturalistic ethics is not only to find some kind of objectivity but also to account for the imperatives expressed as commands. What is the answer to "why should I tell the truth, the whole truth and nothing but the truth"?

According to the new ethics:

1. There are no such properties as good or bad, or right or wrong; that is, objectively there is no ought or ought not.

2. Therefore there is no true or false in ethics, and no evidential grounds of truth but only taste.

3. Therefore "ought" goes back to desire and to desires only.

                                                              (WD, 143–45)

If it is to a Nietzsche's taste to lie, particularly to prove his personal independence of servile submission to fact, and if this is courageous rather than cowardly, then we have Nietzsche's desire of his will to be a superman against Russell's wishes to be honest. And there is no way to decide except by groundless choice.

What can Russell say in disapproval? "When I say 'hatred is bad,' I am really saying, 'Would that no one felt hatred!' I make no assertion: I merely express a certain kind of wish"[14]

But what then can Russell say is scientific ethics? A psychological approach to the point of view of the person judging displaces the logic of self-evident axioms. Therefore ethics can be studied empirically. Now this meant at the time of "Scientific Method in Philosophy" (1914) the extension of evolutionary theory from the origin of species to the explanation of human values. How do ethical notions arise?

Evolutionary ethics, which Russell defends in *Mysticism and Logic*, is based upon the survival of the species.[15] Cooperation of members of the tribe is a natural basis for the good, and evil is any threat to survival, as from a hostile tribe. The enemy is then obviously wicked. Ethical notions then can never be impartial, as required in science (*ML*, 108–9).

Russell does not push his science of ethics to the relativistic extreme of denying the search for truth inherent in the scientific method. So far, we have accounted only for "political objectivity." Beyond this is the possibility of an ideal observer, whose vision is that of the scientist liberated from any partial loyalty. What this means, as in Spinoza's *Ethics,* is that moral judgment concerns only human nature and has no meaning "in . . . the world at large." Therefore scientific philosophy must ignore "ethical notions" in its "submission to fact." The divorce of fact from value is taken so seriously that it is even called *"the essence of the scientific temper"* (*ML*, 109, italics added).

Russell's naturalistic ethics is as antimetaphysical as his intuitionistic ethics. Nearly all past metaphysical systems have been biased toward human values. Scientific philosophy requires a neutral stance. That is, human ends are not to be exalted into the purpose of the cosmos. Most hierarchical views place man "a little lower than the angels" (Psalms 8:5), and the moral motive of belief in God is to sustain human dignity. All this is so wrong that Russell defines philosophy as "an unusually ingenious attempt to think fallaciously."[16]

It is not only theistic ethics, now revived as "divine command morality," that is impugned. The fallacy of non sequitur mars every metaphysical ethical system. Kant's metaphysic of ethics postulates immortality and God to allow for rewards of the righteous in a future life. Russell argues against both Hegel and Bergson because their metaphysical ethics are similarly designed to continue the Christian condemnation of the wicked as disobedient to God. What Bergson condemns is acting mechanically, and what he praises is acting organically. The wicked must suffer, according to Bergson's *Laughter,* a hell "even more terrible than moral condemnation. They become subject to ridicule" (*SE*, 92).

Among "false theories as to the nature of things" Russell includes behaviorism, whose founder was John Watson. The non sequitur is even more outrageous: "Since the only thing we can do is to cause matter to move, we ought to move as much matter as possible;

consequently art and thought are valuable only in so far as they stimulate the motions of matter" (*SE,* 93).

A reader who has never confronted the variety of moralities should read "Styles in Ethics" to see whether he can yet affirm which virtues are truly good and which alleged sins or vices are truly evil. As in ancient and Renaissance skepticism, there is empirical evidence against any actual universal standard.[17] As rational ethics had collapsed, so also empirical ethics.

The "subjectivity" of values is most forcefully argued in *Religion and Science* (1936). It is not merely that there is relativity of values, virtues, conscience, and every other ethical term, but that all of them are *nothing but* the expression of desire. Since ethics is itself the expression of a desire, as "an attempt . . . to escape from subjectivity" ethics is absurd (*RS,* 234).[18] Everything that is said, including what Russell himself had believed thirty years earlier, "that happiness is preferable to unhappiness, friendliness to unfriendliness, and so on," is beyond any kind of evidence, beyond reason and argument, and utterly "outside the realm of truth and falsehood" (*RS,* 243). There is approval of virtue and disapproval of vice, but these are the expression of temperament and education. There are assertions that seem impersonal, as that of belief in "an ordered hierarchy from king to peasant," requiring the virtue of obedience to law, but this is a rhetorical device to universalize the desire of the legislator. The conclusion of the argument is utter skepticism. "Whatever knowledge is attainable must be attained by scientific method; and what science cannot discover, mankind cannot know" (*RS,* 243).

The Normative Moralist
in Spite of His Emotive Theory

When World War I began, Bertrand Russell was already in ethics a subjectivist and a relativist. The theoretical basis on which he could build the conclusion "war is evil" was eroded. It might just as well be Nietzsche's barbaric doctrine that war is a test of strength. Yet Russell, as we shall see in the next chapter, acted with utter courage and clear conscience that there was no doubt that to fight to an ultimate victory was evil. We shall examine the circumstances of the argument in the next chapter.

In countless ways Russell expressed himself with the certainty of one who has moral truth and has knowledge of true virtue. We shall first examine his most famous statement about the good life, and then ask whether there is a contradiction. How can the subjectivist and relativist talk so assuredly about the good?

"The good life is inspired by love and guided by knowledge." This is perhaps the finest summary of Russell's moral teachings, and it has been widely accepted, even by such a caustic Christian theologian as Reinhold Niebuhr, who disapproves of nearly everything else in Russell as "sophisticated silliness."[19]

What I Believe (1925) is easily available both in *Why I Am Not a Christian* and in *Basic Writings.*[20] Russell is declaring that two ends of life he has found to be good in themselves, and both "knowledge and love [are] indefinitely extensible," that is, there can never be too much of them. We are warned not to expect these statements to be proved or even argued, but they are stated with the "hope that as many as possible will agree." Nevertheless we are invited to reflect that if holy men advise public prayer to cure a pestilence, their "love without knowledge" spreads the infection, while on the other hand "the late war afforded an example of knowledge without love." Since wise people seek the good life, they ought to avoid guidance of leaders who lack either knowledge or love, for one of these does not replace the other (*BW*, 372).

It is logical therefore to infer that "both love and knowledge are necessary." Of the two, which is "more fundamental"? Probably since love is the motive, whereas knowledge is the achievement, and because everyone is capable of love, but knowledge is the achievement of a few, and because the emotional drive of love is more powerful than the drive to avoid error and escape ignorance, Russell chooses love. "Love . . . will lead intelligent people to seek knowledge, in order to find out how to benefit those whom they love." Why not then say that love is sufficient? Because "the most genuine benevolence" in medical matters "may do harm" without medical knowledge. "An able physician is more useful to a patient than the most devoted friend." But why not say that knowledge is sufficient? Because extension of the benefits of science depends on benevolence (*BW*, 372).

But, we may object, "love" is most imprecise: "it covers a variety of feelings." Russell does not, as in his logical and analytic writings, seek one meaning, as the definition of "truth." Of meanings of

"love," Russell wants "to include them all." Love is not only "pure
benevolence," the "love thy neighbor as thyself" (Luke 10:27) to
which he frequently appeals, but also "aesthetic delight, pure delight
in contemplation." The formulation then includes as intrinsic goods
what is so appealing in G. E. Moore's ideal, enjoyment of "a land-
scape or a sonata."

The love that is genuinely another sort, other than aesthetic
delight, must include sacrificial devotion to others, as altruistic
concern with the sick, even when, as with helping lepers, they are
repulsive (*BW*, 373–74). Although love has been called a "variety
of feelings," Russell does not mean only "sympathy"; that is only
a part "but leaves out the element of activity that I wish to include"
(*BW*, 373).

There is intellectual delight and altruistic devotion: are they not
poles apart? They can be combined, as in sex love and parental
benevolence; when there is "an indissoluble combination," love is
at its fullest. But in sex love, where there is no secure possession,
jealousy destroys love. "Delight without well-wishing may be cruel:
well-wishing without delight easily tends to become cold and a little
superior."

In this very imperfect world, there are not only jealousy and
cruelty, two of the vices that, along with fear and hatred, Russell
frequently cites as blemishes of character, but certain limits. Although love was said to be in principle "indefinitely extensible,"
we cannot feel delight in ugly people who disgust us. Nor can we
be wholly benevolent. Often "benevolence" is a word to describe
"the desire for another person's welfare," and this is "a pale emotion
nine parts humbug" (*BW*, 373). What this means is that there is
a circumstance when benevolence toward a rival is impossible and
inappropriate. This is when one person wants to marry another. In
this conflict, if instinct is ignored, there will be a subtle vengeance.
In spite of what Santayana and, more strongly, D. H. Lawrence
alleged, Russell was not wholly cerebral and bloodless.

Does Russell describe the good life that can be actually achieved?
Because he has been dealing with ends, he denies that it is "ethical
knowledge," yet he is giving a practical prescription based on common knowledge of human nature in society. But what kind of
knowledge is there that "the good life is one inspired by love and
guided by knowledge"? The "knowledge" here referred to as an
ingredient is "scientific knowledge and knowledge of particular

facts" (*BW*, 374). Ends come only from desire, and there is no knowledge, says Russell, of which end we *ought* to desire: there is science only as to "how to achieve it."

Many read Russell as though he were saying of the good life that this is what we ought to seek, but he would not wish to be classed with authorities—"parents, school-masters, policemen and judges" (*BW*, 374). Can there be a wise person who mediates between individual desires of persons and impersonal scientific knowledge of fact? There can be no "legislative morality." At this point Russell the ethicist interprets Russell the moral philosopher:

When I said that the good life consists of love guided by knowledge, the desire which prompted me was the desire to live such a life as far as possible, and to see others living it; and the logical content of the statement is that, in a community where men live this way, more desires will be satisfied than in one where there is less love or less knowledge (*BW*, 375).

The formulation appeals to broad experience rather than simply to Russell's private desire. The problem is stated: "Love makes [a parent] wish to cure [an ill child], and science tells you how to do so. There is not an intermediate stage of ethical theory, where it is demonstrated that your child had better be cured" (*BW*, 375). Perhaps there is a moral mediation that is not in the strict sense scientific but is nevertheless valid.

The expressions of ends, as various as condemning all war or holding noble the soldier in battle, are but expressive of desire and are a matter of taste. Is it paradoxical for Russell to hold this in theory, yet in practice to express himself describing, as we saw above, the good life? The problem is whether such an expression as "hatred is bad" means only the exclamation "Would that no one felt hatred!" (*P*, 257). The emotivist interpretation is that there is no evidence relevant to the choice of ends, and such are not statements with any reference to fact. My desire is accompanied by the desire that others should desire the same. Yet Russell admits that to be an ethical judgment there must be a statement of a satisfactory moral order that is universal and not merely an expression of my desire.

The problem can also be stated as to the dualism between fact and value. In *What I Believe*, though the expression of desire is the meaning of good, there is mediation between nature and value.

Russell was confronted with the charge of inconsistency and incoherence between his philosophy of man and nature and his philosophy of value. "Undoubtedly we are part of nature, which has
produced our desires, our hopes and fears," and so on (BW, 14–
15). "It is we who create value, and our desires which confront
value. . . . It is for us to determine the good life, not for Nature."
      Russell's "Reply to Criticisms" (1944) deserves careful reading.
Apart from restating the formula for the good life as an expression
of "vehement ethical judgment," he asks what more an ethical
judgment is than an expression of "desires as to the desires of
mankind?"[21] Psychologically, if Russell feels such desires, then why
not, on this theory, express them (PBR, 722)? If it is "the same
kind of objectivity as a judgment of fact," there is no possibility
because "no property, analogous to 'truth,' . . . belongs . . . to
an ethical judgment" (PBR, 723). Therefore all we can do when
there is a moral difference is to try to persuade each other. A man
with strong desires tries to "rouse these desires in other people."
Russell confesses that when he expressed his ethical persuasion he
was preaching. Since Russell has in no way modified the fact/value,
nature/man, science/desire dualisms, these are reexpressed: "The art
of presenting one's desires persuasively is totally different from that
of logical demonstration, but it is equally legitimate" (PBR, 724).
      Russell's famous conclusion presents a dilemma otherwise sum-
marized: "I find my own views argumentatively irrefutable, but
nevertheless incredible. I do not know the solution."[22] Russell agrees
with his critics' unhappiness but not with any of the alternatives
they suggest.

Persuasion, as a method of settling ethical dispute is satisfactory *provided
your desires are good;* if they are evil, rhetoric in their defence is an art of
the devil. But what are "good" desires? Are they anything more than
desires that you share? Certainty there *seems* to be something more. Suppose,
for example, that someone were to advocate the introduction of bull-
fighting in this country. In opposing the proposal, I should *feel,* not only
that I was expressing my desires, but that my desires in the matter are
right, whatever that may mean. (PBR, 724)

So Russell defended himself logically but shares the feelings of
his critics "in feeling I am not satisfied. . . . *While my own opinions
as to ethics do not satisfy me, other people's satisfy me still less*" (PBR,
724, italics added).

Is There a Russellian Solution to the Problem of Moral Knowledge?

Russell, as we have just seen, admits that although logically "irrefutable," his combination of emotivist ethics and moral teaching is "incredible." Is there a solution in his philosophy, even though he said he did not know it?

The neglected question of Russell's moral career and his moral philosophy is what is his theory of virtues and vices? This is the ancient and medieval way that was out of favor during Russell's career, but has been revived during the last decade. Perhaps now in retrospect we can find in Russell himself and his writings a solution he himself never made explicit.

In any popular essay or book of Bertrand Russell we confront a moral philosopher who continues the liberal tradition of his family and who exemplifies the virtues that he once stated as "A Liberal Decalogue." By stating ten commandments he leaves us in no doubt that in the seemingly indicative statements "truthtelling is a virtue" and "envy is a vice" Russell is communicating imperatives "be scrupulously truthful" and "do not feel envious."

A Liberal Decalogue

Perhaps the essence of the Liberal outlook could be summed up in a new decalogue, not intended to replace the old one but only to supplement it. The Ten Commandments that, as a teacher, I should wish to promulgate, might be set forth as follows:

1. Do not feel absolutely certain of anything.
2. Do not think it worth while to proceed by concealing evidence, for the evidence is sure to come to light.
3. Never try to discourage thinking for you are sure to succeed.
4. When you meet with opposition . . . endeavour to overcome it by argument and not by authority, for a victory dependent upon authority is unreal and illusory.
5. Have no respect for the authority of others, for there are always contrary authorities to be found.
6. Do not use power to suppress opinions you think pernicious, for if you do the opinions will suppress you.
7. Do not fear to be eccentric in opinion, for every opinion now accepted was once eccentric.

8. Find more pleasure in intelligent dissent than in passive agree-
    ment, for, if you value intelligence as you should, the former
    implies a deeper agreement than the latter.
9. Be scrupulously truthful, even if the truth is inconvenient, for it
    is more inconvenient when you try to conceal it.
10. Do not feel envious of the happiness of those who live in a fool's
    paradise, for only a fool will think it is happiness.[23]

We can go from rules to virtues by thinking that the kind of
person Russell admired and wanted himself to be was: open-minded,
truthful, encouraging of inquiry, fair in debate and not authoritar-
ian, critical of authority, tolerant, courageous in representing unpopular causes, discerning, candid about arguments against his own
position, unenvious. But why should one attempt such an interpretation of the good habits of persons? The role of the normative
moralist is to elaborate an ideal for human nature, and for every
virtue there is an opposite, a vice. Although the virtues of one
battling evil are heroic and thus challenge another person to emulate
excellence, if one accepts these habits as true virtues, it is the vices
that invariably fascinate us. For every reader of Dante's *Paradise* and
Purgatory there are ten who have gone with him through nine levels
of *Inferno*.

Russell the moral person, as we have seen, never made claims to
have lived up to any conventional code, such as the Ten Commandments of Moses, and wants to appear totally liberated from
consciousness of sin. Once he quipped that there is only one Mosaic
sin he had not committed. "It says, 'Thou shalt not covet thy
neighbour's ox.' Now I never have."[24] Russell did not pretend to
conform to the Seventh Commandment, and if adultery is a major
sin, he did not compound it by hypocritical denial and deceit.
Therefore even faithful religious readers have sometimes expressed
admiration. A reviewer of *Why I Am Not a Christian* concludes that
much of religion is motivated by fear and is therefore cowardly,
whereas Russell's attack is courageous. Just as earlier we noted the
Puritan temper, so the moral position is never hedonism, identifying
pleasure as the good.

His standpoint is austere; one might perhaps go so far as to say that Lord
Russell is a religious man himself and Truth the God to whom he offers
uncompromising and unyielding worship. He is certainly a man of the
very highest moral character, and in his long life he has probably come

closer to the precepts of Jesus about CHARITY and MERCY and STEADFASTNESS and COURAGE than have the great majority of people who call themselves Christians.[25]

Just as earlier we found Russell the supposedly antimetaphysical analyst to be in the end the staunchest friend of metaphysics, so now the ironic turn is that the enemy of conventional morality, the skeptic who abandons absolutism, defends subjective and relative goods, even to the skeptical end of identifying the good only as the desired, is really making an important constructive contribution both to morality and to ethical theory. Intuitionism seemed to lead to ethics as a formal science, but to consider good and bad as qualities leads to the insoluble question of whether the qualities are in the object or in the subject. The whole position was inappropriate for a theory of knowledge based on relations. Russell's option for subjectivism was still coupled with the search for a science of ethics. This led to handing over the data of morality to psychology and sociology, and thus we can describe what people desire and how they satisfy desires, but have no discrimination between good and bad desires, and no account of general moral imperatives. Russell concluded, "I do not know the answer."

In spite of all these shifts of interpretation, Russell continues to hold to such a discrimination as that between kindness and cruelty. He seems to know persons who are kind and that kindness is admirable, and he knows persons who are cruel and that cruelty is abominable. Can we say generally that as persons in relation to other persons, what we know of them are their virtues and vices?

Before we face the theoretical difficulties of how we come to know the good and bad habits of persons, let us consider one virtue in the concrete. When young Russell came up to Cambridge, he was examined in mathematics by Whitehead. Although he had been led to think himself stupid, Whitehead found him brilliant and complemented the painfully shy youth. Whitehead's "kindness did not end" with remembering "his examination ten months earlier. . . . He told all the cleverest undergraduates to look out for me, so that within a week I had made the acquaintance of all of them and many of them became my lifelong friends."[26]

Whitehead was extraordinarily perfect as a teacher. He took a personal interest in those with whom he had to deal and knew both their strong and weak points. He would elicit from a pupil the best of which a pupil was capable. He was never repressive, or sarcastic, or superior, or any of the things that inferior teachers like to be. I think that in all the abler young men with whom he came in contact he inspired, as he did in me, a very real and lasting affection. (*PMem*, 97)

There are several difficulties that must be raised. The first difficulty is, what is a person? The second, how do persons know one another? The third, who is to say which personal traits are good (virtues) and which personal traits are bad (vices)? If these difficulties can be resolved, then we have a theoretical basis for proceeding to the study of society and politics, and to philosophy of religion, because both these critiques are based upon a discrimination between virtues and vices.

What is a person? Generally Russell does not ask this question because the traditional doctrine of the soul as substance led to the skeptical conclusion that the deduction of the soul's immortality is invalid and that there can be no scientific proof that the soul is free and no empirical evidence that there is such a thing. Then, too, when Russell takes his scientific stance, he wants to say that a person is just another thing subject to all the laws of the natural order (*BW*, 368). Thus the sense datum epistemology that works fairly well for material objects like the table (rectangular, hard, brown) and the extension of scientific method is apt to blind us to Russell's philosophy of the person. This is best found in *Principles of Social Reconstruction* (1916).

The human person as agent can be understood by distinguishing three sources of action called the life of instinct, the life of the mind, and the life of the spirit. On each of the three levels there is desire, love, or appetition, and we can understand why Russell speaking of "the good life" as "inspired by love" wanted all forms of love, the sexual drive to reproduce, along with "love of possession, . . . family, . . . country, . . . one's group," the impersonal love of knowledge, and the impersonal feeling expressed in art and the divine imperative of "a mystery half revealed, . . . a hidden wisdom and glory, . . . a transfiguring vision."[27]

The master aim of "a practical philosophy" is the harmony of all three parts, in which each part can play its necessary role.

Instinct, mind, and spirit are all essential to a full life; each has its own excellence and its own corruption. Each can attain a spurious excellence at the expense of the others; each has a tendency to encroach upon the others; but in the life which is to be sought all three will be developed in *co-ordination and intimately blended in a single harmonious whole.* Among *uncivilized* men instinct is supreme, and mind and spirit hardly exist. Among *educated men* at the present day mind is developed, as a rule, at the expense of both instinct and spirit, producing a *curious inhumanity and lifelessness, a paucity of both personal and impersonal desires,* which leads to *cynicism* and *intellectual destructiveness.* Among ascetics and most of those who would be called saints, the life of the spirit has been developed at the expense of instinct and mind, producing an outlook which is impossible to those who have a healthy animal life and to those who have a love of active thought. It is not in any of these *one-sided developments* that we can find *wisdom* or a philosophy which will bring new life to the civilized world. (*PSR,* 144, italics added)

Although the later ideal of the good life meant by "knowledge" science and grasp of fact, in the earlier version, ten years earlier, it is wisdom of the spirit that purifies instinct into a universal impersonal love (*PSR,* 152–53).

In several essays Russell sketched an elaboration of this solution, "Science and Values," the conclusion of *The Scientific Outlook* (1931), and "The Expanding Mental Universe" (1959).[28] Is the only "knowledge" of humans the know-how of mechanistic science that enables us to master natural forces? This is, argues Russell, not adequate to account for science. Because "in its beginnings" people "who were in love with the world" came to understand "the stars and the sea, . . . the winds and the mountains" (*SO,* 262).

The importance of this revision of epistemology is that the kind of knowledge springing from love is not mechanical manipulation. The knowledge of what is loved is enjoyment for its own sake, and this is the knowledge of "the mystic, the lover and the poet."

Scientific knowledge has neglected the love of qualities in the known, and by its division between subject and object, has transferred "color and sound, light and shade, form and texture" to the perceiver. Thus the "beloved has become a skeleton of rattling bones." This is exactly the criticism of science made by Whitehead in *Science and the Modern World* that called attention to the romantic revolt. Russell takes the romantic side also on the superiority of love-knowledge to power-knowledge. This would mean a knowledge of the person's purposes involved in their characters, and presumably a discrimination of their wise from their foolish choice of ends. How else could Russell feel so sure that the ruthless quest of power, particularly springing from hatred, is bad (*SO*, 266–67)? This is a way of knowing that yields religious conclusions. One is that "division in the soul,' between control over nature and metaphysical wonder about nature, "is fatal to what is best in man." Another is that "the worship of Satan" is "the renunciation of love" (*SO*, 264).

This way of knowing finds cooperation in organic wholes, such as a living body, and extends this natural example of unselfishness to the whole human race. We have here again, a bridging of the gulf between natural fact and human value, and we shall have to pick up the quest for unification in the last chapter on religion.

Although generally Russell is known as a critic of organicist thought, his model for thought about the relations between persons is explicitly that of organs of the body that, as the mouth, function by serving all other parts. The future of human society depends upon transcending mechanism: "It is this kind of unification and *expansion of self-interest* that will have to take place if a scientific society is to prove capable of survival. *This enlargement in the sphere of feeling* is being rendered necessary by the new interdependence of different parts of the world" (*EMU*, 393, italics added).

Chapter Seven
Rational Man and Irrational Society: Can Mankind Resolve the Disorders of Our Age?

Russell the Activist: A Man of Liberal Virtues

Bertrand Russell is in one respect at least like the philosophers in his *History of Western Philosophy*. The subtitle gives the reason: *And Its Connection with Political and Social Circumstances from the Earliest Times to the Present Day*. The philosophers best known to the non-technical are those who have made known their views on society, state, and economy, who have expressed strong fears of anarchy or of tyranny, and who have prescribed ways of hope and progress. Russell is in the tradition of Pythagoras, Plato, Aristotle, Augustine, Dante, Thomas Aquinas and William of Occam, who are remembered from the ancient and medieval worlds, as are Machiavelli, Hobbes, Locke, Rousseau, Hegel, Marx, and J. S. Mill from the modern world. Because of their long involvement in public affairs, two philosophers of our age have constantly responded to political crises, and their political conclusions are closer than their philosophies: Dewey and Russell. Because of the connection between theory and practice in their careers, they may be for future generations the best remembered philosophers of the twentieth century, especially of the English-speaking world.[1]

Russell's career in public affairs was motivated by a liberal's concern to replace the evils of bad people and institutions with the benefits of truly virtuous people and institutions. As a young man in his twenties with his activist American bride, Alys, he studied the efforts of the socialist movement to check the evils of laissez-faire capitalism. *German Social Democracy* (1896) was followed twenty years later by pacifist writings in the effort to rid the world of the evils of war. *Principles of Social Reconstruction* (1916) was published in America as *Why Men Fight: A Method of Abolishing the International Duel.*

At the time of President Woodrow Wilson's great hope for a League of Nations, Russell was comparing and contrasting new ways of redesigning society. *Political Ideals* (1917) and *Roads to Freedom: Socialism, Anarchism and Syndicalism* (1918) prepared him far better than any other philosopher for a critical study of Russian communism under Lenin. Russell's left-wing friends in the Labour party were disappointed with his predictions of tyranny and stifling censorship in *The Practice and Theory of Bolshevism* (1920). Russell needed to change little when he republished the book (1965); Soviet Marxism was indeed a fanatical secular religion and its ideology a new creedal orthodoxy. Because ideology is an instrument of power, when Stalin made a pact with Hitler, it did not take Russell by surprise.

In the 1920s Russell shifted emphasis from mathematics and epistemology to some of the pressing problem areas of public life. *The Problem of China* (1922) deals with the decay of the old Confucian order of the empire and the agonizing efforts to switch toward modern scientific and industrial life. *The Prospects of Industrial Civilization* (1923), which he wrote with Dora Russell, his second wife, deals with economic problems. Sexual and family patterns were then being reviewed critically, and Russell became best known for *Marriage and Morals* (1929).[2] The birth of children and the problem of their education led to the Russells' experiments in Beacon Hill School (1927–35), and these were communicated theoretically in *On Education Especially in Early Childhood* (1926), published in America as *Education and the Good Life,* and *Education and the Social Order* (1934), published in America as *Education and the Modern World.*[3]

In the 1930s, when after the financial collapse and during the Great Depression there were many economic and political experiments, Russell contributed *Freedom and Organization—1814–1914* (1934), *Which Way to Peace?* (1936), and *Power: A New Social Analysis* (1938).

World War II, which induced many nations to adopt patterns of planning and control, was the background of *Authority and the Individual* (1949) and *New Hopes for a Changing World* (1952). The atomic bombs dropped on Japan by the United States created an era with new evils to which old ideas seemed unfit. Russell became a prophet of doom who theoretically and actively demanded that world leaders prevent armed conflict more terrible in consequence than anything in past history. *Common Sense and Nuclear Warfare* (1959) was one of many efforts.

Is Russell's career as a political activist and theoretician comprehensible as a whole? It might seem to be merely a collection of causes: socialism and feminism at the turn of the century; pacifism during World War I and even into the Hitler period (1936); an assortment of issues like industrial democracy and workers' rights, permissiveness in rearing children, and tolerance of hitherto forbidden sexual relations, all going under the ambiguous justification of being thought modern; down to what we now call a freeze on nuclear armaments. Nevertheless, the "causes" have a unifying bond as a set of virtues in sharpest contrast to a set of vices. These we have begun to study in the previous chapter on ethics. Russell is consistently the moralist in public affairs, and one approach is to examine carefully the way in which his responses reveal a coherent understanding of the virtues and vices in a liberal perspective.

Is it right to proceed from ethics to politics and to use the moral categories, good and evil, virtue and vice, in interpreting the conflict of passions, creeds, and institutional powers? This is exactly the ordering found in Russell's *Human Society in Ethics and Politics* (1952). It is of course the ordering in Plato and Aristotle, and traditional Christian philosophy as well.

Is it right to regard Russell's political philosophy as a part of the philosopher's activity but not properly philosophy? His political philosophy has been ignored or treated lightly. When Russell himself made a selection of his best essays in 1927, fully two-thirds of them dealt with what Dewey called "the problems of men."[4] There are two major difficulties in guiding the reader in Russell's practical philosophy. The first is that the terrain is a century of world history, and the second is mapping it, which means finding the structure. The first can be resolved by reading the second half of *Basic Writings*, for thirty-two essays are well selected from the twenty-odd books that together constitute this major contribution to wisdom.[5] "The world in which I have lived," writes Russell in the preface, "has been a very rapidly changing world. The changes have been in part such as I could welcome, but in part such as I could assimilate in terms borrowed from tragic drama. I could not welcome wholeheartedly any presentation of my activities as a writer which made it seem as though I had been indifferent to the very remarkable transformations which it has been my good or ill fortune to experience" (*BW*, 7). It is only if we discriminate between good and evil that we can recognize that noble people, because of flaws, fall from greatness. The problem in reading the characters of the drama is to read their virtues and vices.

What is wisdom about? We say it is the ability to state and solve moral problems, and to see them in the context of finding an order that is not tyrannous and a freedom that is not anarchic. The problem is finding a balance between extremes. This is the ancient definition of virtue, the excellence that lies in a mean. We shall not find that Russell exactly continues the Aristotelian theory of the four cardinal virtues, but, in his search for new virtues to replace the old, he has made a valuable contribution to the theory as well as the practice of the virtues of a free man. Although there may not be knowledge of the ends of life, among which freedom and happiness along with truth are ranked so high, there may be wisdom in selecting them. Morality in political and religious philosophy is best conceived as a search for wisdom in the conduct of life. A Platonist would say that wisdom is orientation to the Good.

Russell the Puritan moralist is engaged in the war against evil. What particularly engages all of his hatred, and all his vigorous intelligence, is the challenge of four great evils: poverty, war, stupidity, and utter destruction. He is a liberal with a guilty conscience because capitalism produces, along with great wealth, much misery, and he explores the socialist and communist solutions to poverty. He is an Englishman who loves his native land yet recognizes that nationalism produces war, and he explores pacifist solutions to the problems of violent conflict. He is a lover of historical civilization; yet he recognizes that tradition inhibits intelligence, the chief intellectual virtue, and he explores education as a solution to stupidity. Finally, the advances of physics have provided the new demonic powers of nuclear weapons that threaten utter destruction of all life, and Russell's final phase of combat against Satan is an effort to save humanity from doom.

Russell the Liberal Becoming Socialist but Refusing to Be Communist

Russell's political orientation is liberal, and by that he means that it is wise to secure the maximum of individual liberty com-

patible with social order. Sometimes it is the orderly character of
Victorian England that is his model, and it is his model because it
was relatively disorganized. With the sadness of tragedy he tells of
that vanished age, not only of the sad fate of kings and queens, but
of the excellent ideals of parliamentary government that have become
difficult to continue and to further. It is sad to reflect on faded
ideals, on "the absolute condition of stability which made it an
unquestioned axiom that no dangers were to be expected anywhere
in the world, except an ordered and gradual development towards
a constitution exactly like that of Britain. Was ever an age so
blessedly blind to the future? Cassandra truly prophesied disaster
and was not believed; the men of my grandfather's age falsely prophesied prosperity and were believed."[6]

How a liberal becomes a socialist is told in this way. First, the
inner contradiction of nineteenth-century liberalism was that its
economic theory was laissez-faire, and in the unregulated opportunities for making money, while a few prospered, many suffered.
The rich became richer, while the poor seemed to become poorer.
Even John Stuart Mill, in later editions of *The Principles of Political
Economy,* had to make a place for socialism. Russell is attracted to
"the Probable Futurity of the Labouring Classes" because it is vol-
untary rather than forced, and because it does not concentrate power
of production and distribution in the state (*PMem,* 119). This particular point must never be forgotten because even as Russell was
becoming a socialist he wrote "Pitfalls in Socialism." That is, state
ownership and administration tend toward tyranny.[7] In a strict
sense, then, a liberal cannot be socialist, but these labels are used
loosely.

It is only when we go into the character of Russell's liberalism
and the character of his socialism that we discover why he was never
a trusted member of either political party.[8] He stood for Parliament
both as Liberal candidate in 1907 and as Labour candidate in 1922,
and at other elections also he was always defeated. To put it succinctly, although he loved freedom, it was always with concern for
economic justice, and although he loved economic justice, it was
with equal or greater concern for individual liberty. He never was
a "true believer," one of the faithful. Critical philosophy took prec-
edence over successful politics. He manages, at the very beginning
of "Pitfalls in Socialism" to alienate both liberals and socialists:
liberals, because he refuses to recognize the property rights of stock-

holders; socialists because he sees no gain in state ownership of railways. In two sentences he does this: "I see no reason to believe that any real advance towards democracy, freedom, or economic justice is achieved when a state takes over the railways after full compensation to the shareholders." State ownership would produce "the dead uniformity of state administration," and recognition of stockholders does not advance "economic justice . . . in any degree" (*PI,* 44–45). Both Liberal and Labour would object politically that Russell must have been a Conservative in disguise! But Tories failed to recognize, early and late, what a supreme asset they had in Russell.

Russell does not deny Marx's argument that "by the competition of capitalists, the small men are driven from the field, and sink into the rank of the proletariat."[9] There is a fundamental weakness in individualism of the economic and also the political sort. What Russell does not defend is "the extreme individualist doctrine of the Rights of Man," because it is "totally false in theory, and in practice destructive." Likewise, laissez-faire economics. He cares, as do the Marxists, for social life, but he is convinced that the way to secure it is through democracy, because this is a commitment to equal justice (*GSD,* 166).

How are economic collectivism and political democracy to be accomplished? Not, Russell hopes, by violent revolution but by gradual evolution that allows the new rulers to acquire experience and avoid "foolish and disastrous experiments." Russell's appeal, in his conclusion, is to tolerance and wisdom: on the part of property owners, "friendliness to the working class"; on the part of social democrats, "less uncompromising policy within the Party." The goal is "internal peace of the nation," and this requires "common justice and common humanity" and "every spark of generosity from class-consciousness" (*GSD,* 171). If we seek a positive statement of ideal humanity, this is, as we have already seen, in *Principles of Social Reconstruction* (1916).[10]

It should be very clear that the chief principle of social reconstruction is the moral superiority of "creativity," as we now call "creativeness," over possessiveness. How does Russell arrive at his principle, or at least, how is it justified? "Political Ideals" (1917, a lecture read for him in Glasgow, too close to the seacoast for the government to risk that a pacifist might signal German submarines) uses many justifications. Russell quotes from the Gospel teachings of Jesus and appeals to the principle of growth of all living things, but the fundamental argument is neither theological nor naturalistic. Creativeness leads to a life full of all the virtues of a good person in good institutions, and possessiveness leads to a life full of all the vices of a bad person in institutions that are evil (*PI,* 12–25). Russell is all the more persuasive because he has combined all these appeals, religious and scientific, moral and political.

Why is the Russian Revolution even worse than the French? Because the Russian is like the fanatical "rise of Islam." That is, humanity is considered in the grip of omnipotence, and worse than Allah are "omni-potent material forces."[11] This is a new secular religion, always judged by Russell to be worse than its orthodox theistic predecessors. Russell more than anyone else has led us to think of Russian communism as a fanatical religion incompatible with enlightenment and a scientific culture: "Bolshevism is not merely a political doctrine; it is also a religion, with elaborate dogmas and inspired scriptures. When Lenin wishes to prove some proposition he does so, if possible, by quoting texts from Marx and Engels. A Communist is not merely a man who believes that land and capital should be held in common, and their produce distributed as nearly equally as possible. He is a man who entertains a number of elaborate and dogmatic beliefs—such as philosophic materialism, for example—which may be true, but are not, to a scientific temper, capable of being known to be true with any certainty. This habit, of militant certainty about objectively doubtful matters, is one from which, since the Renaissance, the world has been gradually emerging, into that temper of constructive and fruitful skepticism which constitutes the scientific outlook" (*BPT,* 6).

Russell's pragmatic argument is that dogmatic belief gives advantage only in the short run. If capitalists remain skeptical, they will win in the long run (*BPT,* 6–7).

Lenin and leaders like him do appeal to Russell the Puritan in one respect. That is, they are men dedicated to a single goal, and they have the virtue of the guardians in Plato's *Republic;* they are austere (*BPT,* 27–29). By austerity Russell means that the communist "works sixteen hours a day, and foregoes his Saturday half-holiday. He volunteers for any difficult or dangerous work which needs to be done, such as clearing away piles of infected corpses. . . . He is not pursuing personal evils, but aiming at the creation of a new social order" (*BPT,* 27).

Russell is preaching a grim sermon on "the sins of the fathers visited upon the children of those" who hate and lack kindness (Exodus 20:5). The moral philosophy of history was never made explicit. Marx was perverse: "He didn't want the happiness of the proletariat but the unhappiness of the bourgeoisie. This is the hate element. His philosophy produced disaster. A philosophy which is to do good must be one inspired by kindly feelings and not by unkindly feeling."[12]

Could it be that in history something works not only to punish vice but also to reward virtue? Russell scorns such speculation, but for more than twenty-two years (1914–36) he professed kindness and reconciliation between nations.

Russell the Pacifist and His Theory of Creative Virtues versus Destructive Vices

That war is evil and peace is good is one of the standard beliefs of philosophers, and here we could cite St. Augustine's *City of God,* Hobbes's *Leviathan,* and Kant's *Eternal Peace.* The twentieth century is distinguished by Gandhi's nonviolence. Among Western philosophers the best known for his pacifism is Bertrand Russell.

It is easier to understand how a liberal becomes a pacifist than how a liberal becomes a socialist. Especially in Russell's case there is an ingrained opposition to violence in his "English mind." To such a mind it is self-evident that "kindliness and tolerance are worth all the creeds in the world" (*BPT,* 28).

There are ties between socialism and pacifism in that both place the primacy of concern in humankind rather than any nation or race. Both socialist and pacifist feel entrapped in a system: the socialist in a class structure in which the rich exploit the poor, the pacifist in a nationalist structure in which militarists incite peoples to hate each other as enemies. The socialist fights the vice of greed. The pacifist fights the vice of pride. Each is pleading morally for a "change of heart," as Russell sometimes put it.[13] Both socialism and pacificism express a strong preference for harmony over discord, and are attempts to plot the triumphs of harmony in human affairs. By 1917 Russell's voice proclaimed moral idealism, and a reviewer in the *New Republic* characterized the author of *Why Men Fight:* "Here is a human being who has brought to the consideration of the war an intellect of extraordinary scrupulousness, an imagination penetrated with consciousness of human values, a broad and serious sense of responsibility, a complete emancipation from personal motives and a complete independence of class and party and creed."[14]

The best accounts for understanding Russell's position in World War I are the autobiographical "Experiences of a Pacifist in the First World War" (*PMem*, 30–34); "The Ethics of War" (1915) and other essays gathered into *Justice in War-Time* (1916);[15] *Rex v. Bertrand Russell,* which contains Russell's defense in court;[16] and G. H. Hardy's *Bertrand Russell and Trinity.*[17] A valuable German commentary is Herbert Gottschalk's chapter "The First World War and Prison." The fullest account, with much about Russell's wartime love affairs, is in the *Autobiography, 1914–1944.*[18]

Early in World War I Russell wrote a letter to the London *Nation* in which he put the case against the war. War is commanded by the state and approved by the churches, yet it is a compound of the most obvious vices, murder, hatred, deceit, injustice, hypocrisy, and pride.

The motivation of nations is pride and prestige. War mentality condemns reasoning about consequences because this shows fear. In terms of virtues, military motivation exaggerates courage. A theologian could have written the final sentences: "Nothing stands in [the] way [of settlement by an international court] except the pride of rulers who wish to remain uncontrolled by anything higher than their own will. When this great tragedy has worked itself out to its disastrous conclusion, when the poisons of hate and self-assertion have given place to compassion with universal misery, the nations will perhaps realize that they have fought in blindness and delusion, and that the way of mercy is the way of happiness for all."[19]

That Russell found himself, a Puritan, with Quakers, is entirely comprehensible. These extreme Protestants rely on personal contact of the spirit with God and usually find institutional religion of the churches lax and corrupt. Although we usually talk of Russell as our twentieth-century Voltaire and think of him as representing eighteenth-century rationalism, this liberalism is a layer of consciousness supported by a seventeenth-century Puritan conscience. In a difficult decision, he writes: "I never had a moment's doubt as to what I must do. I have at times been paralyzed by scepticism, at times I have been cynical, at other times indifferent, but when the war came I felt as if I heard the voice of God" (*PMem*, 31). Now the point of separation between utilitarian calculus and obedience to divine command: "I *knew* that it was my business to protest, *however futile* protest might be. My *whole nature* was involved" (italics added).

Russell was not himself a conscientious objector, but as defender of conscientious objection to the war, was found guilty of prejudicing "the recruiting and discipline of His Majesty's forces." Russell's justification was the tradition of British liberty to appeal to conscience against any "human institution" (*RBB*, 38–40).

Russell was found guilty and fined. He refused to pay the fine and the goods in his rooms in Trinity College were seized and offered for public sale. When the first book was auctioned, the bid was sufficient to cover the moneys due the court (£110). Although Russell's friends saved his books, they could not save his lectureship at Trinity College (*BRT*, 40–46).

The rise of rearmed fascist Italy and rearming Nazi Germany in the 1930s confronted his pacifism with severe tests. Which would win—his pacifism held with the tenacity familiar in religious believers or the realism necessary for sober politics? At first faith used reason, as in *Which Way to Peace?* (1936). Russell argued by analogy. If Gandhi uses *satyagraha* (soul-force) against the British in India, why could not the British use passive resistance against Nazi aggression and invasion?

Bertrand Russell's daughter, Katharine Tait, tells much about the hopes of youth in the thirties and the fading of pacifist hope: "It was the first book of his I ever read, and I found it utterly convincing. Surely, I thought, in view of these facts, no government would be mad enough to start another war. But my father was less convinced by his arguments than I, and he never allowed *Which Way to Peace?* to be reprinted, feeling it was insincere. He had no objection to reprints of books maintaining views he had since abandoned, but this one maintained a view he had not really held even while he was writing it. As it became clear to all who followed the news that the Nazis were in no way disarmed by passive resistance, my father began to have second thoughts about his pacifism, and so another field of action was closed to him. . . . He could neither support nor condemn attempts to build up Britain's military power in opposition to Hitler."[20]

Pacifism ended, and the threat of war continued, and after World War II Russell concluded that world government required international military power.

Russell the Educator: Hope of Inculcating the Virtues of a New International Order

Different systems of education are distinguished by the virtues each system encourages in its students. Some moralities, Christian, for example, esteem humility a virtue, whereas Aristotelian ethics counts it as a vice. "Christ enjoins love; Kant teaches that no action of which love is the motive can be truly virtuous" (*BW*, 413). Even if two systems agree about the ingredient virtues, they "differ as to their relative importance. One man will emphasize courage, another learning, another kindliness, and another rectitude. One man, like the elder Brutus, will put duty to the State above family affection; another, like Confucius, will put family affection first. *All these divergences will produce differences as to education.* We must first have some conception of the kind of person we wish to produce, before we can have any definite opinion as to the education which we consider best" (*BW*, 413).

Russell is a lover of English ways, and he can recognize the virtues of public school education, but he also isolates the "virtues." The ironic twist is that virtues turn out to be vices. British people are conspicuously reserved and unexpressive. It is considered bad form to show one's emotions, as do Italians or Irish. Russell asks, why? Is it really better to be reserved? In answer to the first he replies: "Social dealings in private life are filled with fear, especially in Britain. People take pains not to wear their heart on their sleeves for daws to peck at. As far as they can, they keep their emotions to themselves. They will behave in exactly the same way to you whether they like you or dislike you, provided they have no motive of self-interest for making up to you. They are stiff and shy and unspontaneous. They wear an armour designed to conceal the frightened child within" (*BW*, 713). The education of people to be controlled by fear is, in Russell's analysis, to be mastered by a vice. How do we know then that to be reserved is a bad habit, inculcated by bad education? Here Russell moves on to the consequences. "The result is that social intercourse becomes boring, that friendships have little life in them, and that love is only a pale shadow of what it might be."

Russell devoted a whole book to *The Conquest of Happiness*. Here, with regard to reserve, the clear standard by which it is judged a vice is that it conduces to misery and ought therefore to be replaced with openness: "The outer world is bleak, the inner world is stuffy. This is not how human relations should be. They should be free and spontaneous. Vanity should be less touchy and envy less widespread. The habit of reserve not only makes it easy for self-deception to flourish secretly, but also, owing to the energy spent in the purely negative occupation of preventing self-expression, greatly diminishes the fruitful outflow of energy in useful ways. It has the further defect that men are particularly anxious to conceal friendly impulses, since these especially, if known, make them feel that they are vulnerable. Hours of tedium and years of ossification result from this reign of social terror" (*BW*, 713). This is one of the most illuminating analyses to illustrate an ancient truth about vices: just as one virtue leads to and supports the others, so also with the vices. Reserve is accompanied by vanity, envy, self-deception, boredom.

Another British virtue, inculcated especially at those pinnacles of English life, Eton and Oxford, is the observance of good form. Of course, we must think of courtesy as a virtue. But with superstitious reverence for authority, pride in nation or church which seeks to inculcate subservience and narrow patriotism, what is this "worship of 'good form' "? This virtue carried to excess is a vice.

Russell exalts intellect above good manners. What he is rebuking is sometimes called antiintellectualism, along with neglect of "artistic creation" and "vital energy." "The evils of 'good form' arise from two sources: its perfect assurance of its own rightness, and its belief that correct manners are more to be desired than intellect, or artistic creation, or vital energy, or any of the other sources of progress in the world. Perfect assurance, by itself, is enough to destroy all mental progress in those who have it. And when it is combined with contempt for the angularities and awkwardnesses that are almost invariably associated with great mental power, it becomes a source of destruction to all who come in contact with it. 'Good form' is itself dead and incapable of growth; and by its attitudes to those who are without it spreads its own death to many who might otherwise have life" (*BW*, 405–6).

The traditional Socratic question is, can virtue be taught? Russell's answer is emphatically yes, and he goes on to add, that in English public schools, as elsewhere, there are some virtues that are really good in a scientific and international order, but that most "virtues" are really vices. In contrast to the vices that are taught on the playing fields of Eton, what are genuine virtues?

Education in the highest sense, for Russell, is the relation of the teacher to the young. Often he stresses that "the educator should love the young." To be a good teacher "it is necessary also that he should have a right conception of human excellence." This is an excellence for men and women, and there is to be "no distinction whatever between male and female excellences" (*BW*, 418–19). There are different vocational excellences, called by the Greeks *aretai*, and Russell agrees they are habits, acquired, that is, by practice and as different as those of a poet and a postman (*BW*, 418). The imaginative vision of a poet is a vice in a postman and routine punctiliousness is a vice in a poet. But what concerns morality most are the common excellences that "jointly form the basis of an ideal character" (*BW*, 419).

Traditionally in Greek culture the virtues are temperance, courage, wisdom, and justice, and these, the four cardinal virtues, were adopted from Plato by St. Augustine and from Aristotle by St. Thomas Aquinas. These are not the only good habits, for many ancients had piety, and Augustine summed up all four in love. There were added to the four pagan virtues the three Christian or theological virtues from St. Paul: faith, hope, and charity (1 Cor. 13). In this ancient tradition, Russell gives in his list "vitality, courage, sensitiveness, and intelligence," without suggesting there are no others.

Why is vitality put first among the virtues, as most basic? "It is a safeguard against envy because it makes one's own existence pleasant. As envy is one of the great sources of human misery, this is a very important merit in vitality" (*BW*, 419). In other places envy is analyzed as a mortal sin because it takes the form of substituting for excellent work of one's own the absorption with another's success, even the attempt to steal it, or to ruin its renown, or to destroy the person who is envied.[21]

Courage is the second virtue, and contrasts to fear, which Russell often analyzes as the root of vice. By courage is not meant mere "absence of fear," especially when there is a rational basis for fear. False "courage" is the appearance of courage produced by threat of shame and disgrace. "Fear should be overcome not only in action but feeling, and not only in conscious feeling, but in the unconscious as well." This is the existentialist anxiety made famous among us through Paul Tillich's *Courage to Be*. Russell does not go into the fear of death and annihilation, nor does he have any answer to the

ultimate threat of nonbeing. But he does recognize that trench
warfare produced shell shock, a complete inability to function, and
that fear motivates rulers to erect a "whole system of oppression
and cruelty" and may produce in an otherwise controlled aristocracy
acts of vengeful repression againt rebellion. Thus cruelty is "an
offshoot of cowardice, and deserves the same contempt as is bestowed
upon the more obvious forms of that vice."

The third virtue is sensitiveness and sympathy. Why Russell did
not develop them to the extent he developed vitality and courage
is a mystery. He could have considered traditional justice and wisdom, which certainly have a great place in his ideal for an international society; a systematic survey would require careful exploration
of the intertwinings of justice with mercy, and wisdom with knowledge. Perhaps we must turn elsewhere in Russell to make good the
gaps. There is a development of Christ's teaching, always fundamental to Russell's morality, "Love thy neighbour as thyself" (Luke
10:27)—provided it is coupled with intelligence, as in his formula,
"the good life is inspired by love and guided by knowledge." This
is developed in Russell's educational morality as the cultivation of
the "capacity for abstract sympathy," a virtue "as rare as it is important" (BW, 423).

It should by now be obvious that vitality must be kept from
decay by intelligence, that true courage is never apart from knowledge of the dangers, that sympathy to be universal must be general
and therefore abstract. The moral virtues therefore must be guided
by intelligence. But what does Russell mean by the last virtue in
his quartet? Curiosity, as in a cat or a child, is necessary but not
sufficient. Curiosity, leading us when young to peek into drawers
and cupboards, may develop into trying "to peer through curtains
after dark" or to gossip about what we find out about our neighbors.
This is of "no very high value," and malice rather than love of
knowledge is evident when "one gossips about other people's secret
vices, but never about their secret virtues" (BR, 425, order reversed).

Intelligence is not developed under certain conditions. It is dis-
couraged as a danger to character, a threat to faith, or a deficiency
of charm and sexual attractiveness. Indeed it may seem unlike conventional virtue to call intelligence a virtue at all. This is one of
the great defects, writes Russell of Christian teaching as contrasted
to that of the pagan Greeks. When the church teaches "that nothing
matters except 'virtue,' . . . 'virtue' consists in abstinence from a

certain list of actions arbitrarily labelled 'sin.' So long as this attitude persists, it is impossible to make men realize that intelligence does more good than an artificial conventional 'virtue' " (*BW*, 424). Although Russell stresses knowledge, evidently there is intelligence about the true ends of life. Sometimes the choice of ends is made, as in David Hume's philosophy, solely as the result of passions. This could not be Russell's critical philosophy. If morality concerns ends and intelligence is the crowning virtue, there must be wisdom to guide us. Those who trust a set of rules are morally ignorant and stupid.

The second barrier to true intelligence is lack of information. Intelligence cannot be merely ability to gain knowledge, but must be actual knowledge. Aptitude is acquired only by exercise, and information helps train the intelligence; hence they are closely interrelated. "Ignorant adults are unteachable; on such matters as hygiene or diet, for example, they are totally incapable of believing what science has to say" (*BW*, 424). There is no limit on or excess of knowledge. The ability to know is never worn out by much acquisition, nor does a person reach the weariness of Koheleth's "much study is a weariness of the flesh" (Eccles. 12:12). "The more a man has learnt, the easier it is for him to learn still more—always assuming he has not been taught in a spirit of dogmatism" (*BW*, 424).

This caveat against what we call ideology leads us to the third block to intelligence. Many alert people, with a high degree of orderliness, even gifted in deductive reasoning, get caught in "systems." It should be obvious from Russell's experience with liberals, socialists, communists, and pacifists, and of course with anti-Semitic fascists, that they fall prey to excessive reverence for some authority. Russell finds particularly offensive the workings of the faithful and the patriotic dominated by "habits of reverence towards God and religion, and of respect for the civil and religious institutions of the country" (*BW*, 426). Here again is the rebel preaching that a necessity of the good life is to "be emancipated from the herd" (*BW*, 427). But note carefully the "herd" may be a minority, even a tiny dissenting group, such as followers of Trotsky among communists, a small sect that typically considers Lenin and Stalin to have a false version of the Gospel of Marx.

The danger of becoming enslaved by a system is particularly evident to original philosophers who observe their disciples, and it is the prime reason that Russell, like many philosophers, rejoices in not having disciples. "All sorts of intellectual systems—Christianity, Socialism, Patriotism, etc.—are ready, like orphan asylums, to give safety in return for servitude. A free mental life cannot be as warm and comfortable and sociable as a life enveloped in a creed: only a creed can give the feeling of a cozy fireside while the winter storms are raging without" (*BW*, 426–27). Russell might well have referred to the cowardice of crawling back into an intellectual womb. "Courage is essential to intellectual probity, as well as to physical heroism" (*BW*, 426).

Russell the educator is a citizen of the world inculcating the virtues necessary to the creation of a new international order.

The Prophet of Doom and His Condemnation of the Wicked

The last of the four great evils as seen by Russell is total annihilation of life. He had fought misery, war, and stupidity, and in the period after World War II he had even greater certainty it was nuclear war that mankind must prevent. Increasingly he identified himself as the voice of human reason, and he expected the heads of state, especially the chiefs of the Soviet and the American states, to listen to reason. As the danger of all-out war became greater and as he could count on fewer years, his voice became shrill, and he depended on others to prepare his messages. Often the young men around him fixed on the United States as the incarnation of evil, or as one Moslem leader later called it, "the Satan nation."

Always before, in combating evil, he had reservations about liberalism, about socialism, about pacifism, about the extent of freedom in education. Although students early noted in him a tendency to dogmatism, it was nearly always tempered by skepticism. But when he fixed upon Lyndon Johnson as the captain of the forces of evil in the Vietnam War, there must, Russell determined, be a trial on the pattern of the Nuremberg trials of the Nazis, so rigged that there must be a condemnation of the criminal. Anticommunist liberals, chief of whom was and still is Sidney Hook, called attention to the failure to allow the accused to state his side. Some chose to palliate the intellectual failure and moral lapse as senility or even madness. To comprehend the last phase, one may consult the sources to be found in Ralph Schoenman's *Bertrand Russell, Philosopher of the Century.*[22]

Russell's political beliefs can be learned from hearing him and seeing him perform in conversation. There are videotaped interviews made in 1959 that communicate what he thought evil and wrong in human nature and institutions, and how he thought things could be set right. The interviews have also been published in a book called *Bertrand Russell Speaks His Mind.* If it is at all possible, one should, to make Russell's acquaintance, look at and listen to the films of his television dialogues.[23]

Chapter Eight

Russell's Religion: Could His God Be the Ground of Order?

The Labyrinth of Russell's Religion

Had Russell been a moralist only, or a prophet only, there would be no such complexity as we find in his religion and in his philosophy of religion. By now the full force of the complexity of Russell the man and Russell the philosopher should have emerged. Because religion is the most comprehensive area of human interest, as compared to science, economics, morality, art, even politics, it has both the greatest opportunity to integrate life, when the synthesis is successful, and the greatest danger of collapse, when synthesis fails. If Russell were only a frustrated metaphysician, a failure at synthesis, and only an analytic piecemeal dealer in paradoxes and arguments, he would be far less interesting than he is in his most famous essays. These are "A Free Man's Worship" (1903), "Why I Am Not a Christian" (1927), "Has Religion Made Useful Contributions to Civilization?" (1930), and "Can Religion Cure Our Troubles?" (1954). These are all available in a handy collection, *Why I Am Not a Christian,* edited by Paul Edwards to show the antireligious secularism of Russell. One might conclude either from humanist advocacy or antihumanist denunciation that Russell is the most eminent religious humanist of the twentieth century.[1] We shall have to consider the hypothesis that Russell's personal career demonstrates a case of the emotional exhaustion of Christianity, its logical, moral, and political collapse. Particularly since Russell was outrageously slandered by church leaders and prevented from teaching at City College of the City of New York in 1940,[2] Russell's writings are ammunition for those who, with the militant atheists, consider religion a holdover from primitive man and barbarous periods and that it now represents only superstitious beliefs and fanaticism that block the progress of civilization. Russell is often compared to Voltaire, famous for his imperative against Catholicism, *"écrasez l'infame!"* (wipe out the infamy!).

One way to make Russell's religious career, or antireligious career, if you will, a fascinating introduction to philosophy is to ask whether the secular humanist interpretation is adequate.

The opposite interpretation is best represented, at least for the beginning of our dialectic, by Katharine Tait's hypothesis that her father Bertrand Russell was essentially a religious man. In another age, she argues, he would have been a monk in a monastery and be remembered as a saint: his whole philosophic career can be most comprehensively read as a "search for God." We have already pondered the conclusions of *Problems of Philosophy* (1912) and of *Principles of Social Reconstruction* (1916) and the interpretation of Russell's pacifism as an application of Christ's Gospel. "The Essence of Religion" (1912), not found in *Why I Am Not a Christian* but reprinted in *Basic Writings,* states an emotionally positive case. Russell was quite constant throughout his whole career in holding that the most valuable aspect of any person is his personal religion, and it is a grave defect to have none. We cannot say that this means that Russell had any experience of the God of Judaism or Christianity except that the summons to oppose World War I came "as . . . the voice of God." Yet certainly he joined no church, preached no creed, practiced no code such as the Ten Commandments, but indeed did quite the opposite. But he had passionate devotion to the whole of mankind, expressed sympathy with each person suffering loneliness, and found the greatest joy in contemplation. Although indeed a scoffer, he also professed "cosmic piety."

Russell's relation to religion generally was a hate-love relationship, but we must guard against putting him down in our psychiatric case book as simply schizophrenic. There is a moral interpretation that is far more valuable as a hypothesis. Stated very simply, there is bad religion and good religion. The bad religion, and it can be very bad, is known for its vices. The good religion, and it can be very good, is known for its virtues. Therefore we need, continuing Russell's ethics and politics, to discriminate between the good and bad habits of persons and institutions by applying theories of virtues and vices to religious persons and institutions. We find in Russell more system than he is given credit for, and indeed more than he even knew he had. This makes the reader hungry for more than the

few essays we have already mentioned and for more thorough development of a criteriology of religious phenomena, that is, a set
of standards by which to judge religions good and bad, beyond his
two books *Mysticism and Logic* (1912) and *Religion and Science* (1935).

We have developed, in the previous chapters on ethics and politics, the conflicts between good and evil, and identified the great
evils of misery, war, stupidity, and annihilation; the question remains, what of religion? Is it the fifth great evil, and the worst of
all because it is involved in the other four, or is it the great good
because it is identified with the solutions to the evils? A dialectical
reading of Russell, because "religion" is so complex a set of attitudes,
beliefs, insights, judgments, habits, and social relations, finds him
on both sides. When religion is the solution, he loves it, and when
religion is the problem, he hates it. This is far from crazy; it is
most rational and wise.

On one hand religion provides the worst obvious examples of
failed logic, failed mathematics, failed epistemology, failed metaphysics, failed ethics, and failed politics. Sometimes it seems that
Russell combed literature to select horrible examples with which to
shock bishops out of their gaiters. If we wished to train Christian
debaters, we could do the trick in reverse by writing a tract on the
fallacies of atheism and use Russell's arguments as examples of
fallacies.

Philosophy of religion is the most comprehensive discipline of
philosophy, and although all the areas have aspects that are logical,
epistemological, ontological, moral, aesthetic, and political, it is
in religion that the problems become most acute. Sometimes it
seems that philosophy of religion, even more than metaphysics, is
all problems and no solutions. There is always the temptation to
use "God" as the solution, and to think that no matter how many
problems are left over from all the other areas, somehow they are
going to be all resolved on a higher level of insight sometimes called
"faith." Indeed there is a theological strategy that shows the difficulties, unsolved problems, and collapse on the level of reason,
and then invokes a saint or a prophet with a revelation, and asserts
that "God" provides the answer that man seeks. When we say that
reason fails, this is skepticism, and then the less we know, the more
we must take on faith. This is dogmatism. Not only defenders of
religion sometimes fall into a combination of skepticism and dogmatism; Russell himself was criticized for being the mirror opposite

of an apologist. That is, when engaged in debate, he became absolutely certain that there is no evidence for God and no benefit from believing.

It is significant that the most positive statements of personal religion came in the period 1912–16, and the negative statements, beginning with *What I Believe* (1925), which seems to some more "What I Do *Not* Believe," set the tone of attack on religious institutions, as in *Why I Am Not a Christian,* from 1927 on. Does this mean that we should consider the early statements puerile or juvenile and count the late as mature and wise? No. The reason is that in "Reply to Criticisms" Russell reaffirmed the early approach: "What makes my attitude towards religion complex is that, although I consider some form of personal religion highly desirable, and feel many people unsatisfactory through lack of it, I cannot accept the theology of any well known religion, and I incline to think that most churches at most times have done more harm than good."[3] Which side of the story should we recommend? Of his personal religion, in 1943 he still found "the one in *Social Reconstruction* (Chapter VII)" *least unsatisfactory (RC,* 726). There are good reasons Russell developed the negative side later: the pacifist period was one in which Russell encountered all the evils, especially church religions in league with nations in prosecuting war; he discovered how few professing Christians apply Christ's teachings to war; the postwar period was one of sober reflection on the moral failure of Christian civilization and the rise of the secular fanaticisms, fascism and communism; it was a period in which science seemed the healthy and progressive aspect of the West; and he had the opportunity in China to study philosophies that conduce to peace and stability. The West progressed while China stagnated, but the price seemed high. Is Christianity, daughter religion of Judaism, the poison? "From the Jews we derive fanatical belief, which its friends call 'faith'; moral fervor, with the conception of sin; religious intolerance, and some part of our nationalism."[4] Russell, as did his friend Santayana, tended to say what they disliked about Protestants by referring disparagingly to "the Jews," and to ascribe only good things in Western civilization to "the Greeks" (*PC,* 196). This kind of talk, common in Nietzsche, is not only inconsistent with Russell's high regard for the Judeo-Christian concept "love of neighbor" but plays into the hands of anti-Semites.

It is illuminating to think of the search for God in the tradition of the Jews and the tradition of the Greeks. As contrasted in Hebraism and Hellenism, these are the ways of action and contemplation. The prophet hears the voice of God and takes appropriate action to do good and oppose evil. The context is history in which the future may be salvation or damnation of people. The mystic, by contrast, sees the ideal form behind the imperfect copies that appear, and by intellectual ascent frees himself step by step from the finite rising to the infinite, or from the temporal into the eternal.

Both of these religions, the prophetic and the mystical, are well developed in Russell. Each finds beautiful expression. Very few celebrations of the contemplation of beautiful forms can match "The Study of Mathematics."[5] Very few documents of action against war and for peace can match Russell saying "as if I heard the voice of God."[6] We have spoken of "the religion of Russell" when we should have said "the religions of Russell." Part of the trouble is that at times his personal religion is that of the activist, at times that of the contemplative. From the activist perspective, the contemplative is merely aesthetic, avoiding the moral obligations of a rough-and-tumble world by retreating into an ivory tower. From the contemplative perspective, the activist is troubled about an imperfect world, bothered with trifles, pursuing a vain course of political maneuvers that will hardly improve affairs on the whole, and will never surely bring inner contentment. Interpreters of Russell sometimes find his way that of Mary, sometimes that of Martha (Luke 10:38–42), and as in the partly Hellenic, partly Hebraic Christian blending, there remains an unresolved tension.[7]

The profound conflict in Bertrand Russell is that if he had been satisfied with identifying God as the perfection of forms, he could have been a mystical logician-mathematician and told his story as the discovery of beauty, even Beauty, as God present whenever we discover order and structure. Russell is also the moralist and prophet who must heed a moral imperative. But had he only identified the discovery of God as a person's faithfulness to conscience, he could have preached his God as did his friend and ally in the antinuclear cause, Albert Schweitzer.[8]

Why couldn't he settle down and be a happy Hellenic mystic or thunder away against evils and act as a Hebraic prophet? Because there are the demands of the austere intellectual. Not only Beauty and Goodness appeal to the worshiper in Russell. There is also Truth.

We can understand why Russell considers only the highest standards of rigor in demonstrations. Religion demands complete trust and commitment. This cannot be given to anything merely probable or likely. Absolute trust can be given only to the Absolute, teaches Kierkegaard. Russell is as passionately religious as the Danish Pascal whose insight was that "purity of heart is to will one thing." Russell expressed himself as devoted to Truth, and this comes close to being a unifying principle, for here is both the motive of science and the first moral principle, therefore the religious foundation of both theory and practice. "Better the world should perish than that I, or any other human being, should believe a lie. . . . But that is the religion of thought, in whose scorching flames the dross of the world is burnt away" (*ML*, 72–73).

What must we then say of Russell as a religious man? He was a person of profound religious experience, yet one who failed to recognize that he had much in common with prophets of Israel, such as Isaiah; saints and teachers of the Catholic faith, such as Augustine; and founders of new religions, such as Buddha. How can a Voltaire be put in such company? Russell has much to say on his discovery of the religious message of sympathy or love.

After hearing Gilbert Murray read part of his then unpublished translation of the Hippolytus of Euripides, which includes a hymn to Love (Eros), Russell, with others, found "Mrs. Whitehead undergoing an unusually severe bout of pain." Whitehead, together with the Russells, suffered great anxiety about her heart trouble and her increasing invalidism.

She seemed cut off from everyone and everything by walls of agony, and the sense of the solitude of each human soul suddenly overwhelmed me. Ever since my marriage, my emotional life had been calm and superficial. I had forgotten all the deeper issues, and had been content with flippant cleverness. Suddenly the ground seemed to give way beneath me, and I found myself in quite another region. Within five minutes I went through some such reflections as the following: the loneliness of the human soul is unendurable; nothing can penetrate it except the highest intensity of the sort of love that religious teachers have preached; whatever does not spring from this motive is harmful, or at best useless; it follows that war is wrong, that a public school education is abominable, that the use of force is to be depreciated, and that in human relations one should penetrate to the core of loneliness in each person and speak to that.[9]

But if Russell reports such a profound experience, how did he slip into secularist propaganda and make common cause with humanists? As a young man he rejected Voltaire, or any approach to religion that is "external, . . . coldly critical, . . . remote from the emotions" as well as the optimistic metaphysics of Leibniz or Bradley. How could he have joined the scoffers to make "fun of the whole thing from a common sense, semi-historical, semi-literary point of view," which he concluded was "hopelessly inadequate" (*Ai*, 285)?

The antireligion is anti−bad religion, which is very bad because it is really vice masquerading as virtue. It was the Puritan in Russell who righteously turns iconoclastic. In the name of Truth he must denounce the moral falseness of hypocrisy. If people are like the philosophic combination of the tender and the tough, how helpful to teach the tender, universal sympathy, by talking tough. Russell in Trinity College found he could hurt people by his "somewhat brutal statement of unpleasant truths." States of the world made him "caustic," and one side of realism was "the practice of describing things which one finds almost unendurable in such a repulsive manner as to cause others to share one's fury" (*Ai*, 84).

The famous American theologian Reinhold Niebuhr once wrote "Can Schweitzer Save Us from Russell?" What we are to be saved from, in Judeo-Christian language, is the Evil One, Satan, and in picturing Russell, it is as a philosopher ever "more cynical in his view of life and . . . more ruthless in stating the tenets of his religion of despair."[10] The theologian is probably referring to "A Free Man's Worship" (1903) but mentions only *What I Believe* (1925), which was published two years before *Why I Am Not a Christian* (1927). The latter was clearly even more offensively prejudiced against what the theologian regards as the Biblical truths of Christianity, and the pity of this antagonism is that we have no deeper account from Niebuhr than his one-sided response to what he regarded as Russell's one-sidedness. Dialogue could have been fruitful for many reasons, chief of which was Niebuhr's agreement with Russell that the optimism of Idealism was inadequate to characterize reality. That is, the theologian has to agree with the facts of Russell's pessimism: "So much of the world seems blind and cruel and capricious; so much of life seems to defy the pat dogmas of God's omnipotence. Neglected truths have a way of revenging themselves upon their destructors." The theologian, agreeing with the facts, cannot agree with Russell's conclusion that "the universe reveals no purpose and encourages none of the hopes with which men have been wont to beguile their life" (*CSSUR*, 1093).

Why does Niebuhr call Russell's philosophy of religion a "religion of despair"? Traditional religious thought bases man's hope on God the Creator who rules nature, guides history, rewards the righteous who obey God's law revealed in Scripture, and punishes the wicked. All that is left of religious metaphysics is the struggle of good against evil in the human sphere, and the only faith is in what man discovers, for there is no God to reveal His truth to man. Man discovers orders, according to Russell's metaphysics, but no order of orders, or ultimate ground of order. The theologian's anxiety is that he can't live a life of religious faith on that thin basis. Russell's response: that is all anyone can honestly claim.

The whole truth about Russell's religion can only be surmised from the little that he tells us of his adolescent struggle to find reasons to believe in God, immortality, and freedom, his account of his Puritan upbringing and revolt against divine command morality, his investigation of mysticism which attracted his religious feelings, his rejection of proofs of the existence of God (especially in Leibniz), his pacifism partly based on Christ's teachings. When one learns these autobiographical facts and reads "The Essence of Religion," one would surely conclude that Russell was himself a deeply religious man. This we are told emphatically by his daughter Kate in *My Father, Bertrand Russell.*

It may be objected that Russell's morality was based on an optimistic view that man's intellect, applied to nature and yielding technological control over nature, was the secret of human salvation. In many cases indeed Russell did think the Biblical view of man as sinner was that of the unenlightened who had not taken account of Darwin, Marx, and Freud. Although Russell never subscribed to any theory of original sin, what difference is there between this cornerstone of Augustinian and Calvinist theology and what Russell found true of human nature? It comes to the same grim fact that humans are perverse. Russell does not continue the optimistic Enlightenment view of man as essentially good, but sides, in principle, though never admitting it, with neoorthodoxy made famous by Karl Barth and Reinhold Niebuhr.

In 1951 Russell published the preface to Gustav Herling's *A World Apart.* [11] The Polish author took his title from Dostoyevsky's

House of the Dead to characterize slave labor camps, to which Stalin condemned him, along with thousands of Poles. Not only Russian communists but Western Stalinists, then called fellow travelers, denied that there was any such horror as "hard labor and starvation in the Arctic cold."

Fellow travelers who refuse to believe the evidence of books such as Mr. Herling's are necessarily people devoid of humanity, for if they had any humanity they would not merely dismiss the evidence, but would take some trouble to look into it.

Communists and Nazis alike have tragically demonstrated that in a large proportion of mankind the impulse to inflict torture exists, and requires only opportunity to display itself in all its naked horror.

Then follows a theme familiar to us in the assessment of human sinfulness: beware, as Leo Baeck said, of falling into hatred of the persecutor. Rabbi Baeck made a practice of praying for the Nazis. Russell puts this point philosophically and morally:

I do not think that these evils can be cured by blind hatred of their perpetrators. This will only lead us to become like them. Although the effort is not easy, one should attempt, in reading such a book as this one, to understand the circumstances that turn men into fiends, and to realize that it is not by blind rage that such evils will be prevented. I do not say that to understand is to pardon; there are things which for my part I find I cannot pardon.

I hope [*A World Apart*] will . . . rouse in its readers not useless vindictiveness, but a vast compassion for the petty criminals, almost as much as for their victims, and a determination to understand and eliminate the springs of cruelty in human nature that has become distorted by bad social systems.

If this "root of radical evil," as Kant renamed "original sin," was something Russell had at first ignored, he was forced to recognize it through running a school. Liberals had ignored sin in their Enlightenment theory of human progress being achieved through freedom alone. But Russell had had much experience of the depth of human evil in World War I, which uncovered what is vicious and malicious. In the end Russell's religious experience includes not only the contemplative's Beauty, Truth, and Goodness but also the moral imperative to face the evil in oneself.

Promethean Defiance of a
Purposeless Material Universe

Russell's realistic revolt against monism and idealism is sometimes discussed only as a matter of real external relations, pluralism of many real particulars and universals, and the correspondence theory of truth in propositions of the same structure as facts. When we explored these in logic, epistemology, and ontology, we neglected the theological depth of the revolt, though in ethics we encountered the belief in real good as contrasted to real evil. In considering political theory we found this based upon the real evils of misery, war, stupidity, and annihilation. Russell's revolt against metaphysical optimism that denied real evil became a revolt against Christian theology of the nineteenth century because most Protestant thinkers had become idealists in metaphysics.

Russell had made a close study of three metaphysicians who had reached positive religious conclusions. These were Leibniz, Bradley, and McTaggart, and all reached optimistic conclusions. With regard to evil, it is either only apparent and not real, or it is proximate and not ultimate. We may not then appeal to actual experience of the world and say that it is not good, for there is reality which is the true world, as religious faith expresses it, "a heavenly city" other than this corrupt world. [12] The relation of the temporal progress of the world to this absolute as a "future state of things is 'a harmony which must someday become explicit.' " Can metaphysics give us this comfort for our present ills (*WNC*, 96–97)? "Christianity and all previous optimisms have represented the world as eternally ruled by a beneficent Providence, and thus metaphysically good" (*WNC*, 98).

How can we trust such a theory of God guiding and directing the course of events when this is satisfying to human hope? For example, is it not suspect as "a device by which to prove the future excellence of the world—prove, for example, that good men would be happy after death" (*WNC*, 99)?

If there is no ground of religious belief but human wish, then the value of religion is the "emotion," for there can be nothing cognitive, because there is nothing experienced. If God is timeless, and "all experience equally is in time . . . [then] no experience is experience of the Deity" (*WNC*, 102). "The gulf fixed between Appearance and Reality is so profound that we have no grounds, so far as I can see, for regarding some experience as nearer than others to the perfect experience of Reality" (*WNC*, 102). The only value of the beatific vision, to which some philosophizing leads, is then in the "philosophizing, not of philosophy" (*WNC*, 102).

Russell therefore has grounds for not philosophizing in an optimistic way. "The desire to find comfort in metaphysics has, we must all admit, produced a great deal of fallacious reasoning and intellectual dishonesty" (*WNC*, 103). As for consolations of philosophy, they "are flowers to be gathered by the way, but they do not constitute a reward for its attainment, since, by all that appears, the flowers grew only at the beginning of the road and disappear long before we have reached our journey's end" (*WNC*, 102).

Russell personally sought the comfort that religious people promise from the practice of their faith, and suffering intense loneliness in an unrewarding marriage, he "tried to take refuge in pure contemplation; I began to write *The Free Man's Worship*. The construction of prose rhythms was the only thing in which I found any real consolation."[13]

Exactly why is belief in God a consolation? Although there is evil "in this mad monstrous world," if we fathom it, we discover "a hidden purpose . . . and the purpose is good." This is something which we must reverence beyond the visible world. This is most clearly expressed as the belief "that God intended harmony to come out of chaos by human efforts." One version of this is that if there is sin, it is occasion for forgiveness, and therefore "the future might be better." But this version of sacred history, put in the mouth of Mephistopheles, is all a cruel trick man's imagination and hope play on him: the world reverts to chaos, and the process of ordering is repeated. This is Russell's anticipation of the myth of Sisyphus, two generations before Camus. The feeling is of existential annihilation, but it is in the name of science, probably referring to entropic loss of all order, that the process is called purposeless and "void of meaning."

A Free Man's Worship is Russell's Book of Job. The despair of righteous Job is that although he had not sinned, and his God was altogether righteous, yet he was punished by God as though he had sinned. Russell knows he lives in a beautiful world. "I lay awake through long nights, hearing first the nightingale, and then the chorus of birds at dawn, looking out upon sunrise and trying to find consolation in external beauty." Yet he suffers the intense loneliness he had seen in Mrs. Whitehead's agony (*Ai*, 225). The cruel trick played by nature is that man, favorite child of his mother, alone gifted with the discernment of good and evil, intelligence, and freedom, is subject in the end to the inexorable fate of "resistless forces" (*WNC*, 107).

This may well be the end of the purposeful cosmos thought out by Plato and Aristotle, a metaphysics used to support the Providence of the Creator God of the Bible, but it is not the end of all religion. There is the intensity of a dualism like that of Zoroaster. The prophet of ancient Persia postulated two deities, of Light and of Darkness, of Truth and of Deceit. The summons is to fight for the good god against the evil god. Russell postulates the God of love over against the God of power. In colorful terms he pictures the slave's worship over against the free man's worship. The first springs from fear and is cowardly; the second springs from man's confidence and is brave. The bad is vicious: "The religion of Moloch [detested by the prophets of Israel as a devil demanding of parents the sacrifice of their children] is in essence the cringing submission of the slave, who dares not, even in his heart, allow the thought that his master deserves no adulation" (*WNC*, 108). The worship of the force of matter is idolatry, failure to "maintain our own ideals against a hostile universe" and to submit to evil (*WNC*, 109). The good religion is virtuous:

Let us preserve our respect for truth, for beauty, for the ideal of perfection which life does not permit us to attain, though none of these things meet with the approval of the unconscious universe. If power is bad, as it seems to be, let us reject it from our hearts. In this lies man's true freedom: indetermination to worship only the God created by our own love of the good, to respect only the heaven which inspires the insight of our best moments. In action, in desire, we must submit perpetually to the tyranny of outside forces; but in thought, in aspiration, we are free, free from our fellow man, free from the petty planet on which our bodies impatiently crawl, free even, while we live, from the tyranny of death. Let us learn, then, that energy of faith which enables us to live constantly in the vision of the good; and let us descend, in action, into the world of fact, with that vision always before us. (*WNC*, 109–10)

This is the heroic religion of Prometheus who defied Zeus (*WNC*, 110). It is austere as Stoicism in heeding duty and enduring pain. It has Christian wisdom, "exceeding that of the Promethean philosophy of rebellion," in gaining "the virtue of resignation" (*WNC*, 110). Although this religion begins in despair, it gains joy and tenderness that "gladden the pilgrim's heart" (*WNC*, 112). It is creative of the "beauty of tragedy" and of sympathy with "fellow sufferers" (*WNC*, 113–15).

The essay, in spite of the effort to find a religion without dogma, that is, without propositions about the world, nevertheless makes two great commitments that are never examined. One is that the "world of fact" is "not good," and that as "omnipotent matter" demonstrates the cruel indifference to human suffering of the devil deity (*WNC*, 108, 115). The problem may be stated: is it matter as such that is the principle of evil, as these evils have been typified as such vices as cowardice? The second problematical assertion is whether, because there is no harmony between the world of fact and the world of ideals, it is "man [who] created God, all-powerful and all-good, the mystic unity of what is and what should be" (*WNC*, 108).

The Platonic Liberal and
the Essence of Religion

Several critics have pointed out absurdities in Russell's *Free Man's Worship*. Several turn upon what Russell's critical thought had to say about matter and the whole dualism between matter and mind. But touching on whether Promethean indignation is wise, Russell in this case is his own best critic. "The Essence of Religion" (1912) came nine years later, during the period of the happy love affair with Lady Ottoline when he wrote *Problems of Philosophy* (*Ai*, 312–19). [14] Perhaps Lady Ottoline laughed at the heroic pose of defying the physical universe. *A Free Man's Worship* is heroic and humorless as a Wagner opera. Perhaps also she taught her lover Bertie to enjoy life rather than to condemn "the world." And among the things to be enjoyed is beautiful worship.

In "The Study of Mathematics" Russell had spoken like a monk, which he sometimes dreamed of becoming, to escape "the dreary exile of the actual world." [15] The other side of Platonic austerity is "the true spirit of delight, the exaltation, the sense of being more than a man, which is the touchstone of the highest excellence" (*PE*, 73). If poetry as well as mathematics is the way of expressing this joy, why not use the rich metaphysical treasures of religious symbolism? In the "Essence of Religion" we may have a reflection of Lady Ottoline's nonorthodox but nevertheless ardent Christian theism. "Christianity enjoins love of God and love of man as the two great commandments. [Luke 10:27] Love of God differs, however, from love of man, since we cannot benefit God, while we cannot regard man as wholly good. This love of God is more contemplative and full of worship, while love of man is more active and full of service" (*BW,* 574). Again, "there is a worship which can only be given to an actually existing object, and another worship which can be given to what merely has its place in the world of ideals; these two kinds may be distinguished as worship of the actual and worship of the ideal. The two are combined in worship of God, since God is conceived as both actual and complete embodiment of the ideals" (*BW,* 569).

Rather than an extra-human that is at best indifferent, why not a universe communicating something of supreme worth? A way of knowing by sympathy in the lover and poet can be developed by the mystic. What Russell reports is "a quality of infinity, like light breaking through from some greater world beyond. Sudden beauty in the midst of strife, uncalculating love, or the night wind in the trees, seem to suggest the possibility of a life free from the conflicts and pettiness of our everyday world, a life where there is peace which no misfortune can disturb. The things which have this quality of infinity seem to give an insight deeper than the piecemeal knowledge of our daily life. . . . [This is] a life in harmony with the whole" (*BW,* 567).

The conclusion of this "experience of sudden wisdom. . . , the source of what is essential in religion," is that humans make "contact with a deeper, truer, more unified world. . . . Behind a thin veil, it sees the glory of God, dimly as a rule, sometimes with dazzling brightness" (*BW,* 567). This is as close as he comes to an intuition in the cosmos of the ground of order or what theists call the Mind of the Maker.

In correcting optimism, *A Free Man's Worship* moved to pessimism. In correcting the pessimism, Russell achieved the moderate position of meliorism. [16] William James once defined his meliorist position as "evil is good—to overcome." The world can be made better, however bad we find it, and it is our duty to improve it. Certainly this is the religion sustaining the political philosophy. Although earlier we spoke of Russell's moral solutions to political problems, these are also religious solutions. People like Catholic saints (St. Francis, for example) and Quakers attempt "a gradual incarnation" of the divine into human life. Among Jews, it is Spinoza's key to wisdom, "the intellectual love of God."[17] Russell concludes *Principles of Social Reconstruction:* "By contact with what is eternal, by devoting our life to bringing something of the Divine into this troubled world, we can make our own lives creative even now, even in the midst of cruelty and strife and hatred that surround us on every hand."[18]

Voltairian Defiance of the Church

Different as are *A Free Man's Worship* and *The Essence of Religion,* each is a good religion. In the Promethean indignation with matter, it is the worship of the good; in the Platonic vision it is the active incarnation of the good. Is there any way in which the next step, *Why I Am Not a Christian* can be interpreted as an advance? Both of the two previous essays considered religion as a private matter, internal to the religious person. But religions are social, and no view that omits the institution is adequate. In the earlier essays Russell is the Protestant who continues the tradition of identifying religion as the relation of the individual soul to God—even when he has ceased to believe in God. Russell's religion is often the practice of the absence of God. In the latter essays, chief of which is *Why I Am Not a Christian,* he is still the Protestant, but now denouncing the institutions that cannot prove there is a God and cannot transform the vices of people into virtues. With little logic and less mysticism, Russell the prophet denounces the tyranny, superstition, deceit of the churches, their creeds and their codes. Their cults are ignored as irrelevant, even though previously he had stressed worship. The orientation of *A Free Man's Worship* and *The Essence of Religion* is to nature, whether hostile, indifferent, or harmonious. The orientation of *Why I Am Not a Christian* is largely to history: why has the Christian metaphysical vision done no better intellectually with its evidences of God, and failed morally to produce a world of love, justice, equality, and peace?

Why I Am Not a Christian represents an advance in that it recognizes religion as a social network of relations, not merely the individual's apprehension of the eternal, the infinite, the ideal, as Russell variously calls the divine. It fits Russell's entry into the political order to recognize that Christianity is a part of European and world history. The important thing to look for is the basis of the judgment that most or all of the institutional manifestations called "religion" in history are so bad that the religion of churches is the fifth great evil of mankind.

We can study stages in Russell's relation to mysticism, from "Mysticism and Logic" to "The Mystic Vision" of five years later, 1919. [19] The original statement was partly positive in that the "highest eminence . . . it is possible to achieve in the world of thought" is the "true union of the mystic and the man of science" (*SPBR*, 19). Yet can the mystic vision square with the piecemeal arduous search for fact (*SPBR*, 55)?

Mysticism comes off worse in the second essay, because it is judged the opposite of basic realism. [20] The mystic is faulted in two ways. First, the mystic's reliance on feeling allows him to impose his subjectivity upon the world. Second, the mystic is so overwhelmed by patriotic fervor that he may urge those who love their enemies to kill them. [21]

The first half of *Why I Am Not a Christian* is a negative appraisal of the proofs for the existence of God. The most careful study Russell made of the proofs was in *The Philosophy of Leibniz* (1900), and subsequent to the rejection of all proofs is a debate with Father Copleston S.J., author of the famous *History of Philosophy*, broadcast in 1948 by the British Broadcasting Corporation. [22] Happily this debate is available on audiotape and it is a delight because Father Copleston knows Russell's position as well as the traditional arguments which are cosmological. Russell rejects the five ways of Thomas Aquinas, because he considers them fallacious. Since the time of Hume and Kant, modern philosophers have known the criticisms, and Russell has nothing new to contribute.

The argument of *Why I Am Not a Christian* shifts from frustration with knowing whether God exists to moral disgust that those who profess Christ don't follow his "very excellent maxim" (*WNC*, 14). There is a delightful taunt: "I have no doubt that the present Prime Minister [Stanley Baldwin], . . . is a most sincere Christian, but I should not advise any of you to go and smite him on one cheek. [Luke 6:29] I think you might find that he thought this text was interpreted in a figurative sense" (*WNC*, 14). The point about Christianity as moral guide in history is that it has sanctioned all kinds of abominations. "In the so-called ages of faith, when men really did believe the Christian religion in its completeness, there was the Inquisition, with its tortures; there were millions of unfortunate women burned as witches; and there was every kind of cruelty practiced upon all sorts of people in the name of religion" (*WNC*, 20).

Why has the Christian religion proved to be so bad? Russell gives his analysis: religion is based on fear, all kinds of fear and terror, and men have turned to a conception of God as omnipotent power and slavishly worshiped the cosmic despot. Religion is then based on the vices of cowardice and slavish demeaning of human life and stupid dishonesty about the world (*WNC*, 22–23). No wonder then, as Russell adds in "Has Religion Made Useful Contributions to Civilization?" that he traces "cruelty, timidity, and stupidity" to the influence of religion (*WNC*, 29). The religion he condemns is not the good personal religion motivated by hope and love, but the bad religion, and he ends by stating the good as the norm by which we know the bad to be bad: "A good world needs knowledge, kindliness, and courage, it does not need a regretful hankering after the past or a fettering of the free intelligence by the words uttered long ago by ignorant men" (*WNC*, 21).

Russell would wish a future heaven on earth, that he thinks science and technology now make it possible for free people to create. We have a hell on earth, and he characterizes the evils "war, pestilence, and famine," as three of the four horsemen of the Apocalypse, (Revelation 9) death being the fourth. Russell is fighting the evil one, and this is religion itself: "Religion prevents our children from having a rational education; religion prevents us from removing the fundamental causes of war; religion prevents us from teaching the ethic of scientific co-operation in place of the old fierce doctrines of sin and punishment. It is possible that mankind is on the threshold of a golden age; but, if so, it will be necessary first to slay the dragon that guards the door, and this dragon is religion [Revelation 2:20]" (*WNC*, 47).

This is a familiar mode of writing. It goes back to the Apocalypse in which there is a great final battle between the forces of good and the forces of evil, the latter including dragons and devils, and especially the favorite "Babylon" (Revelation 11–12) which for Protestants used to mean "Rome" or Roman Catholics, and especially the pope. Russell's style of denouncing "religion" is, in this precise sense, religious. His friend D. H. Lawrence tells an intimate story of being educated in the denunciation of evil in *The Apocalypse.*

What Russell sometimes means by "religion" is the *good* religion of the virtues, summarized in "The Essence of Religion" as "worship, acquiescence, and love." The *bad* "religion" which he denounces is summarized as "the three human impulses . . . fear, conceit, and hatred." "Religion" is one of those curious general words used to collect imaginatively either the virtues or the vices. The procedure is open to the obvious logical objection, as one Christian critic observed, that it is based on the fallacy of selecting instances.[23] Russell did not deny the charge.[24] Should we go further and say, with T. S. Eliot, that Bertrand Russell still remained a "Christian"?[25] It is, after all, an old prophetic custom inculcated in generations of Puritans to denounce the worshipers of idols as the Bible says, "those who go a whoring after [false or strange] gods" (Exodus 34:15–16).

Prophetic religion is based upon not only turning people against the old religion because it is bad but also, in the name of the Lord, turning people toward the new religion because it is good.[26] Russell ends *Why I Am Not a Christian* with the fervor of a Messiah. The good world that is to come "needs a fearless outlook and a free intelligence. It needs hope for the future, not looking back all the time toward a past that is dead, which we trust will be far surpassed by the future that our intelligence can create" (*WNC,* 23).

The Final Tragedy of Bertrand Russell:
His Failure to Found a New Religion

Just before the inconclusive victory of World War I, Russell wrote: "The war has left throughout Europe a mood of disillusionment and despair which calls aloud for a new religion, as the only force capable of giving men the energy to live vigorously."[27] What if Russell, instead of launching various attacks upon established religion, had devoted his powers to saying what this "new religion" should be? Because of the esteem of creativeness over destruction, it might have been far better for Russell not to have written his antireligious essays, which would not be to say that existing religion is equal to the tasks of redeeming mankind from the evils of poverty, war, stupidity, and annihilation. The enormity of evil in the hearts and institutions of mankind exceeds the capacities of the rival religions in their vast intellectual lag behind the sciences and in their philosophical barbarism. The religions are as tribalistic as the states are nationalistic.

Russell knew what is needed: the promise of "glorious things: an end of the injustice of rich and poor, an end to economic slavery, an end of war;" the promise of

an end of the disunion of classes which poisons political life and threatens our industrial system with destruction, . . . an end to commercialism, that subtle falsehood that leads men to appraise everything by its money value, and to determine money value often merely by the caprices of idle plutocrats. It promises a world where all men and women shall be kept sane by work, and where all work shall be of value to the community. . . .

In place of palaces and hovels, futile vice and useless misery, there is to be wholesome work, enough but not too much, all of it useful, performed by men and women who have no time for pessimism and no occasion for despair. (*BPT*, 15)

Russell could have devoted his last decade to thinking out the principles of a world religion. As a moralist he recognized that government may be a means to human happiness, and that indeed world government with an international military force was a necessity for survival, but that real happiness depends on the heart of man. He never failed to take the same side as the so-called world religion. There is a complementarity between the Western theistic religions, Judaism, Islam, and Christianity, and the Eastern impersonal cosmic pieties, such as Confucianism, Taoism, much of Buddhism and some Hinduism. The best expression of the possibility of integrating the wisdom of the East with the wisdom of the West is in *Has Man a Future?* (1961).[28]

From millenia of struggle with natural forces, famine, and flood, we find in the Joseph story the idea of the ever-full granary (Genesis 41:47–57) and in the Noah story the threat of flood (Genesis 6–9). "Against inundations two methods were attempted: the Chinese, at the dawn of their history, built dykes along the Yellow River, while Western Asia, as appears in the story of Noah, thought the best protection was a virtuous life. . . . To this day, the two types of theory, Chinese and West-Asian, have persisted in uneasy antagonism, but with a gradually increasing prevalence of the Chinese point of view. Quite recent developments have shown that a virtuous life (not quite in the traditional sense) is as necessary to survival as dykes" (*HMF*, 9). This is the old Russell, the religious liberal, who sees the moral point rather than mocking, as did the freethinker, the literal expression.

It should not be strange that the most profound expression of the human situation comes in one of his last books, *Has Man a Future?* It is an expression of hope in a stable world with creative adventures to replace violent conflicts that threaten to end history. Russell is opposing "pride and rapacity" and expressing humility and indeed repentence and begging the god Osiris, Judge of the Underworld, for his forgiveness. The religion of theism, the proposition that the relation between man and the ultimate is between a finite and sinful person and an infinite righteous person, evidently in the end is a mode of symbolism that has its use—even if metaphysically absurd. Why should a "just and inexorable judge" forgive humankind? People are limited by circumstance and only recently have emerged from ignorance. And now the new knowledge has "intoxicated [us] with our new power over nature" and we pursue power over fellow human beings. Russell has rewritten what Protestant worship calls a "general confession" and ends by appealing to the prophetic wisdom against strife. The future is to be created by humans in the transcendent image of shining beauty.[29]

Lord Osiris, we beseech Thee to grant us a respite, and a chance to emerge from ancient folly into a world of light and love and loveliness. (*HMF*, 13–14)

The old prophetic preacher expects from his congregation a loud "Amen."

Notes and References

Preface

1. *Russell: The Journal of the Bertrand Russell Archives* 37–40 (1980–81):94.
2. *The Encyclopedia of Philosophy,* ed. Paul Edwards (New York: Macmillan, 1967), 7:235–58.
3. "On the Notion of Order," *Mind* 10 (1901):30–51; cited hereafter as ONO.
4. *Logic and Knowledge: Essays 1901–1950,* ed. Robert C. Marsh (London: George Allen & Unwin, 1956), 270.
5. Paul A. Schilpp, *The Philosophy of Bertrand Russell* (Evanston: Library of Living Philosophers, 1944), 716. The philosophers referred to who have stressed structure are Hiram McClendon and Grover Maxwell.

Chronology

1. Alys Russell's 1948 BBC broadcast "How to Enjoy Life at Eighty," *Listener,* 11 November 1948, 722–23; and Beatrice Webb, *Our Partnership* (London: Longmans, Green & Co., 1948).
2. H. G. Wells, *Experiment in Autobiography* (New York: Macmillan Co., 1934), 654.
3. "The Philosophy of Bergson," in *History of Western Philosophy* (New York, 1945).
4. G. H. Hardy, *Bertrand Russell and Trinity,* foreword by C. D. Broad (1942; reprint, London: Cambridge University Press, 1970).
5. *Current Biography, Who's News and Why,* ed. Maxine Block (New York: H. W. Wilson Co., 1940), 700–702 and *Current Biography,* 1951, 542–45; *The Bertrand Russell Case,* ed. John Dewey and Horace Kallen (New York: Viking, 1941).
6. Sidney Hook in *New York Times Book Review,* 2 January 1949, 8.
7. *Fact and Fiction,* pt. 4, "Peace and War" (London: G. Allen & Unwin, 1961).
8. *New Statesman,* 7 November 1957; *Look,* 21 January 1958; *The Vital Letters of Russell, Krushchev and Dulles* (London, 1958); *The Basic Writings of Bertrand Russell* (London: G. Allen & Unwin, 1961), 726–28.
9. Ernest Gellner, *Words and Things* (London: Gollancz, 1959).
10. *Obituaries from the Times, 1961–1970* (Reading: Newspaper Archive Developments Limited, 1975), pp. 691–94.

Chapter One

1. Ronald W. Clark, *The Life of Bertrand Russell* (London, 1975), 20. Other accounts of the Russells begin only in the fifteenth century: *Encyclopaedia Britannica*, 11th ed., s.v. "Russell Family."

2. *Encyclopaedia Britannica*, 14th ed., s.v. "Russell."

3. Ibid., 11th ed., s.v. "Russell, John Russell, 1st Earl."

4. "Lord John Russell," in *Portraits from Memory and Other Essays* (London, 1956), 109–13; cited hereafter as *PMem.*

5. Bertrand and Patricia Russell, *The Amberley Papers: The Letters and Diaries of Lord and Lady Amberley,* (London, 1937); cited hereafter as *AP.*

6. The best account of Russell's vices is Sidney Hook's essay in *Encounter* 62, no. 3 (March 1984):9–20. The conclusion, succinctly summarized, is that Russell was vain, lusty, greedy, dishonest, ungrateful, cruel, cynical, and malicious.

7. "Knowledge and Wisdom," in *PMem,* 160–64.

8. "Death of Kate, Rachel, and Amberley," in *AP,* 2:566–76.

9. "My Mental Development," in *The Philosophy of Bertrand Russell,* ed. Paul Arthur Schilpp (New York: Tudor, 1951), 3–20; cited hereafter as *PBR.*

10. *My Philosophical Development* (London, 1959); hereafter cited as *MPD.*

11. "Alfred North Whitehead," in *PMem,* 92–97. In Russell's writings there is no parallel to the encomium for his old mentor.

12. *The Autobiography of Bertrand Russell,* vol. 1, *1872–1914;* vol. 2, *1914–1944;* vol. 3, *1944–1969* (Boston, 1967–69); hereafter cited as *Ai, Aii,* and *Aiii.*

13. Alan Wood, *Bertrand Russell: The Passionate Sceptic* (London, 1957).

14. Ronald W. Clark, *The Life of Bertrand Russell* (London, 1975).

15. Beatrice Webb, *Our Partnership* (London: Longmans, Green & Co., 1948), generously quoted in H. W. Leggett, *Bertrand Russell, O.M.* (London: Lincoln-Prager, 1949), 20–26.

16. Katherine Tait, *My Father, Bertrand Russell* (New York, 1975); cited hereafter as *MFBR.* Dora Russell, *The Tamarisk Tree: My Quest for Liberty and Love* (New York: G. P. Putnam's Sons, 1975); cited hereafter as *TT.*

17. *Marriage and Morals* (London, 1929), chaps. 10–12, "Marriage" and "Prostitution"; and "Trial Marriage," 105–33.

18. Herbert Gottschalk, *Bertrand Russell: A Life,* trans. Edward Fitzgerald (New York: Barnes and Noble, 1967); cited hereafter as *BRL.*

19. *German Social Democracy* (London: George Allen & Unwin, 1965).

20. *The Practice and Theory of Bolshevism* (London, 1920).

21. "Why I Am Not a Communist," in *Basic Writings, 1903–1959,* ed. Robert E. Egner and Lester E. Denonn (London, 1961), 479–81.

22. *Authority and the Individual, With a Terminal Essay "Philosophy and Politics"* (Boston: Beacon Press, 1949); cited hereafter as *AI.*

23. *Dear Bertrand Russell: A Selection of His Correspondence with the General Public 1950–1968,* ed. by Barry Feinberg and Ronald Kasrils (Boston: Houghton Mifflin, 1969), 3–24; cited hereafter as *DBR.*

Chapter Two

1. *A History of Western Philosophy* (New York, 1945), 37; cited hereafter as *HWP.* Other accounts of Russell's relation to the Pythagorean tradition will be considered in chap. 2.

2. *Mysticism and Logic* (London: G. Allen & Unwin, 1950), 1. Among the most significant of Russell's autobiographical accounts are, in chronological order, "Logical Atomism" in *Contemporary British Philosophy,* ed. J. H. Muirhead (London, 1924), 359–83; Introduction to *Selected Papers of Bertrand Russell* (New York, 1927), ix–xix; "My Mental Development," in *PBR,* 3–20; *PMem;* "My Religious Reminiscences," in *The Rationalist Annual,* 1958, in *Basic Writings,* ed. Egner and Denonn, 31–36; *MPD;* and all three volumes of his autobiography, particularly when compared and contrasted.

3. John Dewey, *The Quest for Certainty* (New York: Minton Balch, 1929).

4. *The Problems of Philosophy* (New York, 1959), 7; cited hereafter as *PP.*

5. *PBR,* 19–20.

6. *MPD,* 20, 21.

7. *Bertrand Russell Speaks His Mind* (London, 1960), 11.

8. *Introduction to Mathematical Philosophy* (London, 1918), xi.

9. For example the criticism of Edgar S. Brightman, "Russell's Philosophy of Religion," in *PBR,* 537–56.

10. The solemn bibliographies commonly omit Philip E. B. Jourdain, *The Philosophy of Mr. Bertrand Russell* (London: G. Allen and Unwin, 1918), and Myra Buttle, *The Bitches' Brew: The Plot against Bertrand Russell* (London: C. A. Watts & Co., 1960).

11. T. S. Eliot, *Collected Poems* (New York: Harcourt, Brace, 1930, 1936), 35–36.

12. There is considerable literary interest in the "synthesis of Apollo and Apollyon," and in the identification of Mr. Apollinax with "Priapuss in the shrubbery / Gaping at the lady in the swing." The lascivious god has a "notably erect penis." See Floyd C. Watkins, "T. S. Eliot's Mysterious 'Mr. Apollinax,' " *Research Studies* 38 (September 1970):193.

13. *PMem,* 92.

14. On Russell's personal induction into Euclid, see virtually every autobiographical account. On Euclid as providing the model of "a rigorous deductive order," see *Wisdom of the West* (London: Rathbone; New York: Crescent, 1959), 98–99.

15. Russell's best account of the various forms of the ontological argument is in *Philosophy of Leibniz* (London: G. Allen & Unwin, 1937), 172ff.

16. Wood, *Passionate Sceptic.* It is very common for readers of Russell to suspect in him, underneath the guise of openmindedness and even skepticism, an assurance of certainty. The issue was formulated by one of Russell's former students at Harvard: Raphael Demos, "Mr. Russell and Dogmatism," *Journal of Philosophy* 42 (25 October 1945):589–94. This led to a response from Henry D. Aiken, idem. 43 (11 April 1946):214–17. Flora Lewis, "The Tragedy of Bertrand Russell," *Look* 31 (4 April 1967):30ff.

17. Originally in *Proceedings of the Aristotelian Society,* n.s. 12 (1912):1–24, reprinted in *LK,* 103–24.

18. Ronald Jager, *The Development of Bertrand Russell's Philosophy* (London, 1972), 77.

19. James K. Feibleman, "A Reply to Bertrand Russell's Introduction to the Second Edition of the *Principles of Mathematics,*" in *PBR,* 155–74, with Russell's response, 686–90.

20. "Logic as the Essence of Philosophy," in *OKEW,* 48–49.

21. *The Principles of Mathematics,* 2d ed. (London, 1937), 43. The rejection of the view is on p. x, again *MPD,* 159–60. The commentary of Elizabeth R. Eames, *Bertrand Russell's Theory of Knowledge* (London, 1969), chap. 5, "Realism," is most helpful.

22. "My Mental Development," in *The Basic Writings of Bertrand Russell,* ed. Egner and Denonn, 46; cited hereafter as *BW.*

23. Languages as different as Sanskrit, English, and Hebrew have a range of meanings of "truth" that makes pertinent Pontius Pilate's question, "What is truth?" See James Hastings, "Truth," *A Dictionary of the Bible* (Edinburgh: T. & T. Clark, 1902), 4:816–20.

24. *Wisdom of the West,* 408: in the original illustrated edition, ed. Paul Foulkes (London: Rathbone; New York: Crescent, 1959), 343.

25. "The Influence and Thought of G. E. Moore," a symposium of reminiscences by four of his friends, Part 1 by Russell (others by Leonard Woolf, Morton White, John Wisdom), *Listener,* 30 April 1959, 755. The others here and elsewhere refer as does Woolf to Moore's "Passion for Truth," 756–57.

26. "Meinong's Theory of Complexes and Assumptions," *Mind* 13 (1904):52. This is reprinted in *Essays in Analysis,* ed. Douglas Lackey (New York: George Braziller, 1973), 21–76.

27. *The Principles of Mathematics*, 2d ed. (London, 1937), 48; cited hereafter as *PMath*.

28. "Dewey's New Logic," in *PBR*, 146 (with Dewey's reply, 544–49).

29. A. J. Ayer, *Bertrand Russell* (New York: Viking Press, 1972), 59–68, carries us through about seven different stages of development.

30. *Aiii*, 60.

31. *The Analysis of Mind* (London, 1921), 278.

32. On appropriateness, see ibid., chap. 13, "Truth and Falsehood," especially pp. 255–59.

33. *Sceptical Essays* (London, 1928), 61.

34. *Philosophy* (New York, 1927), 254; cited hereafter as *P*.

35. *Education and the Good Life* (New York: Boni & Liveright, 1926), 158; cited hereafter as *EGL*.

Chapter Three

1. "On the Notion of Order," *Mind*, 10 (1901):51; cited hereafter as *ONO*.

2. *A Critical Exposition of the Philosophy of Leibniz*, 2d ed. (London, 1937), 169–70; cited hereafter as *PL*.

3. *Principia Mathematica* (Cambridge, 1910–13); cited hereafter as *PM*.

4. *BW*.

5. *MPD*, 65–101.

6. *Introduction to Mathematical Philosophy*, 2d ed. (London: 1920), cited hereafter as *IMP*.

7. *ONO*, 30–51.

8. A particularly good essay on the complex and long-sustained debate is Timothy Sprigge, "Russell and Bradley on Relations," in *Bertrand Russell Memorial Volume*, ed. George W. Roberts (London: George Allen & Unwin, 1979), 150–70.

9. *PMath*, pt. 4, "Order," especially chap. 24, "The Genesis of Order," chap. 25, "The Meaning of Order," chap. 26, "Asymmetrical Relations," 199ff. Paul G. Kuntz, "Order," *New Catholic Encyclopedia* (New York: McGraw-Hill, 1967), 10:720–23; and *The Concept of Order* (Seattle: University of Washington Press, 1968).

10. *An Essay on the Foundations of Geometry*, Foreword by Morris Kline (1897, reprint, New York, 1956); cited hereafter as *EFG*.

11. "On the Relations of Number and Quantity," *Mind* 6 (1897):335; cited hereafter as *RNQ*.

12. *Mysticism and Logic*, p. 86; cited hereafter as *ML*.

13. *OKEW*, 159.

14. "The Philosophical Importance of Mathematical Logic," *Monist* 23 (October 1913):481–91.

15. Josiah Royce, *Logical Essays* (Dubuque, Iowa: Wm. C. Brown Co., 1951). Whitehead's articles on mathematics are reprinted in *Essays in Science and Philosophy* (London: Rider & Co., 1948).

16. Charles S. Peirce, "The Order of Nature," in *Chance, Love and Logic,* ed. Morris R. Cohen and John Dewey (London: Kegan Paul, Trench, Trubner, 1923), 106–30.

17. On the centrality of structure in Russell's philosophy, the fullest account is Hiram J. McLendon, "Uses of Similarity of Structure in Contemporary Philosophy," *Mind* 64, no. 253 (January 1955):79–95.

18. A. N. Prior, "Russell, Bertrand Arthur William: Logic and Mathematics," *Encyclopedia of Philosophy* 7:245.

19. *Human Knowledge: Its Scope and Limits* (New York: Simon & Schuster, 1948), 281; cited hereafter as *HK.*

20. "Logical Atomism," *Contemporary British Philosophy,* 1st ser. (1924), 378; cited hereafter as *LA.* Also in *LK,* 321–43.

21. *Analysis of Matter,* (New York: Dover, 1954), 254; cited hereafter as *AMat.*

22. *BPR,* 672–74.

Chapter Four

1. *PMath,* xiv.

2. The best brief account is Morris Weitz, *Introduction to Twentieth-Century Philosophy: The Analytic Tradition* (New York: Free Press, 1966), 1–11. The same author has a detailed critical account, "Analysis and the Unity of Russell's Philosophy," in *PBR,* 57–121, and the general article "Analysis, Philosophical," in *Encyclopedia of Philosophy,* ed. Paul Edwards (New York: Macmillan, 1967), 1:97–105.

3. "Meinong's Theory of Complexes and Assumptions," in *Essays in Analysis;* cited hereafter as *EA.*

4. *Oxford English Dictionary* (Oxford: Clarendon Press, 1961), 1:305. Thomas Hobbes, in *Elements of Philosophy Concerning Body* "There is . . . no method by which we find out the causes of things but is either compositive or resolutive, or partly compositive, and partly resolutive. And the resolutive is commonly called analytical method, as the compositive is called synthetical." Knowledge "that anything is" begins our search for "the causes of anything." By "parts" Hobbes means not "parts of the thing itself, but parts of its nature," i.e., not "head," etc., but "figure, quantity, motions, sense, reason, and the like," accidents compounded together *(The English Works of Thomas Hobbes* [London: John Bohn, 1839], 1:66–67).

5. *PMath,* 141.

6. *HWP,* 744–45.

7. Ludwig Wittgenstein, *Tractatus Logico-Philosophicus* (London: Routledge & Kegan Paul, 1922), 7:189.

8. *LA,* 375.

9. *Inquiry into Meaning and Truth,* (London, 1940), 327, 336; cited hereafter as *IMT.*

10. See Weitz, "Analysis, Philosophical," in *Encyclopedia of Philosophy,* 97. By discovery of categories I mean of the most fundamental relations. See the next chapter on metaphysics.

11. Paul A Schilpp, ed., *The Philosophy of John Dewey* (New York: Tudor, 1951), 142.

12. A. J. Ayer, *Language, Truth, and Logic* (New York: Dover, 1946), 57ff.

13. Henry Veatch, "The Philosophy of Logical Atomism: A Realism Manqué," in *Essays on Bertrand Russell,* ed. E. D. Klemke (Urbana: University of Illinois Press, 1970), 102–17.

14. *The Scientific Outlook,* (New York: W. W. Norton, 1962), 69; cited hereafter as *SO.* Occasionally writers on Russell have recognized the hypothetico-deductive aspect of Russell's analytic method. See Grover Maxwell, "The Later Bertrand Russell: Philosophical Revolutionary," in *Bertrand Russell's Philosophy,* ed. George Nakhnikian (New York: Barnes & Noble, 1974), 69–70.

15. *OKEW,* 190.

16. *AMat,* 2.

17. *MPD,* 103.

18. *LK,* 341, italics added. Also found in *LA,* 379. The valuable comments of Ronald Jager, *The Development of Bertrand Russell's Philosophy* (London, 1972) is one of the rare commentaries that endeavors to do justice to the complexity of Russell's "analysis" (41f).

19. Russell begins a celebrated essay in the *American Journal of Mathematics* by retelling what is called the Epimenides: "Mathematical Logic as Based on the Theory of Types" (1908) (*LK,* 59).

20. See Ronald J. Butler, "The Scaffolding of Russell's Theory of Descriptions," *Philosophical Review* 63, no. 3 (1954):350–64.

21. See Yehosua Bar-Hillel, "Types, Theory of," *Encyclopedia of Philosophy,* 7:168–72.

22. "On Denoting," reprinted in *LK,* 41–56. Analytic philosophers often praise this as Russell's finest essay and extol it as the model of analysis.

23. A very entertaining and informative account of the break between Russell and Oxford philosophers in 1959 is found in Ved Mehta's "A Battle against the Bewitchment of Our Intelligence," originally in the *New Yorker,* now the first chapter in *Fly and the Fly-Bottle* (Boston: Little, Brown, 1962).

24. Introduction to Ludwig Wittgenstein, *Tractatus Logico-Philosophicus*, with a new translation by D. F. Pears and B. F. McGuiness (London: Routledge & Kegan Paul, 1961), ix–xxii. The original translation by Russell has the introduction under the same title, 7–23.

25. Paul G. Kuntz, "Order in Language, Phenomena, and Reality," *Monist* 49, no. 1 (January 1965):107–36.

26. *PMem*, 154–59.

27. Ernest Gellner, *Words and Things* (London: Victor Gollancz, 1959), 13–15.

28. Russell's point that "common sense" often protects antiquated science is made by Michael McClosky, "Intuitive Physics," *Scientific American* 248, no. 4 (April 1983):122–30.

29. H. D. Lewis, *Clarity Is Not Enough: Essays in Criticism of Linguistic Philosophy* (London: G. Allen & Unwin, 1963).

Chapter Five

1. *MPD*, 41.

2. *ML*, 1.

3. *HWP*, 730.

4. See note 14 to chapter 1.

5. *BW*, 241.

6. *LK*, 323.

7. *Ai*, 84, 184–85. The most eloquent expression of the "sublime" conception of the whole is in *Problems of Philosophy* (New York: Oxford University Press, 1959), pp. 141–43.

8. Russell's rejection of Kant was first expressed at length in his fellowship dissertation, *An Essay on the Foundations of Geometry* (Cambridge: Cambridge University Press, 1897; New York: Dover, 1956), and remained in *HWP*, in chapters on Kant and the post-Kantians.

9. *SO*, 95.

10. There are various editions of *The Philosophy of Logical Atomism:* Monist 29 (1919); University of Minnesota, n.d.; *LK*, 175–281.

11. Russell's knowledge of the Aristotelian tradition and of the non-Aristotelian scholastics and the anti-Aristotelian humanists was not deep. The detailed firsthand acquaintance was with Leibniz.

12. *A Critical Exposition of the Philosophy of Leibniz* (Cambridge: Cambridge University Press, 1900); 2d ed. (London: G. Allen & Unwin, 1937).

13. *Wisdom of the West* (Greenwich, Conn., 1959), 274; cited hereafter as *WW*. The original is far better illustrated, perhaps thanks to the editor, Paul Foulkes.

14. *OKEW*.

15. As well as the original edition of *Principia Mathematica* there is a paperback edition. Alfred North Whitehead and Bertrand Russell, *Principia Mathematica* to section 56 (Cambridge: University Press, 1964).

According to the new logic of Russell, to use "exists" of a proper name, as in "God exists," abuses the "is" of existence. "There is an x" is the proper logic, with x characterized by predicates. This latter is a description without existential import. Thus confusion is avoided by "a correct symbolism" which philosophy lacked before *Principia Mathematica*. The position is stated confidently: "The difficulties connected with it are difficulties resulting from bad symbolism, and are solved by a correct symbolism—solved so radically that everything said by philosophy on the subject is seen to be meaningless rubbish. The difficulties connected with identity and diversity said to be metaphysical categories of selfhood in idealistic thought are not solved" in traditional philosophy. When such philosophy is based upon mind and matter, "muddle-headed notions," concealed by questions of idealism versus materialism, it is necessary for the logician to protest that "nothing real can possibly be either mental or material."

Among other logical errors of metaphysicians is their handling of "the nature of infinity and continuity." This challenge rests on the claim that only professional mathematicians have a right to these concepts. A metaphysician can't therefore rightfully protest.

16. *IMT*.

17. *The Bertrand Russell Case*, ed. John Dewey and Horace M. Kallen (New York, 1941, 1972). An excellent brief summary is by Paul Edwards in his *Encyclopedia of Philosophy* 7:238.

18. The fullest account of Russell's relation to logical positivism is in *HWP*.

19. *HK; Human Society in Ethics and Politics* (London, 1954); cited hereafter as *HS*.

20. "Science and Metaphysics," review of E. W. Hobson, *The Domain of Natural Science*, Gifford Lectures 1921–22, *Nation and Athenaeum* 33, no. 23 (8 September 1923):716; cited hereafter as *S&M*.

21. "Is Science Superstitious?" review of E. A. Burtt, *The Metaphysical Foundation of Modern Physics* and A. N. Whitehead, *Science and the Modern World*, *Dial* 81 (September 1926):179–86; cited hereafter as *SS*. Also in *Sceptical Essays* (London, 1928), chap. 3.

22. "Relativity and Religion," review of A. N. Whitehead, *Science and the Modern World*, *Nation and Athenaeum* 39 (29 May 1926):206–7.

23. "Physics and Metaphysics," *Saturday Review of Literature* 4 (26 May 1928):910–11.

24. Charles Hartshorne, "Whitehead and Russell," in *Insights and Oversights* (Albany, N.Y.: SUNY Press, 1982).

25. *Dear Bertrand Russell*, 129.

26. Russell sometimes objects to the whole notion of category: "I do not myself believe that the term 'category" is in any way useful in philosophy, as representing any clear idea" (*HWP*, 200). On the other hand in chap. 23, "Substance," *AMat*, he speaks of a category as that which is "forced upon us by the general nature of either facts or value" (238). One reason for not taking Russell's whole attack very seriously is that he blames Fichte's insane "rationalistic totalitarianism" on the search for categories without making the connection very clear (*HWP*, 707–18). On the other hand, if one thinks systematically of "substance, quality, quantity, space, time," etc., one finds that Russell, in *Problems of Philosophy*, goes systematically through the questions: What is there? how much? of what sort? how related? where? when? etc. In other words, the progression of his thought is clear because he uses the traditional categories.

Chapter Six

1. Several commentaries on Russell's ethics are needed to map the full extent of the practical and theoretical problems. The fullest is Lillian W. Aiken, *Bertrand Russell's Philosophy of Morals* (New York, 1963); Frederick Copleston, S.J., *A History of Philosophy* (London: Burns and Oates, 1966), 8:471ff; Ronald Jager, *The Development of Bertrand Russell's Philosophy* (London, 1972), chap. 10, "Ethics and Religion," 462ff; W. I. Matson, "Russell's Ethics," in George W. Roberts, *Bertrand Russell Memorial Volume* (London: George Allen & Unwin, 1979), 422–27; Paul Edwards, "Russell, B. A. W.: Ethics and the Critique of Religion," (New York: Macmillan, 1967), 7:251–56.

2. One of the most interesting theological responses to Russell is that of Reinhold Niebuhr, "Can Schweitzer Save Us from Russell?" *Christian Century* 42 (7 May 1925):600–601. On the controversial aspects of Russell's career, there are several policies. One may say that questions of sex are beyond the competence of a philosopher (Copleston, 472). One may present Russell's critics as ignorant and stupid bigots (Edwards, ed., WNC). One may say that, although his counsel might be misunderstood, that it was basically only a rational argument (Hao Wang, *From Mathematics to Philosophy* [London: Routledge & Kegan Paul, 1974], 347). None of these is as honest and forthright as Russell himself.

3. *Sceptical Essays*, 121; cited hereafter as *SE*.

4. *In Praise of Idleness, and Other Essays* (London, 1935), 9; cited hereafter as *IPI*.

5. Ralph Barton Perry, *Puritanism and Democracy* (New York: Vanguard Press, 1944).

6. George Santayana, "The Philosophy of Mr. Bertrand Russell," in *Winds of Doctrine* (New York: Charles Scribner's, 1913), 138–54.

7. Letter to Lady Ottoline Morrell, 27 August 1918, quoted by Clark, *Life of Bertrand Russell.* This critical biographer selects this passage as the motto of his study.

8. *AI,* quoted in *BW,* 358.

9. "The Meaning of Good," review of George Edward Moore, *Principia Ethica* (Cambridge: At the University Press, 1908), *Independent Review* 11 (March 1904):331; cited hereafter as *MG.*

10. Originally in journal articles, reprinted in *Philosophical Essays.* The most readily available reprint is Wilfrid Sellars and John Hospers, eds., *Readings in Ethical Theory* (New York: Appleton-Century-Crofts, 1952), 1–32.

11. "The Ethics of War," *International Journal of Ethics* 15 (January 1915):127–42.

12. *Philosophy,* p. 230; cited hereafter as *Ph.*

13. Santayana, *Winds of Doctrine,* 143.

14. *P,* 257. See note 21 below.

15. *ML.*

16. "Philosophy's Ulterior Motives," in *Unpopular Essays,* (New York, 1950). 45; cited hereafter as *UE.*

17. "Styles in Ethics," in *Our Changing Morality,* ed. F. Kirchwey (New York: A. & C. Boni, 1924), 1–24; also reprinted in *BW,* pp. 345–50.

18. *Religion and Science,* (London, 1935) 231; cited hereafter as *RS.*

19. Reinhold Niebuhr, "Reason vs. Belief," review of *Bertrand Russell, Why I Am Not a Christian,* ed. Paul Edwards, *New York Times,* Book Review, 22 September 1957, 6, 30.

20. *What I Believe,* 'Today and Tomorrow Series' (New York: Dutton; London: Kegan Paul, 1925); also reprinted in *BW,* 367–90.

21. Russell's Reply, 722ff, to Justus Buchler, "Russell and the Principles of Ethics," in *PBR,* 514–17.

22. *Observer,* 6 October 1957, a response to Philip Toynbee's review of *Why I Am Not a Christian.*

23. *Aiii,* 60. From the *News Chronicle,* 1 April 1954.

24. *Bertrand Russell Speaks His Mind,* (London, 1960), 62; cited hereafter as *BRSHM.*

25. *Listener,* 31 October 1957, 709.

26. *PMem,* 92.

27. *Principles of Social Reconstruction,* (London, 1916), 142–44; cited hereafter as *PSR.*

28. "The Expanding Mental Universe," *Saturday Evening Post,* 18 July 1959, reprinted in *Adventures of the Mind,* ed. Richard Thruelson and John Kober (New York: A. A. Knopf, 1959); also in *BW,* 391–98.

Chapter Seven

1. Of the essays that deal with Russell's political and social philosophy in *PBR*, only Sidney Hook's on "Philosophy of History," pp. 645–78, is now worth studying. Of greatest value is Jager, *Development of Bertrand Russell's Philosophy*, chap. 9, 425–60. In the *Bertrand Russell Memorial Volume* are two excellent essays: Antony Flew, "Russell's Judgment of Bolshevism," 428–53, and Benjamin R. Barber, "Solipsistic Politics: Russell's Empiricist Liberalism," 455–78.

2. Although some critics of Russell have said his philosophy was all motivated by sex, he has estimated that of the total amount of his writing, about 1 percent deals with this fascinating aspect of life. Russell's autobiography is extraordinarily candid about the number of affairs, but always discreet about the details.

3. For details of his educational practices, there is Joe Park, *Bertrand Russell on Education* (Columbus, Ohio, 1963). There is a companion volume, *Alfred North Whitehead on Education*, also in the Studies in Educational Theory of the John Dewey Society.

4. *Selected Papers of Bertrand Russell* (New York: Modern Library, 1927). Some books about Russell pay little attention to his practical philosophy and can justify this practice by many statements that this is not properly philosophy, in the strict sense of the term.

5. *BW*.

6. *PMem*, 112–13.

7. *Political Ideals*, (London: G. Allen and Unwin, 1963), 45, 48–49, 52; cited hereafter as *PI*.

8. In cleaning up the ambiguities about the meaning of "socialism," the best source is Flew, cited above in note 1.

9. *German Social Democracy*, (London: 1965), 13; cited hereafter as *GSD*.

10. *PSR* was published in America as *Why Men Fight*.

11. *Bolshevism: Practice and Theory* (London, 1916), 3; cited hereafter as *BPT*. We have cited the original 1920 edition rather than the 1949 second edition, which is *The Practice and Theory of Bolshevism*.

12. "A Life of Disagreement," *Atlantic Monthly* 190 (August 1952):54. The same points are made many times, eminently in "Why I Am Not a Communist" (*BW*, 479–81).

13. "Is a Permanent Peace Possible?" *Atlantic Monthly* 115 (March 1915):127–42, reprinted in *Justice in Peacetime* (1916).

14. F. H., "Beneath the Battle," review of *Why Men Fight*, in *New Republic* 10, no. 118 (3 February 1917):24.

15. *Justice in War-Time* (London: G. Allen and Unwin; Chicago: Open Court, 1916); cited hereafter as *JWT*.

16. "Rex v. Bertrand Russell," reprinted in *The Cambridge Mind: Ninety Years of the Cambridge Review, 1879–1969,* ed. Eric Homberger (London: Jonathan Cape, 1970), 35–40; cited hereafter as *RBR.*

17. G. H. Hardy, *Bertrand Russell and Trinity: A College Controversy of the Last War* (Cambridge: At the University Press, 1942). There is a second edition with foreword by C. D. Broad (1970); cited hereafter as *BRT.*

18. *Aii.* Herbert Gottschalk, *Bertrand Russell: A Life,* trans. Edward Fitzgerald (New York, 1967), 41–48. Although crude on the philosophy, this concentrates on the degree to which Russell was successful in his predictions of future history. There is a book, Jo Vellacott, *Bertrand Russell and the Pacifists of the First World War* (New York: St. Martin's Press, 1981).

19. "The Ethics of War," *Ethics* 25 (January 1915):142.

20. Tait, *My Father,* 119–20.

21. "Oh, envy, yes. It's a terrible source of unhappiness to a great many people" (*BRSHM,* 92).

22. Ralph Schoemman, ed., *Bertrand Russell: Philosopher of the Century: Essays in His Honour* (London: George Allen & Unwin, 1967).

23. The transcript of the films by Van Con Productions, distributed by Telemat Sales, Ltd.

Chapter Eight

1. *Why I Am Not a Christian,* ed. Paul Edwards (New York, 1957), contains a preface by Russell, in which he significantly writes: "There has been a rumor in recent years to the effect that I have become less opposed to religious orthodoxy than I formerly was. This rumor is totally without foundation. I think all the great religions of the world—Buddhism, Hinduism, Christianity, Islam, and Communism—both untrue and harmful" (p. v.). The matter of religion that is not "rigid systems" or "fanaticisms," responsive to evidence and dedicated to cooperation, which Russell professes, is ignored by both Russell and his editor (cited hereafter as *WNC*).

2. Edwards has the best readily available account in an appendix to *WNC,* 207–59.

3. *PBR,* 726.

4. *The Problem of China,* (London, 1922), 196; cited hereafter as *PC.* Two chapters in *BW* are "Chinese and Western Civilization Contrasted" (from *PC*) and "Eastern and Western Ideals of Happiness." The passage occurs in *BW,* 548, in the context of the study of Western vices and Eastern virtues. It is most significant that Russell reluctantly admits vices in the Chinese and never attacks Confucianism or Taoism or any Chinese philosophy or religion as he does all others, even Buddhism.

5. "The Study of Mathematics," *New Quarterly*, November 1907, reprinted in *Philosophical Essays*, rev. ed. (London, 1966), chap. 3, and *ML*, chap 4.

6. "Experiences of a Pacifist in the First World War," in *PMem*, 31.

7. Russell is quoted on both sides of the controversy about whether a philosopher should be a contemplative or an activist. See John G. Slater, "The Philosopher's Duty in These Times," *Russell* 5, no. 35–36 (1979–80):55–57; S. Nixon, "The Duty of a Modern Philosopher," *Russell* 5, no. 37–40 (1980–81):43–46.

8. Herbert Spiegelberg, "The Correspondence between Bertrand Russell and Albert Schweitzer," *International Studies in Philosophy* 12 (1980):1–45.

9. *Ai*.

10. Niebuhr, "Can Schweitzer Save Us from Russell?" 1093–1095; cited hereafter as *CSSUR*.

11. Gustav Herling, *A World Apart* (New York: New American Library, 1952).

12. "Seems, Madam? Nay, It Is," a previously unpublished essay from 1899, in *WNC*, 94–103.

13. *Ai*, 225. The intense unhappiness is specified: "About twice a year I would attempt sex relations with [Alys], in the hope of alleviating her misery, but she no longer attracted me, and the attempt was futile" (228).

14. Russell pays Lady Ottoline the highest compliments for her influences on him (*Ai*, 317). One of the cleverest tributes is:

> Said Lord Russell to Lady Cecilia,
> I certainly wish I could feel ya,
> Your data excite me,
> It would surely delight me
> To sense your unsensed sensibilia.

Clark, *Life of Bertrand Russell*, 215.

15. *Mysticism and Logic*, 61.

16. An excellent neglected critique is R. F. Alfred Hoernlé, "The Religious Aspect of Bertrand Russell's Philosophy," *Harvard Theological Review* 9, no. 2 (1916):157–89. I do not know how Russell responded to this constructive criticism.

17. Very helpful studies may shortly be published: Kenneth Milton Blackwell, "Bertrand Russell's Spinozistic Ethic of Impersonal Self-Enlargement" (Ph.D. diss., University of Guelph, 1981), and Stephen Nathanson, "Russell's Scientific Mysticism." The best comprehensive published

study is Jager, *Development of Bertrand Russell's Philosophy*, 484–507. Russell was a very serious student of religious philosophies, and many essays deserve reprinting. For example, Russell's "The Mystic Vision," review of A. Clutton-Brock, *What Is the Kingdom of God? Athenaeum*, no. 4651 (20 June 1919):487–89; cited hereafter as *MV*.

18. *PSR*, 169. The references favorable to Franciscan and Quaker Christianity occur on pp. 138–40.

19. "Mysticism and Logic," unfortunately omitted from both *BW* and *WNC*, was published by Russell himself just after "A Free Man's Worship" in *Selected Papers*, 19; cited hereafter as *SPBR*.

20. "Religion and Metaphysics," a review of McTaggart, *Some Dogmas of Religion, Independent Review* 9 (1906):109–16. There is a significant development of the evil of omnipotence (113). Russell develops his criticism of the arguments of mysticism, but holds to the value of mysticism in personal religion in "Mysticism," chap. 7, *RS*, 171–89. This clearly shows the erroneous interpretation of Russell as a secularist. When Russell expresses hatred of bad religion, it is in defense of good religion, not the alternative of no religion at all.

21. Hardy, *Bertrand Russell and Trinity*, 9.

22. *Critical Exposition of the Philosophy of Leibniz*, 172–90. "The Existence of God—A Debate," in Paul Edwards and Arthur Pap, *A Modern Introduction to Philosophy*, rev. ed. (New York: Free Press, 1965), pp. 473–90; cited hereafter as *EGD*. Audiotape Cassette PMC 056, "A Debate on the Existence of God," shortened version of above, produced by the Open University, 28 minutes.

23. Herbert G. Wood, *Why Mr. Bertrand Russell Is Not a Christian: An Essay in Controversy* (London: S.C.M. Press, 1928); Cecil Henry Douglas Clark, *Christianity and Bertrand Russell: A Critique of the Essay, "Why I Am Not a Christian"* (London: Lutterworth Press, 1958); George Samuel Montgomery, *Why Bertrand Russell Is Not a Christian; An American Opinion* (New York: Dakotan, 1959).

24. Edgar S. Brightman, "Russell's Philosophy of Religion," in *PBR*, 537–56.

25. T. S. Eliot, "Why Mr. Bertrand Russell Is a Christian," *Criterion* 6, no. 2 (August 1927):177–79. Perhaps the best thing in this critique is the note that Russell fails to distinguish the "fear" of God and the "fear" of bankruptcy, and the like. He "would agree that it is . . . better to fear God than to fear insolvency or the disapproval of one's neighbours; I do not know whether he could be induced to agree that the proper fear of God may make us more indifferent to these unworthy terrors." A theologian "would observe that there is a good and a bad fear of God." Eliot is equally instructive on Russell's atheism as "Low Church," or what

we have called Puritan Protestant, and a variety of Christianity. Eliot then has an explanation for Russell's religion: the religion of a Whig (179).

26. See also F. E. Sparshott, review of *Portraits from Memory* and *Why I Am Not a Christian, Tamarack Review* 6 (1958):90–94.

27. *BPT,* 15.

28. *Has Man a Future?* (Baltimore, 1961), 9; cited hereafter as *HMF.*

29. The irony of Russell the seeker for God who denounced Christianity is more poignant in that his children, along with others in his school, were taught to mock the nonexistent gods of ancient Egypt (see Tait, *My Father,* 87–88). Among the letters on religion, Russell notes that two of his three children became "earnest Anglicans" (Feinberg and Kasrils, *Dear Bertrand Russell,* 20). In the light of the dialectic that turns children by antireligion into religion, he writes "I am not at all sure that one should take any positive steps to keep [children] inorthodox" (21).

Selected Bibliography

Lester E. Denonn provides the most convenient bibliography: "Bibliography of the Writings of Bertrand Russell to 1941," in *The Philosophy of Bertrand Russell*, ed. Paul A. Schilpp, 3d ed. (New York: Tudor Publishing Co., 1951), 743–802. More complete is Werner Martin, *Bertrand Russell: A Bibliography of His Writings* (München: K. G. Saur; Hamden, Conn.: Linnett Books, 1981). Kenneth Blackwell of the Russell Archives, McMaster University, Hamilton, Ontario, is preparing what will be the most complete bibliography.

The difficulty in compiling a complete bibliography is that Russell wrote for the general public, and his essays are scattered through hundreds of journals. Because his writings were directed at people with different interests and needs, a bibliography that helps the reader select among his books and articles is most useful. Because classification is also difficult, I have arranged the following listing chronologically.

PRIMARY SOURCES

1. Original Works

German Social Democracy. London: Longmans, Green & Co., 1896.

An Essay on the Foundations of Geometry. Cambridge: Cambridge University Press, 1897. Reprint. New York, Dover, 1956.

A Critical Exposition of the Philosophy of Leibniz. Cambridge: Cambridge University Press, 1900. 2d ed. with a new preface. London: George Allen & Unwin; New York: Humanities Press, 1937.

The Principles of Mathematics. Cambridge: Cambridge University Press, 1903. 2d ed. with a new introduction. London: George Allen & Unwin; New York: W. W. Norton, 1938, 1950.

With Alfred North Whitehead, *Principia Mathematica*. Cambridge: Cambridge University Press, 1910–13. 2d ed. with a new preface, 1935. *Principia Mathematica* to *56, Cambridge: Cambridge University Press, 1964.

Philosophical Essays. London: George Allen & Unwin, 1910.

The Problems of Philosophy. London: Williams & Norgate; New York: Henry Holt & Co., 1912. The Home University Library is now published by the Oxford University Press. New York: Oxford University Press, 1959.

Our Knowledge of the External World as a Field for Scientific Method in Philosophy. Chicago: Open Court, 1912. Revised ed. London: George Allen & Unwin, 1929; New York: W. W. Norton Co.; New York: Humanities 2, 1949; Mentor, New York: New American Library, 1960).

Principles of Social Reconstruction. London: George Allen & Unwin, 1916. 2d ed., 1920. As *Why Men Fight: A Method for Abolishing the International Duel.* New York: Century Co., 1916. 2d ed. London: A. & C. Boni, 1930.

Justice in War-Time. London: George Allen & Unwin; Chicago: Open Court, 1916. 2d ed. 1924.

Political Ideals. New York: Century Co., 1917. Reprint. London: George Allen & Unwin, 1936.

Mysticism and Logic and Other Essays. London: Longmans Green & Co., 1917.

Roads to Freedom: Socialism, Anarchism and Syndicalism. London: George Allen & Unwin, 1918. As *Proposed Roads to Freedom; Socialism, Anarchism and Syndicalism.* New York: Henry Holt and Co., 1919.

Philosophy of Logical Atomism. In *Monist,* 1918–19, Vol. 28, 495–552, LVol. 29, 33–63, 190–222, 344–80. Reprinted at the University of Minnesota, n.d. In Robert C. Marsh, ed., *Logic and Knowledge: Essays 1901–1950.* 175–281. London: George Allen & Unwin, 1956.

Introduction to Mathematical Philosophy. London: George Allen & Unwin, 1919.

Bolshevism: Practice and Theory. New York: Harcourt, Brace & Co., 1920. 2d ed. London: George Allen & Unwin, 1949. As *The Practice and Theory of Bolshevism.* London: George Allen & Unwin, 1920.

The Analysis of Mind. London: George Allen & Unwin, 1921.

The Problem of China. London: George Allen & Unwin; New York: Century Co., 1922.

Introduction to Ludwig Wittgenstein, *Tractatus Logico-Philosophicus.* London: Routledge & Kegan Paul, 1922, 7–23.

With Dora Russell. *The Prospects of Industrial Civilisation.* London: George Allen & Unwin, 1923. 2d ed., 1959.

The ABC of Atoms. London: Kegan Paul, 1923.

Icarus or the Future of Science. London: Kegan Paul, 1924.

"Logical Atomism." In *Contemporary British Philosophy: Personal Statements,* 1st ser. Edited by J. H. Muirhead. London: George Allen & Unwin, 1924, 356–83.

The ABC of Relativity. London: Kegan Paul, 1925. Rev. ed. Edited by Felix Pirani. London: George Allen & Unwin, 1958.

What I Believe. New York: E. P. Dutton; London: Kegan Paul, 1925. Reprint. In *Basic Works.* Edited by Robert P. Egner and Lester E. Denonn. London: George Allen & Unwin, 1961, 367–90.

Why I Am Not a Christian. London: Watts & Co., 1927. Reprint. In *Little Blue Books.* Girard, Kansas: Haldeman-Julius Publications, 1927. In *Why I Am Not a Christian.* Edited by Paul Edwards. New York: Simon & Schuster, 1957. In *Basic Writings.* New York: Simon & Schuster, 1957. Reprint. 1961. Paperback ed., 1962.

The Analysis of Matter. London: Kegan Paul, 1927. Reprint. London: George Allen & Unwin, 1955.

An Outline of Philosophy. London: George Allen & Unwin, 1927. As *Philosophy.* New York: W. W. Norton, 1927.

Sceptical Essays. London: George Allen & Unwin, 1928. New ed. 1960.

Marriage and Morals. London: George Allen & Unwin, 1929.

The Conquest of Happiness. London: George Allen & Unwin, 1930.

The Scientific Outlook. New York: W. W. Norton, 1931. Reprint. London: George Allen & Unwin, 1949.

Education and the Social Order. London: George Allen & Unwin, 1932. As *Education and the Modern World.* New York: W. W. Norton, 1932.

Freedom and Organization. London: George Allen & Unwin, 1934. As *Freedom versus Organization 1814–1914.* New York: W. W. Norton Co., 1934.

In Praise of Idleness. London: George Allen & Unwin, 1935. Reprint. New York: Barnes & Noble, 1961.

Religion and Science. Home University Library. London: T. Butterworth-Nelson; New York: Henry Holt, 1935.

Which Way to Peace? London: Michael Joseph, 1936.

With Patricia Russell. *The Amberley Papers; The Letters and Diaries of Lord & Lady Amberley.* New York: W. W. Norton; London: Hogarth Press, 1937, 1940.

Power: A New Social Analysis. New York: W. W. Norton, 1938.

An Inquiry into Meaning and Truth. London: George Allen & Unwin, 1940.

"Reply to Criticism." In *The Philosophy of Bertrand Russell.* Edited by Paul A. Schilpp. Evanston and Chicago: Northwestern University Press, 1944.

A History of Western Philosophy. New York: Simon & Schuster, 1945. As *History of Western Philosophy.* London: George Allen & Unwin, 1946.

Human Knowledge: Its Scope and Limits. London: George Allen & Unwin, 1948.

Authority and the Individual. London: George Allen & Unwin, 1949.

Unpopular Essays. London: George Allen & Unwin, 1950.

Impact of Science on Society. New York: Columbia University Press, 1951. Reprint. London: George Allen & Unwin, 1952.

New Hopes for a Changing World. London: George Allen & Unwin, 1951.

Satan in the Suburbs and Other Stories. London: George Allen & Unwin; New York: Simon & Schuster, 1953.

Nightmares of Eminent Persons and Other Stories. London: Bodley Head; New York: Simon & Schuster, 1954.

Human Society in Ethics and Politics. London: George Allen & Unwin, 1954.

John Stuart Mill. London: Oxford University Press, 1955.

Portraits from Memory and Other Essays. London: George Allen & Unwin, 1956.

Understanding History and Other Essays. New York: Philosophical Library, 1957.

Common Sense and Nuclear Warfare. London: George Allen & Unwin, 1959.

My Philosophical Development. London: George Allen & Unwin, 1959.

Wisdom of the West. Edited by Paul Foulkes. New York: Doubleday, 1959.

Bertrand Russell Speaks His Mind. London: Arthur Barker, 1960.

Fact and Fiction. London: George Allen & Unwin, 1961.

Has Man a Future? New York: Simon & Schuster, 1962.

Unarmed Victory. New York: Simon & Schuster, 1963.

With Christopher Farley, Ralph Schoenman, and Russell Stetler. *War Crimes in Vietnam.* London: George Allen & Unwin, 1967.

The Autobiography of Bertrand Russell. 3 vols. Boston: Little, Brown, 1967–69.

2. Anthologies and Collections

Selected Papers of Bertrand Russell. New York: Modern Library, 1927.

Bertrand Russell's Dictionary of Mind, Matter and Morals. Edited by Lester E. Denonn. New York: Philosophical Library, 1952.

Logic and Knowledge: Essays 1901–1950. Edited by Robert C. Marsh. London: George Allen & Unwin, 1956.

Why I Am Not a Christian and Other Essays. Edited by Paul Edwards. London: George Allen & Unwin, 1957.

The Vital Letters of Russell, Kruschev and Dulles. London: MacGibbon & Kee, 1958.

Good Citizen's Alphabet. Illus. by F. Themerson. London: Glaberbocchus, 1953.

Bertrand Russell's Best: Silhouettes in Satire. Edited by R. E. Egner. London: George Allen & Unwin, 1958.

Basic Writings, 1903–1959. Edited by Robert E. Egner and Lester E. Denonn. New York: Simon & Schuster, 1961.

Dear Bertrand Russell: A Selection of His Correspondence with the General Public, 1950–1968. Edited by Barry Feinberg and Ronald Kasrils. London: George Allen & Unwin, 1969.

Bertrand Russell's America 1896–1945. Edited by Barry Feinberg and Ronald Kasrils. London: George Allen & Unwin, 1973.

Essays in Analysis. Edited by Douglas Lackey. New York: George Braziller, 1973.

SECONDARY SOURCES

1. General Works

Ayer, A. J. *Russell.* London: Fontana-Collins, 1972.

Clark, Ronald William. *The Life of Bertrand Russell.* London: Jonathan Cape and Weidenfeld & Nicolson, 1975.

Jager, Ronald. *The Development of Bertrand Russell's Philosophy.* London: George Allen & Unwin, 1972.

Saintsbury, Richard Mark. *Russell.* London: Routledge & Kegan Paul, 1979.

Watling, John. *Bertrand Russell.* London: Oliver & Boyd, 1970.

Wood, Alan. *Bertrand Russell: The Passionate Sceptic.* London: George Allen & Unwin, 1957.

2. Collections of Essays

Klemke, E. D. *Essays on Bertrand Russell.* Urbana: University of Illinois Press, 1970.

Nakhnikian, George, ed. *Bertrand Russell's Philosophy.* New York: Barnes & Noble, 1974.

Pears, D. F. ed. *Bertrand Russell: A Collection of Critical Essays.* Garden City, N.Y.: Doubleday, 1972. This contains a valuable bibliography by Harry Ruja, pp. 357–87.

Roberts, George W., ed. *Bertrand Russell Memorial Volume.* London: George Allen & Unwin, 1979.

Schilpp, Paul Arthur, ed. *The Philosophy of Bertrand Russell.* Evanston: Library of Living Philosophers, 1944.

Schoenman, Ralph, A. J. Ayer, et al., eds. *Bertrand Russell: Philosopher of the Century.* London: George Allen & Unwin, 1967.

3. Special Problems

Russell, Dora Winifred Black. *The Tamarisk Tree: My Quest for Liberty and Love.* London: Eleck/Pemberton, 1975. The best on Russell's misunderstandings with his wives, in this case, his second.

Gottschalk, Herbert. *Bertrand Russell.* London: Baker, 1965. A German appreciation of Russell's political foresight.

Hardy, Godfrey Harold. *Bertrand Russell and the Trinity.* 1942. Reprint. London: Cambridge University Press, 1970. An invaluable study by a great mathematician showing how war fever misleads professors into persecuting a fellow academic.

Kallen, Horace M., and John Dewey. *The Bertrand Russell Case*. 1941. Reprint. New York: Da Capo Press, 1972. Evidence showing how an academic's civil rights are violated by religious bigotry.

Lewis, John. *Bertrand Russell: Philosopher and Humanist*. New York: International Publishers, 1968. Naive Marxist ideology.

Park, Joe. *Bertrand Russell on Education*. Columbus: Ohio State University Press, 1963. Elementary and simpleminded.

Perry, Leslie R. *Bertrand Russell, A. S. Neill, Homer Lane, W. H. Kilpatrick: Four Progressive Educators*. London: Collier-Macmillan, 1967. Russell as one of several educational reformers.

Tait, Katharine. *My Father, Bertrand Russell*. New York: Harcourt Brace Jovanovich, 1975. A profound study of Russell's religious difficulties by his daughter.

Vellacott, Jo. *Bertrand Russell and the Pacifists in the First World War*. New York: Martin's Press, 1981. A careful examination of conscientious objection to World War I.

4. Advanced Works

Aiken, Lillian W. *Bertrand Russell's Philosophy of Morals*. New York: Humanities Press, 1963.

Ayer, A. J. *Russell and Moore: The Analytical Heritage*. Cambridge: Harvard University Press, 1971.

Clack, Robert J. *Bertrand Russell's Philosophy of Language*. The Hague: Martinus Nijhoff, 1969.

Eames, Elizabeth Ramsden. *Bertrand Russell's Theory of Knowledge*. London: George Allen & Unwin, 1969.

Fritz, Charles Andrew. *Bertrand Russell's Construction of the External World*. London: Routledge & Kegan Paul, 1952.

Götlind, Erik. *Bertrand Russell's Theories of Causation*. Uppsala: Almquist & Wiksell, 1953.

Grattan-Guiness, I. *Dear Russell-Dear Jourdain: A Commentary on Russell's Logic Based on His Correspondence with Philip Jourdain*. New York: Columbia University Press, 1977.

Jackson, Mary Louise. *Style and Rhetoric in Bertrand Russell's Work*. Frankfurt and Bern: Peter Lang, 1983.

Linsky, Leonard. *Referring*. London: Routledge & Kegan Paul, 1967.

Pears, David. *Bertrand Russell and the British Tradition in Philosophy*. London: Collins, 1972.

Santayana, George. "The Philosophy of Bertrand Russell." In *Winds of Doctrine*. New York: Scribner's, 1912.

5. Periodicals

In the journals of the English-speaking world, Russell has been the most frequently and sometimes heatedly discussed philosopher of the twentieth century. The leading periodical for our purposes is now *Russell: The Journal of the Bertrand Russell Archives*. It began spring 1971 and is published at McMaster University, Hamilton, Ontario. It is edited by Kenneth Blackwell.

Index

Abelard, Peter, *Sic et Non,* 62
Absolute, the, 139
abstract/concrete, 79, 94
absolutism/relativity of good and right, 103
abstractions of science, 92
action/contemplation, 138, 147, 168n7
agent/spectator, views of perception, 70
agnosticism and atheism, 9
Alexander the Great, 8
altruism, 108
Amberley, Viscount, and Lady Katherine, 1;
  Analysis of Religious Belief, The, 2
ambiguity of language, 68
analogy, required in metaphysics, 93
analysis, Chapter 4, passim; defined, 56;
  conceptual/real, 57; kinds of (grammatical,
  logical, metaphysical, causal), 56, 160n2,
  n4, 161n14, n18, *see* bad grammar; relational, 60
analysis/synthesis, 56, 62
anarchism, opposite, evil to tyranny, 8
Anglicans and Anglicanism, 4, 9
Anglo-American philosophy, 55, 56, 90
anticommunism, 132
anti-Puritan motivation, 96–97
anti-Semites, 137
anxiety: Angst, 90; fear of non-being, 129–
  30
Apocalypse, 150–151
a priori moral truths, 103, 104, 106; *see also*
  truth self-evident of logic and ethics
Aquinas, St. Thomas, 26, 33, 117, 129,
  149
aretai, excellences, 129; *see* virtues
Aristotle, 17, 30–32, 37, 81–85, 117, 119,
  145, 162
asymmetry/symmetry, 33–34, 47
atomism, 58, 60; *see also* whole/part
Augustine, St. Aurelian, of Hippo, 23, 117,
  124, 129, 139
austerity, 123
awe before natural grandeur, 78; *see also*
  cosmic piety
Ayer, A. J., 27, 55, 61, 68, 71, 86, 159;
  Language, Truth and Logic, 68, 86

Bacon, Francis, 30
bad grammar of Aristotelian logic, 81
bad religion, 148–49, 150–51
balance, 8, 45; *see* symmetry
balance between excess and deficiency, 120
Baldwin, Stanley, 149
Beauty, 138, 144–45, 146, 147, 153; of
  tragedy, 146
Beauty, Truth, Goodness, 142; *see also*
  Truth, Good
behaviorism in ethics, 105–6
being, "to be": *see* "is"
belief, and theory of belief, 14f; multiple relation theory, 16–17
Bergson, Henri, 105, 155; *Laughter,* 105
Berkeley, George, 18
benevolence, 108
Bible, King James Version: Ecclesiastes,
  131; Exodus, 124, 151; Genesis, 152; Isaiah, 99; Job, 144; John, 24; Luke, 108,
  130, 138, 147, 149; Paul, 63, 129; Revelation, or Apocalypse, 150–51; *see also*
  Jesus, Ten Commandments, Hebraic
  prophet, love of neighbor, God
Bosanquet, Bernard, 85
Buddha, Gautama, 76
Buddhism, 9

Camus, Albert, 144
Cantor, Georg, 39, 62, 63
Carlyle, Thomas, 15
categories, choice of, 89
categories, discovery of, 60, 161n10; natural
  kinds, 70; Kantian, of mind, 79; moral,
  in interpreting public life, 119; problem
  of, 93, 164n26; of substance and attributes, Aristotelian, 81
causal connection, knowledge of, 51
causal efficacy, 92
causality, 57, 61
cause, causal order, 46, 52
certainty, quest for, 11–12, 13, 14, 15, 29
chance, 44–45, 52; defined, 52
chaos, 45, 144; *see* order/disorder
character, 129; *see also* virtues
children, education of, 6, 9, 118

Chinese humanism, 152
Christian ethics, 95, 100, 105, 130–31
Christianity, 8–9, 134, 137, 149–50
Cicero, 82
civil disobedience, 7, 98–99
clarity, search for, 72–73
Clark, Ronald William, *Life of Bertrand Russell,* 3
class, 47; class of all classes not members of themselves, 62; null-class, 63; what is a ?, 65–66
coherence theory of truth, 25–26
common sense, 84–85; *see also* reality, robust sense of
communism/anticommunism, 7; *see* anticommunism, Marxism
compassion, 142
complexes, philosophy of, 56
conceptual analysis, 57
Confucian order of China, 118, 167n4
Confucius, 127
connotation, 67
conscience: as divine command, Puritan and Quaker, 98–99, 125–26; as voice of God, 135, 138
conscientious objection, 98
construction, 61–62; vs inferences, 49
continuity, a type of order, 39–40; of space, time, motion, 43
continuum, 40
Copleston, Frederick C., S.J., 149, 169n22; *History of Philosophy,* 149
correlation, 46
correspondence of belief to fact, 16–17
correspondence, mirroring, of world in monad, 48, 49
cosmic order, put in doubt by newer physics, 80
cosmic piety, 13, 27, 76, 104, 115, 116, 135
cosmological argument, 14
cosmology, 78; *see also* metaphysics
cosmos and orderer, 76–77, 80; *see also* cosmological argument for God
courage/cowardice, 112, 132
courage/fear, 129
creativeness/destruction, 151
creativity or creativeness/possessiveness, 122–23
cruelty, 130
curiosity, 130
cycle, cyclical order, 44–45

Dante, 112, 117
definitions of good tautological, 100
denoting and denotation, 66, 67
Descartes, René, 83
desire, interest, preference and attitude, root of ethical judgment, 103, 104; *see* naturalistic ethics, 104
determinism/chance, 92; *see also* causality, causal efficacy
Dewey, John, 25, 55, 95, 117, 119
dialectic: of dialogue, nominalist-realist, 18–19; of metaphysics and antimetaphysics, 76
difference, perceived/real, 79
disorder, 80; mode of order, 46
dogmatism/nondogmatism of metaphysics, 85
dogmatism: moral, of Puritans, 97; of a true believer?, 126, 132, *see* skepticism/dogmatism; of ideologies/constructive skepticism of scientists, 123, *see also* skepticism/dogmatism
Dostoyevsky, Fyodor, *House of the Dead,* 142
dualism: Cartesian, 83, *see also* mind/body; of universal and particular, 19–20, 24; or dochotomies, 89, 110, *see also* fact/value dualism; Zoroastrian, 145
duty, 98

education, moral purpose of, 127–32
Einstein, Albert, 90, 93
Eliot, T. S., 13, 151, 169; "Mr. Appollinax," 157n12
emotivism, 106, 109, 111
emotional expectations of a worldview extra scientific, 92
empiricism/rationalism, 14
England, love of, 7
envy, 129
equality, 45; *see* asymmetry/symmetry
equality/inequality, 5
equilibrium, 45; *see* asymmetry/symmetry
ethics, defined, 100; truth of, 99
Euripides, Hippolytus, 139
events, 80; world of, 93, *see also* process philosophy
evil/good, 99
evil and good, real/apparent, 143
evils, four great, challenging to the Puritan moralist, 120, 132
evolution/revolution, 122, 123
evolutionary ethics, 100, 104–5

fact/value dualism, 92, 109
faith/realism, 126
fallacies, 65, 136
fanaticism, 137
fear, 108, 112, 127, 129, 169n25
fear, religion based on, 150–51
fear, conceit, hatred, 151
forms, Platonic: *see* universals
Francis, St., of Assisi, 148
freedom, 102; *see also* determinism
freedom/discipline, 6
freedom, loss of, under socialism, 8
friendship, 102

Galileo, Galilei, 39
Gandhi, Mohandas, 28, 126
Gellner, Ernest, *Words and Things*, 71
Genghis Khan, 8
God, 4, 5, 14, 15, 23, 38, 77, 80–83, 92,
    105, 125, 134–38, 141–44, 145, 147,
    148, 149, 153 (Osiris), 163; proofs of,
    141, 149; proofs fail, 12, 13, 163n15;
    proofs presuppose objectivity, 26–27,
    169n22
God beyond experience, 143–44
good/bad, 101
good form/bad form, 127, 128
good life, the, 107–9
Gottschalk, Herbert, *Bertrand Russell: A Life*,
    7
grammatical forms misleading, 85
greed, 124
habits, characteristics acquired by practice,
    129
Hardy, G. H., *Bertrand Russell and Trinity*,
    125
harmony, 48, 146, 147; fourfold of Pythago-
    ras, 11; of all parts, aim of practical phi-
    losophy, 114–15
hatred, 142
hatred, envy, cruelty, vices, 102
Hebraic prophet, 138, 145, 151
Hebraism/Hellenism, 138
hedonism: *see* pleasure, ethics of
Hegel, Georg Wilhelm Friedrich, 19, 32,
    58, 68, 76, 79, 86, 105, 117
Hempel, Carl, 73
Heraclitus, 54
Herling, Gustav, *A World Apart*, 141–42
heroic religion of Prometheus, 145–46
heterogeneity of the world/homogeneity of
    words, 68–69

hierarchy: individuals: classes: classes of
    classes, 64–65
hierarchy of languages, 69; *see also* theory of
    types
Hitler, Adolf, 126
Hobbes, Thomas, 18, 117, 124, 160n4
holism, 58, 61; *see also* whole/part
honesty, 101–2; *see also* truthfulness
hope, 153; *see* Messianic hope
Hook, Sidney, 132, 156, 166
humanists and humanism, 12, 27
humanism, secular, 134–35, 140
Hume, David, 92, 131
humility, 72, 127
hypocrisy, 98
hypostatic ethics, 103

iconoclasm, 140
idealists, 55
ideologies and systems, 131–32
idolatry, 145
imperatives, moral, 104; *see also* conscience
incarnation, gradual, 148
individuals, in contrast to social collectives,
    sometimes good, sometimes evil, 8
inference from language to world, fallacy, 50
inference, uncertainty of, 89
infinite/finite, 38
infinity, defined, 39; qualitative, 147
intelligence/ignorance and stupidity, 131
internal/external relations, 32
interpretation, 49–50
intrinsic/extrinsic good, 108
intuitionism/naturalism in ethics, 103, 105
Islam, rise of, 123
is/ought dichotomy, 100
"is," six meanings symbolized, 81, 84

James, William, 25, 26, 28, 55, 61, 147
Jesus Christ, 76, 122, 127, 130
Job, 144
Johnson, President Lyndon, 17, 132
journey, philosophic, 11–13, 31, 54
Judaism, 9, 137–38
justice, 122

Kant, Immanuel, 32, 40, 62, 70, 78–85,
    105, 124, 127, 142, 149, 162
Kierkegaard, Søren, 139
kindness, 113, 124
knowledge: ethical, 108–9, *see also* persons,
    knowledge of; inadequate without love,
    107

laissez-faire capitalism, 117, 122
language and the structure of the world, 68
law of nature, 77
Lawrence, D. H., 108, 151; *The Apocalypse,*
151
Leibniz, G. W. von, 25, 30, 31, 32, 36,
38, 40, 48, 68, 82–83, 86, 140–43,
149, 162
Lenin, Vladimir Ilyich, 8, 123, 131
levels of nature and sciences, 77
Lewis, Hywel David, "Clarity is Not
Enough," 73
liar, paradox of, 63
"Liberal Decalogue, A," 110–12
liberalism, 2–5, 97, 111–12; Chapter 7,
117–33
limit, 39
linear order: *see* series
linguistic analysis, 55, 61, 67, 82; attack
on, 71–74; realism vs, 88
Locke, John, 18, 117
logic: essence of philosophy, 83; of relations,
52
logical analysis, 57
logical atomism, 58–62, 78–79
logical order, 45, 47
logical positivists, 68–73, 75, 86, 106; *see
also* Ayer, A. J.
logics: succession of, 30
love: kinds of, 107; love-knowledge over
power-knowledge, 115; of neighbor, 137,
139; teacher's, of young, 129

Machiavelli, Niccolo, 117
McTaggart, John McTaggart Ellis, 143
mapping, 49, 50
marriage, 6
Marx, Karl, 117, 122, 124, 131
Marxism, 122, 123; Soviet, as a secular religion, 118, 123
Mary/Martha, 138
materialism, 77
mathematical logic: *see* relations, theory of
meaning, types of, 69
meaning of different sorts, 67; *see also* denotation, connotation
Meinong, Alexius, 67
meliorism, 147
mercy/justice, 130
Messianic hope, 151–53
metaphors for world views, 91, 93
metaphysical ethics, alleged fallacy, 105; *see
also* is/ought

metaphysics/analysis, 67–68, 70
metaphysics: critique of, 84; death and rebirth of, 75; rejections of, 61, 81
Mill, John Stuart, 2, 18, 36, 117; *Principles
of Political Economy,* 121
Millikan, Robert A., 80
Milton, John, *The Doctrine and Discipline of
Divorce,* 97
mind/body, without break between, 78; neutral monism, 89
minimum vocabularies, 20–21
moderation, "not too much," 96
modernist rebellion against tradition, 5
monadism, 83; *see also* Leibniz
monism, materialistic/idealistic, 83
Moore, G. E., 25, 28, 100–4, 108, 158;
Principia Ethica, 99
morality/ethics, 95, 102
Moses: *see* Ten Commandments
Murray, Gilbert, 139
music, analysis of, 56
mysticism, 149; logical consequence of
atomism, 58; unsatisfied by logical
atomism, 79, 89; vs logic, 11–12

names, 87
naturalism, ethical, 110
nature discrete or continuous?, 36; *see* organicism, atomism
Niebuhr, Reinhold, 107, 140–41
Nietzsche, Friedrich, 104, 106, 137
nominalists and nominalism, 18, 54–55,
86–87; Russell's argument against, 10,
88; usefulness of nominalism, 37–38, 62,
65
numbers, deduced from relations, 31; defined, 32, 35, 37; problem, "what is a
number?", 36–38

Occam, William of, 18, 38, 54, 117
one-one, one-many, many-one relationships,
47, 50
ontological argument, 14, 82
optimism, 144; vs pessimism, 147
order, belief in, 30
order, definition of, 41–42
order/disorder, 45, 80
order in arts, 51
order, instrinsic/arbitrary, dependence of the
latter on the former, 43, 48
order, liberal, maximum of individual freedom within social order, 120–21

order, modes of: *see* balance; cycle, cyclical order; equality; harmony; hierarchy of languages; levels of nature; series

order, new, springing from dissent, 8

order of orders, ground of order, 141–46

order of things/order of nature, belief in, presupposed by science, 92

order of thought/order of things, 30

order-realism/order-subjectivism, 43, 48

order, subjective, 80

order, theory of, Chapter 3 passim; *see* order, definition of; order, modes of

ordinary language/scientific language, 72

organicism, 56–58; Hegel's, 32; Bradley's, 32; Whitehead's philosophy of, 91; *see also* whole/part

organicist, interdependence of parts of a whole, 116

orthodoxy, rebellion against, 2

other worldliness, 146

Ottoline, Lady, Morrell, 146–47, 165, 168

pacifism, 7, 119, 122, 124–26, 137

paradoxes, 12–13, 55, 62–67

Parmenides, 68, 86

participation of particulars in universal, 20, 87

patriotism, 5, 131

Paul, Saint, 129; *see* Bible

peace and war, 118–19

Peano, Giuseppi, 21, 32, 35

Peirce, Charles Sanders, 46, 55

perception, 56

perception of pattern or Gestalt, 60; *see also* structure

personal religion, 137, 138

persons, 114–15; knowledge of, 113

persuasion in moral discourse, 110

philosophy of religion, 136

piety, 129, 131

Pilate's question, 24

Plato, 11, 12, 17, 22, 38, 54, 68, 70, 78, 86, 117, 119, 129, 145

Platonism, fallacy of, requiring nominalism, 65

pleasure, ethics of, 100

Plotinus, 54

Pope, Alexander, *Essay on Man*, 45

power, over nature/over fellow humans, 153

practical philosophy, 94–96

pragmatic theory of truth, 25–26

pragmatism, Russell's argument against, 26

predicate contained by subject, 25, 82

pride, 124, 125

primitive ideas, Peano's, 32

probability, 46–47, 52

process philosophy of Russell as well as Whitehead, 91

progress, 137, 143, 151–52; belief in, 121, 128; resting on creative emotion, 8; through Christianity denied, 134–35; through communism denied, 123–24; through socialism questioned, 122

Prometheus, 143–46

prophet/mystic, 138

Protestant theology, idealistic and optimistic, 143

Providence, 143

Puritan: characteristics of, 98; morality, 96–99, 104; virtues, 3

purposelessness of nature/teleology, 141; defiance of purposeless material universe, 143

Pythagoras, 11, 12, 24, 31–32, 35, 38, 54, 76, 117, 157

Quakers, 148

qualitative/quantitative, 63

quantity, 36, 40; displaced by order, 48

realism: critical or moderate, 48–49; extreme, 19; vs idealism, 143

reality: of particulars and universals, 18; robust sense of, 64

rebellions, five great, 4–9

reflection, trust/distrust in, 90

relations, 21–23; subjective, based in mind, Bradley's theory, 48, 159n8; temporal/spatial, 88; theory of, 21, 30, 32, 83

relativism, ethical, 106

relativity, 77; of orders, not contradictory to objectivity, 43–44

religion, Chapter 8, 134–53; bad/good, 135–37, 140; fifth great evil, 136, *see* evils, four great; of despair, 140, 141; personal/institutional, 135; private/social, 148

religious experience, 139, 142, 147

reserve, 127–28

respect for law/law breaking, 98

revolutions, English and American, and Puritanism, 98

rhetoric, Ciceronian, of humanists, 82, 110

rhythm, 44; *see* cycle, cyclical order

Rights of Man, 122

Robespierre, Maximilien F. M. I. de, 8

Roman Catholics/Protestants, 150
Rousseau, Jean-Jacques, 117
Royce, Josiah, 41, 55
Russell, Alys, 117, 155, 167
Russell, Bertrand, autobiographical accounts, 157n2

WORKS—BOOKS:

Amberley Papers, 2, 3; *Analysis of Matter*, 47, 50, 89; *Analysis of Mind*, 89; *Authority and the Individual*, 8, 98, 118; *Basic Works*, 31, 107, 135; *Bertrand Russell Speaks His Mind*, 133; *Bolshevism*, 7, 118; *Common Sense and Nuclear Warfare*, 119; *Conquest of Happiness*, 95, 127; *Critical Exposition of the Philosophy of Leibniz*, 81, 83, 149; *Dear Bertrand Russell*, 9; *Education and the Social Order (Education and the Modern World)*, 118; *Education Especially in Early Childhood (Education and the Good Life)*, 28, 118; *Essays on the Foundations of Geometry*, 35; *Essence of Religion*, 148; *Freedom and Organization*, 118; *Free Man's Worship*, 7, 8, 144, 146; *German Social Democracy*, 7, 117; *History of Western Philosophy*, 11, 82, 89, 94, 117; *Human Knowledge: Its Scope and Limits*, 46, 47, 52, 89; *Human Society in Ethics and Politics*, 89, 119; *Introduction to Mathematical Philosophy*, 31, 33, 41, 44, 47, 64; *Justice in War-Time*, 125; *Marriage and Morals*, 118; *My Philosophical Development*, 3, 18, 31, 35, 54, 64, 71; *Mysticism and Logic*, 136; *New Hopes for a Changing World*, 118; *Notion of Order*, 44; *Our Knowledge of the External World*, 17, 39, 84; *Philosophy of Logical Atomism*, 81; *Political Ideals*, 118; *Portraits from Memory*, 2, 3; *Power, A New Social Analysis*, 118; *Principia Mathematica*, 11, 31, 32, 50, 65, 84, 85; *Principles of Mathematics*, 25, 33, 54, 57, 65, 66; *Principles of Social Reconstruction (Why Men Fight)*, 114, 118, 135, 137, 148; *Problem of China*, 118; *Problems of Philosophy*, 12, 15, 18, 20, 27, 135, 146; *Prospects of Industrial Civilization*, 118; *Religion and Science*, 106, 136; *Rex vs. Bertrand Russell*, 125; *Roads to Freedom*, 118; *Sceptical Essays*, 28; *Scientific Outlook*, 115; *Which Way to*

Peace?, 118, 126; *Why I Am Not a Christian*, 107, 112, 134–37, 140, 148, 149, 151; *Wisdom of the West*, 24

WORKS—ARTICLES:

"Can Religion Cure Our Troubles?", 134; "Denoting," 66; "Elements of Ethics," 99, 102; "Essence of Religion," 135, 146; "Ethics of War," 125; "Expanding Mental Universe," 115; "Free Man's Worship," 134; "Has Religion Made Useful Contributions to Civilization?", 134, 150; "Is Science Superstitious?", 89; "Knowledge and Wisdom" (from *Portraits from Memory*), 2; "Logic as the Essence of Philosophy," 84; "Mathematics and the Metaphysician," 39, 84; "Mysticism and Logic," 149; "Mystic Vision," 149; "Notion of Order," 31; "Physics and Metaphysics," 90, 93; "Pitfalls in Socialism," 121; "Recrudescence of Puritanism," 96; "Relations of Universals to Particulars," 18; "Relativity and Religion," 90; "Reply to Criticisms," 110; "Russell's Philosophy of Religion," 157; "Scientific Method in Philosophy," 84; "Study of Mathematics," 84, 146, 147; "Styles in Ethics," 106; "Transatlantic Truth," 25; "Why I Am Not a Christian," 9, 134

Russell, Dora, 4; *The Tamarisk Tree*, 4
Russell, Lord John, 1; *Life of Lord William Russell*, 1
Russell, Lord William, 1

Santayana, George, 97–98, 103–4, 108; *Winds of Doctrine*, 103
Schoenman, Ralph, *Bertrand Russell: Philosopher of the Century*, 133
Schweitzer, Albert, 138
science/religion, 76; *see also* science/theology
science/theology, reconciliation rejected, 80
secular ideologies and fanaticism, 9
secularism, 95, 169n20
self-interest, 101–2
series, serial order, 34, 43
sex-love, 108
sexual relations, 4–5, 6
sexual revolution, 95
similarity, 82, 87, *see also* universals; of qualities/of relations, 46–47
simple/complex, 59

simples, 56, 59, 60
sin, 131; original, 141–42
skepticism/dogmatism, 15, 17, 136
Smuts, General Jan Christian, 48
socialism, 7–8, 117, 121; Fabian, 7
space, Euclidian/non-Euclidian, 36
space-time, 77; four-dimensional, 91; *see also* spatio-temporal
spatial order, 35–36
spatio-temporal order, 51
spectator/agent, different views of person, 51
Spinoza, Baruch, 8, 13, 68, 83, 86, 94; *Ethics,* 105
spontaneity, 128
Stalin, Joseph, 131, 142
structure, 46–50, 86, 160n17; of the world, knowledge of, 88, 155
subject/predicate logic, 20, 32, 87
subjectivism, ethical, 106
subsistence/existence, 62, 82
substance, Aristotelian, concept rejected, 87; primary and secondary, 82; substance defined, 82
substance replaced by relation as category of categories, 52
syllogism, syllogistic logic, 32, 82–83
symbolic logic: *see* relations, theory of
symmetry 47; *see also* asymmetry
sympathy, 130
synthesis, goal of Hegelian dialectic of thesis/antithesis, 79
synthetic a priori truths, 70
system, metaphysical, failure to produce a, 75

Tait, Katharine Russell, 4, 126, 135, 170; *My Father, Bertrand Russell,* 4, 141
tautologies, reduction of logic and mathematics, to tautologies, 71
temporal asymmetry, 70–71
Ten Commandments, 96, 111–12, 112, 135
Tennyson, Alfred Lord, 15
theodicy in history?, 124
theory of types: *see* hierarchy of languages
Tillich, Paul, 129
time order/space order, 33
totalitarianism, 120–24
tragedy, 13, 120, 151
true/false, 15–16; inherent in propositions, 25; objectivity, 22
Truth, 23, 121, 138, 139, 141, 144, 147, *see also* Good, Beauty; as name of God, 112, 138, 141, 145, 147, *see also* Gandhi

truth: quest for, 24–25, 27–28, 78, 101, 104; self-evident, of logic and ethics, 100, 101; theory of, 70, *see* a priori truth, correspondence, coherence, pragmatic theory of; shifts in theory, 27–28
truthfulness, 28–29, 76, 98, 112

unity of world, 85; *see also* cosmos, whole
universal characteristic, 82; *see also* Leibniz
universal, defined, 87
universals/particulars, 17–24, 54
universe: *see* whole
utilitarian calculus of pleasures, 36
utilitarianism, universal hedonism: *see* pleasure, ethics of

value, man-made/natural, 110
vanity, 128; *see also* pride
verbs, neglected in formal logic, 84
vices: *see* fear; greed; hatred, envy, cruelty; jealousy; pride; violence
vices, Russell's, 156n6
vices of war, 125
Vico, Giovanni Batista, 84
virtues: *see* austerity; courage; duty; friendship; honesty; justice; kindness; moderation; reserve; truthfulness; vitality; work; worship, acquiescence, love
virtue, theories of: *see* conscience, creativity, good form, habit, happiness, love, moderation
virtues, common/vocational, 129
virtues, four cardinal, traditional, 129; Russellian, 129
virtues, in relation to, happiness, contrasted theories, 102
virtues, liberal, implicit in commandments, 112
virtues, moral/intellectual, 130
virtues, Russell's, 111–13, 124–25
virtues that are vices, 127, 128, 129, 130
virtues, theological, 129
virtue/vice, 2; Platonic, 12; Puritan dichotomy of, 97, 119
vitality, 129
Voltaire, 125, 135, 139, 140, 148

war, moral problem of, 106
Watson, John, 105
Watts, Isaac, 56
Webb, Beatrice, 3, 155
Whitehead, Alfred North, 3, 11, 32, 41, 80, 89, 113–14, 115, 156; *Process and*

Reality, 91, 93; *Science and the Modern World,* 89, 90, 92, 115, 156

Whitehead, Evelyn (Mrs. A. N.), 139, 145

whole, no propositions about, 84

whole/part, categories of, 56–58, 60; *see also* complexes, simples

whole, vision of, 79

wisdom, 2, 6, 10, 115, 120

Wittgenstein, Ludwig, 55, 58, 71, 72, 73; *Philosophical Investigations,* 71; *Tractatus Logico-Philosophicus,* 59, 71

women, 2–3

Wood, Alan, *Bertrand Russell: The Passionate Sceptic,* 3

Wordsworth, William, 15, 57

work ethic, 96

world government, 126

world of being, 67

world of universals, perfect order, 23

world religion, 152

worship, acquiescence, love, 151

Zeno, 40, 62

Zoroaster, 145

DATE DUE